Latin American
Science Fiction Writers

LATIN AMERICAN
SCIENCE FICTION WRITERS

An A-to-Z Guide

EDITED BY DARRELL B. LOCKHART

GREENWOOD PRESS
Westport, Connecticut • London

Library of Congress Cataloging-in-Publication Data

Latin American science fiction writers : an A-to-Z guide / edited by Darrell B. Lockhart.
    p. cm.
    Includes bibliographical references and index.
    ISBN 0-313-30553-6 (alk. paper)
    1. Science fiction, Latin American—History and criticism—Dictionaries.
2. Science fiction, Latin American—Bio-bibliography—Dictionaries.
3. Authors, Latin American—Biography—Dictionaries. I. Lockhart, Darrell B.
PQ7082.S34L38 2004
863'.087620998'03—dc22   2003058416
    [B]

British Library Cataloguing in Publication Data is available.

Library of Congress Catalog Card Number: 2003058416
ISBN: 0-313-30553-6

First published in 2004

Greenwood Press, 88 Post Road West, Westport, CT 06881
An imprint of Greenwood Publishing Group, Inc.
www.greenwood.com

Printed in the United States of America

The paper used in this book complies with the
Permanent Paper Standard issued by the National
Information Standards Organization (Z39.48-1984).

10 9 8 7 6 5 4 3 2 1

Contents

Preface

This volume represents an attempt to provide a comprehensive inventory of Latin American science fiction writing. My interest in such a project stems from at least two primary motivating factors: first, a personal fondness for a genre that has provided me with a great source of entertainment over the years; and second, the desire to engage in the more intellectual enterprise of literary history and interpretation in relation to the science fiction of Latin America. The principal goal of this sourcebook is likewise twofold. On the one hand, it is meant to underscore the vastness and diversity of this body of writing, present a profile of its development over the years, and serve as a point of departure for future research. This leads to its second goal, which has to do with how science fiction historically been has been perceived within the literary environment. In Latin America, perhaps more so than elsewhere, science fiction has long been considered to be a lesser form of literature. This, in spite of the fact that Latin American writers have long been practicing (since at least the eighteenth century) the genre as a means of cultural expression. Therefore, this volume seeks to position science fiction writing as a major presence in Latin American literature, an authentic and unique cultural discourse worthy of greater scholarly attention and analytical inquiry.

The organization of *Latin American Science Fiction Writers: An A-to-Z Guide* is intended, as stated above, to provide an overview of the genre. The introduction provides a brief historical summary of the development of the genre in Latin America, while the sourcebook itself is organized on an author-by-author basis. Entries on the individual practitioners of science fiction writing are arranged alphabetically by the author's actual surname, or the pseudonym by which he/she is best known. The country listed in each heading is not necessarily the author's country of birth, but rather the country with which he/she is associated as a writer. The volume contains entries on 70 writers, prepared by the collective efforts of 20 contributors. The majority of the authors included are from Argentina, Mexico, and Cuba. Every effort was made to ensure that the volume is as all-inclusive as possible. Nevertheless, any project such as this is fraught with a number of difficulties from the outset. It is simply logistically impossible to include every worthy author, and I will avoid attempting any kind of list of authors who for whatever reason did not make it into the final manuscript. Suffice it to say that there are at least as many authors excluded as there are included here. The one consolation is the hope that this will further stimulate academic activity to fill these voids. Women authors are well represented in this volume, which reflects the fact that there are many who cultivate science fiction in Latin America. Finally, this volume concludes with a bibliography of literary anthologies and criticism divided geographically by country.

One of the major obstacles facing the project was locating enough scholars who share a common interest and concern for Latin American science fiction and who were willing and able to contribute to this effort. From the beginning this was meant to be a collaborative project among colleagues, who are scattered throughout North and South America. Therefore, contributors were asked to suggest authors who should be added to (or removed from) the original list of names that went out with the call for contributions. The result was a flood of suggestions that resulted in an ongoing dialogue about the nature and parameters of science fiction in Latin America. Again, far more names were proposed than could be realistically accommodated. The often problematical designation "Latin America" is not invoked here as a totalizing term. I am aware, of course, of the dangers of "lumping together" the diverse regions, realities, identities, and so on that comprise that nebulous territory we call, for lack of a better name, "Latin America." In general terms, any author from a Spanish- or Portuguese-speaking country of the Americas was eligible for inclusion. I decided not to include Latino authors from the United States, more for practical reasons that politically motivated ones. Contributors were given rather lax guidelines to follow in the preparation of the entries with regard to content and approach. However, each was asked to organize the entry by first providing a brief biographical sketch on the author wherever possible, followed by a summary of the author's literary contribution and impact pertaining to the genre, and ending with a bibliography of primary and secondary sources (in many cases there are no secondary critical sources). The authors included in this volume range from the canonical to the virtually unknown, from those who adhere closely to the conventions of science fiction (in its various styles) to those who incorporate only certain elements in the creation of their texts. This is meant to showcase both the wide-arching magnitude of Latin American science fiction as well as its influence on other, more mainstream literary discourses.

This endeavor is part of a broader undertaking to examine popular-genre literature in Latin America. This volume, together with its companion volume *Latin American Mystery Writers: An A-to-Z Guide*, seek to broaden the scope of Latin American literary and cultural studies. Science fiction and mystery fiction—both forms of so-called popular literature (often considered inferior)—are uniquely equipped to offer critical appraisals of society. The parameters of each genre allow for the creation of ingenious parodies and allegories of all the social, political, and economic components of contemporary life. In Latin American countries, where life is often affected by political unrest, social upheaval, and economic crisis, these two genres have found fertile narrative ground.

Lastly, I would like to acknowledge all the individuals who made this volume possible—first and foremost the contributors who embraced this project with enthusiasm and without whom it would not have become a reality. I am especially grateful to everyone involved for their patience, as this project has taken several years to come to fruition. I would also like to thank my research assistant Eric Rojas for his invaluable help in the preparation of this volume, particularly for translating many of the essays into English. Pedro Gómez and Carolyn Russum also provided much-needed assistance with translations. My thanks also to Robert Kowkabany for his excellent work as copyeditor of the manuscript.

Introduction

DARRELL B. LOCKHART

Cuando completé el invento se me ocurrió, primero como un simple tema para la imagi-nación, después como un increíble proyecto, dar perpetua realidad a mi fantasía senti-mental . . .

(When I finished the invention it occurred to me, first as a simple flight of the imagi-nation, and then as an incredible project, to give perpetual reality to my sentimental fantasy . . . [Adolfo Bioy Casares, *La invención de Morel*, translation mine])

One of the defining characteristics of science fiction (SF) writing in Latin America is its position as a marginal discourse. Such a position is readily observed in the fact that most readers, either from Latin American countries or elsewhere, are entirely unaware of the vastness of this literary universe (if I may use the pun). It is vast both in the sense of the enormity of the body of works that exists and in the period of time over which it has been produced. The decentered position of SF within the expansive boundaries of Latin American literature does not neces-sarily indicate that historically it has been marginalized for political or ideologi-cal reasons by institutionalized powers of culture that determine canon-forma-tion. Science fiction is not viewed as a unified subversive or counter-hegemonic discourse, as are bodies of minority literature like Afro-Latin American, Jewish, or gay and lesbian writing. Indeed, SF writers don't form an identity collective outside the common interest they share in the genre.

This does not mean that SF literature is merely a benign entertainment. Much to the contrary, SF writing more often than not is a highly motivated vehicle for communicating trenchant social commentary. It is, of course, commonly recog-nized that SF is not about the future, but is an allegory of the present. The char-acteristic displacement of reality (either in time, space, or circumstances) that SF writing undertakes makes the genre particularly equipped as a discourse of social protest. Science fiction is marginalized more in the sense that it has been eclipsed by the major trends in Latin American literature, from the fantastic (arguably an early manifestation of SF) to social realism, and especially by the extremely overdetermined use of magical realism that exploded in the 1960s, producing a mushroom cloud of marketing that sold it as the "authentic voice" of Latin America.

As if recovering from a nuclear winter, new forms of life are emerging in Latin American literature and history is being reexamined in an effort to recover lost remnants in a postmagical-realist era. Science fiction writing, once considered a minor genre not to be taken seriously—much like detective fiction—and associated with such "objectionable" terms as "pulp literature" and "popular culture," is now being reevaluated in the light of cultural studies. The stigma of being labeled a "science fiction (or detective fiction) writer" was enough to keep many authors away from the genre, causing them to write behind the mask of a pseudonym or use any number of euphemisms to describe their work as other than SF. Likewise, many authors chose to experiment with such genres, but did not dedicate the majority of their efforts to it. This is another factor that has contributed to the marginal status afforded to SF writing. With the postmodern crumbling of cultural hierarchies and highbrow ideals of art, many young science fiction writers feel freer to declare themselves as such and focus their energies on the promotion and production of SF.

It is now fairly widely accepted that the eighteenth-century Franciscan friar Manuel Antonio de Rivas (included here) wrote what in retrospect may be considered the first science fiction work of Latin America. His text "Sizigias y cuadraturas lunares ajustadas al meridiano de Mérida de Yucatán por un anctítona o habitador de la luna" (Syzygies and Lunar Quadratures Arranged to Mérida de Yucatán's Meridian by an Anctitone or Moon Inhabitant [this is an abbreviation of the longer title]) is dated 1775. His narration of a voyage to the moon, along with other "heresies," caused him to be shunned by his brethren and put on trial by the Inquisition in Mexico. In the nineteenth century, it is the Argentine author Eduardo Ladislao Holmberg who is credited with writing some of the foundational texts of Latin American science fiction. These include, principally, his space-voyage narrative "Viaje maravilloso del señor Nic-Nac" (The marvelous journey of Mr. Nic-Nac, 1875) and the robot story "Horacio Kalibang o los autómatas" (H. K. or the automatons, 1879) (see his entry in this volume). The late nineteenth and early twentieth centuries also saw the proliferation of literature of the fantastic, and several authors associated with Latin American Modernism are considered to be founding figures of contemporary SF writing: Amado Nervo (Mexico), Horacio Quiroga (Uruguay), and Leopoldo Lugones (Argentina) are included in this volume for their contributions to the genre in its earliest stages. From these early examples, Latin American SF has continued to produce narratives of speculation, utopian and dystopian visions of society, stories of space travel, and cyberpunk. This volume contains information on a broad gamut of writers who have contributed to the genre, from the foundational figures—some of whom are being rescued from obscurity—to the established masters of Latin American SF, to the newcomers who are defining the future. One is tempted to engage in yet another survey of the history of SF writing in Latin America, yet this would be a rather tautological exercise, since it has been done numerous times before (see the bibliography at the end of this volume). One of the very functions of this book is to provide an aggregated record of that history, though the primary goal is to arrive at a more meaningful evaluation of Latin American SF by stimulating further research.

One of the striking characteristics of Latin American SF is its capacity for survival under adverse conditions. By this I mean that science fiction has had to struggle to make itself visible and accessible in a publishing world that is profit-driven. This has been accomplished by the often heroic efforts of energetic promoters of the genre, whether through the creation of magazines that historically have had great difficulties surviving, small publishing houses, or, most recently and perhaps most successfully, through the development of on-line journals and forums of all sorts, in addition to several international science fiction-fantasy organizations (Bell and Molina-Gavilán provide an inventory of these sources in the introduction to their *Cosmos Latinos*). One of the best and most comprehensive approaches to Latin American SF can be achieved through the examination of the many literary anthologies that bring together authors and texts that otherwise would go unpublished. Such anthologies are instrumental in identifying how science fiction is conceived—in other words, what texts are considered to pertain to the genre and why. In some cases this can prove to be surprising, which points to the diversity of Latin American SF that operates with much wider parameters than its North American counterpart. Literary anthologies can also be helpful in establishing the vivacity of science fiction in a given country. For example, in Argentina, there are many anthologies of SF writing/writers that date from the 1960s up to the year 2000. However, there are very few differences among them. Most of the authors and even the same texts are recycled, with few innovations by new authors. Perusing these anthologies, one would get the impression that there is a rather small, tight-knit community of SF authors in Argentina—which hardly is the case. By comparison, the many literary anthologies that have sprung up in Mexico during the past 15 years or so include a much wider range of authors and texts. This may be due in large part to the fact that a good portion of them are the published results of literary contests. This is the case, for example, with Federico Schaffler's three-volume *Más allá de lo imaginado* (Beyond imagination, 1991–94), which showcases stories by many upcoming, talented writers—only a few of which manage to continue publishing their work. This seems to be a distinguishing characteristic between Argentina and Mexico: that Argentine authors more often than not publish their work(s) first and then are anthologized, while in Mexico, writers first have a short story anthologized and then work toward publishing a book of their sole authorship. Either way, anthologies provide a good source for surveying SF writing at a glance. In Buenos Aires and Mexico City, science fiction (like most literature of the twentieth century) is an urban phenomenon. However, in Mexico, this trend is now changing. Some of the best science fiction is being produced in the northern border-states of the country. Federico Schaffler, José-Mauricio Schwarz, and Gabriel Trujillo Muñoz have been at the forefront of creating a body of literature that is uniquely defined by the realities of the U.S.–Mexico border region. Schwarz's anthology *Frontera de espejos rotos* (Border of shattered mirrors, 1994) is but one excellent example. Any of Trujillo's SF texts also utilize this space as the central setting for his fiction and serve to challenge the hegemony of Mexico City as the only viable center of literary production in the country.

Almost 20 years ago, David William Foster identified SF writing as one of the more significant areas of Latin American cultural production that had gone understudied (*Alternate Voices* 136–43). It would seem that his call for corrective research agendas to fill this void is slowly being addressed. While there have been several studies on the genre of science fiction to come out of Latin American over the years, the earliest of them consisted primarily, if not exclusively, on SF writing outside of Latin America. Among such books one may list the Argentine publications *El mundo de la ciencia ficción: sentido e historia* (The world of science fiction: Meaning and history, 1992) by Pablo Capanna, and *Escalera al cielo: utopía y ciencia ficción* (Stairway to heaven: Utopia and science fiction, 1994) edited by Daniel Link. Both contain only minimal information on SF in Argentina. The book *Ficção Científica: Ficção, Çiência ou uma Épica da Época* (Science fiction: Fiction, science or an epic of the epoch, 1985) by Brazilian Raul Fiker contains no information whatsoever on Brazilian or Spanish American SF writing. Likewise, Luis A. Vaisman's lengthy article "En torno a la ciencia-ficción: propuesta para la descripción de un género histórico" (About science fiction: Proposal for the description of a historical genre) published in the *Revista chilena de literatura* (Chilean journal of literature, 1985) doesn't mention a single Latin American author. In Mexico, Gabriel Trujillo Muñoz wrote the extensive *La ciencia ficción: literatura y conocimiento* (Science fiction: literature and knowledge, 1991), which contains, as an appendix, an essay on Latin American SF. More recently, Ramón López Castro published *Expedición a la ciencia ficción mexicana* (Expedition to Mexican science fiction, 2001), and though the title sounds promising, it contains little new information and consists mainly of a comparative survey, with significant discussion on North American or European authors.

There is a noticeable shift from these initial efforts to identify the major influence of foreign models, to one that focuses on Latin American SF writing and its homegrown roots. There have been several useful essays, books, and bibliographies published that provide useful surveys of SF literature. Most research has focused primarily on Argentina and Mexico, since these are the two major literary poles that have produced the largest body of SF literature. This is not surprising, since both countries have historically been at the forefront of literary production in Latin America. Brazil, of course, is a cultural and literary powerhouse on par with both, but given its linguistic isolation, it is often considered as an island unto itself. One is reminded, for example, that Buenos Aires and Mexico

City were the centers of Spanish American Modernism due in large part to their urban cosmopolitanism. Brazil and Cuba have also produced a significant amount of science fiction, with other countries beginning to follow suit.

The overwhelming amount of new information on SF writing has thus far served the useful purpose of identifying authors and texts and tracing the historical development of the genre in Latin America. Individuals such as Pablo Capanna and Elvio Gandolfo rather thoroughly have mapped out the terrain of the genre in Argentina—and one may add to their efforts those of Angela Dellepiane and Antonio Planells. Mexican critics have thus far done the best job of providing a history of SF within their country. Gabriel Trujillo Muñoz followed up his previously mentioned study with two comprehensive books, *Los confines: crónica de la ciencia ficción mexicana* (The limits: Chronicle of Mexican science fiction, 1999) and *Biografías del futuro: la ciencia ficción mexicana y sus autores* (Biographies of the future: Mexican science fiction and its authors, 2000). His monographs provide an excellent survey of SF literature in Mexico, from its earliest beginnings to the latest writers of cyberpunk. It should be mentioned that Trujillo is also a prolific author of science fiction. In addition, Miguel Ángel Fernández Delgado and Andrea Bell have made significant contributions to the study of SF literature in Mexico. While these are all rather recent studies, Ross Larson merits recognition as having begun to trace the roots of Mexican science fiction in the 1970s. Braulio Tavares and Roberto de Sousa Causo have been instrumental in defining the parameters of contemporary SF in Brazil, while Daína Chaviano (one of Cuba's leading SF writers) and Juan Carlos Toledano have contributed similar efforts with regard to Cuba. Campo Ricardo Burgos López has provided the first overview of science fiction in Colombia in his "La narrativa de ciencia ficción en Colombia" (Science fiction narrative in Colombia, 2000). On a broader scale, the bibliography "Cronología de CF latinoamericana 1775–1999" (Chronology of Latin American SF 1775–1999) compiled through the joint efforts of Yolanda Molina-Gavilán, Miguel Ángel Fernández Delgado, Andrea Bell, Luis Pestarini, and Juan Carlos Toledano, offers an exhaustive list that includes literary texts, magazines, and criticism from almost every Latin American country. It bears repeating that these appraisals, histories, and bibliographies are all important for the significant contribution they have made to the establishment of a solid foundation for the study of Latin American SF. The purpose of this volume is to build on that foundation and provide a comprehensive—though certainly not all-inclusive—source that will aid in furthering the examination of this literary corpus.

In spite of the ever-growing bibliography on Latin American SF, to date there have been only scant critical analyses of this literature, mostly in the form of scattered articles on single texts. It would seem that the time has come to advance the study of Latin American SF to a more theoretical level—to undertake semiotic analyses of SF as a cultural discourse, for example, and begin to develop a deeper critical understanding of the phenomenon of SF writing in its uniquely Latin

American configurations. In fact, this has already commenced to some degree. Yolanda Molina-Gavilán's book *Ciencia ficción en español: una mitología moderna ante el cambio* (Science fiction in Spanish: A modern mythology in the face of change, 2002) is the first comprehensive, theoretically grounded examination of Latin American SF as a cultural product and vehicle of ideology (she also includes Spanish authors in her study). She has also been able to delineate what is unique about Latin American science fiction. While several other critics have pointed to a variety of elements that SF writing contains and the ways by which it differs from North American and European models—namely, differences deriving from so-called hard science and technology—Molina-Gavilán has more thoroughly theorized Latin American SF. Her text is a foundational work in the field and will long serve as a model for the kind of scholarship that needs to be undertaken in the future.

Science fiction has a long history of presence and participation in Latin American literature, where it has developed it own singular style. While its origins, at least in part, stem from foreign models, Latin American writers have been able to endow SF literature with their own set of characteristics and codes that enable them to speak with a unique voice. Indeed, the multiple voices and visions of SF provide a perspective on the social realities of Latin American countries, unlike that of any other literary discourse. Moreover, it is as "authentic" a representation of Latin America as any other literary discourse. That SF is capable of locating culture in different spaces, times, and planes of reality is one of its greatest accomplishments. Viewing the present from these different vantages allows the reader to see reality from a critical distance. Science fiction displaces reality but hardly avoids it; it distorts the actual but leaves it recognizable. Latin American SF is not magical but it is real. The reader may journey to the future or the past, to utopian paradises or hellish worlds of cataclysmic disaster, to the outer reaches of space or the center of the Earth, through time and parallel universes, meet alien races or the humans of tomorrow, enjoy the comforts or suffer the consequences of advanced supertechnologies—but all-the-while be looking in a mirror of the present. Above all, Latin American SF is both entertaining and thought-provoking, which after all is the primary function of any literature. The epigraph taken from Bioy Casares's classic tale *La invención de Morel* (*The Invention of Morel*, 1940) sums up the nature of this body of writing quite nicely. At the same time, it signals that the image-making machine of Latin American SF—like Morel's invention—will continue to perpetually project reality through the lens of fantasy.

Works Cited

Bell, Andrea, and Yolanda Molina-Gavilán. "Introduction: Science Fiction Literature in Latin America and Spain," in *Cosmos Latinos: An Anthology of Science Fiction from Latin America and Spain*, eds. and trans. Andrea Bell and Yolanda Molina-Gavilán. Middletown, CT: Wesleyan University Press, 2003, 1–19.

Burgos López, Campo Ricardo. "La narrativa de ciencia ficción en Colombia," in *Literatura y cultura: narrativa colombiana del siglo XX*, 3 vols, vol 1: La nación moderna, ed. María Mercedes Jaramillo, Betty Osorio, and Angela I. Robledo. Bogotá: Ministerio de Cultura, 2000, 1: 719–50.

Capanna, Pablo. "La ciencia ficción y los argentinos." *Minotauro* (Segunda época) 10 (1985): 43–56.

———. "Estudio preliminar," in *Ciencia ficción argentina: antología de cuentos*. Buenos Aires: Aude Ediciones, 1990, 9–32.

———. *El mundo de la ciencia ficción: sentido e historia*. Buenos Aires: Ediciones Buena Letra, 1992.

Causo, Roberto de Sousa. "Science Fiction During the Brazilian Dictatorship." *Extrapolation* 39.4 (1998): 314–23.

Dellepiane, Angela B. "Critical Notes on Argentinian Science-Fiction Narrative." *Monographic Review/Revista monográfica* 3.1–2 (1987): 19–32.

Fernández Delgado, Miguel Ángel. "A Brief History of Continuity and Change in Mexican Science Fiction." *New York Review of Science Fiction* 99 (1996): 18–19.

———. "Los cartógrafos del infierno en México." *Complot internacional* (Mexico) 1.8 (1997): 14–17.

———. "Páginas olvidadas de la historia de la ciencia ficción mexicana." *Memoria de la III Convención Nacional de la Asociación Mexicana de Ciencia Ficción y Fantasía* (1997): 27–35.

———. "Hacia una vindicación de la ciencia ficción mexicana." *Artifex* 20.21 (1999): 25–30.

Foster, David William. *Alternate Voices in the Contemporary Latin American Narrative*. Columbia: University of Missouri Press, 1985.

Gandolfo, Elvio E. "Prólogo: la ciencia ficción argentina," in *Los universos vislumbrados: antología de ciencia ficción argentina*, ed. Jorge A. Sánchez. Buenos Aires: Andrómeda, 1995, 13–50.

Larson, Ross. "La literatura de ciencia ficción en México." *Cuadernos hispanoamericanos* 284 (1974): 425–31.

———. *Fantasy and Imagination in the Mexican Narrative*. Tempe: Center for Latin American Studies, Arizona State University, 1977.

Link, Daniel, ed. *Escalera al cielo: utopía y ciencia ficción*. Buenos Aires: La Marca, 1994.

López Castro, Rafael. *Expedición a la ciencia ficción mexicana*. Mexico City: Lectorum, 2001.

Molina-Gavilán, Yolanda. *Ciencia ficción en español: una mitología moderna ante el cambio*. *Latin American Studies*, vol. 16. Lewiston, NY: Edwin Mellen Press, 2002.

Molina-Gavilán, Yolanda, et al. "Cronología de CF latinoamericana 1775–1999." *Chasqui* 29.2 (2000): 43–72.

Planells, Antonio. "La literatura de anticipación y su presencia en Argentina." *Revista interamericana de bibliografía/Inter–American Review of Bibliography* 40.1 (1990): 93–113.

Schaffler, Federico, ed. *Más allá de lo imaginado: antología de ciencia ficción mexicana*, 3 vols. Mexico City: Consejo Nacional para la Cultura y las Artes, 1991–94.

Schwarz, Mauricio-José, and Don Webb, eds. *Frontera de espejos rotos*. Mexico City: Roca, 1994.

Tavares, Braulio. "Stories of the Will-Happen: Science Fiction in Brazil." *Foundation* 77 (1999): 84–91.

Trujillo Muñoz, Gabriel. *La ciencia ficción: literatura y conocimiento*. Mexicali, Mexico: Instituto de Cultura de Baja California, 1991.

———. *Los confines: crónica de la ciencia ficción mexicana*. Mexico City: Grupo Editorial Vid, 1999.

———. *Biografías del futuro: la ciencia ficción mexicana y sus autores*. Mexicali, Mexico: Universidad Autónoma de Baja California, 2000.

Vaisman, Luis A. "En torno a la ciencia-ficción: propuesta para la descripción de un género histórico." *Revista chilena de literatura* 25 (1985): 5–27.

Latin American
Science Fiction Writers

José B. Adolph (b. 1933)

PERU

José Bernardo Adolph was born in Stuttgart, Germany, in 1933. Since 1938 he has resided in Peru, and in 1974 he became a Peruvian citizen. He is a professional journalist who completed his studies at the Universidad Mayor in San Marcos, Lima. He has performed multiple jobs in the field of journalism including being editor-in-chief of the following publications: *Dominical* (the Sunday supplement of the newspaper *El comercio* [Commerce]), the newspaper *Correo* (Post), the magazine *Caretas* (Masks), and the newspaper *Ultima Hora* (Last hour).

Adolph is one of Peru's most prolific writers. Among his numerous books, aside from those that pertain to science fiction, are the short-story collections *La batalla del café* (The battle of the café, 1984), *Un dulce horror* (A sweet horror, 1989) and *Diario del sótano* (The basement newspaper, 1996), as well as the novels *La ronda de los generales* (Generals on patrol, 1973) and *Dora* (1989). He has also written a number of plays, which are collected in *Teatro* (Theater, 1986). Adolph has received numerous awards from several different literary competitions in Peru. For example, in 1982, he received First Prize for Novel, sponsored by the city of Lima, in 1983 he won placed first in the short-story competition organized by the magazine *Caretas*; and in 1990, the second prize in the short-story competition "Copé." He is a professor of German at the Goethe Institute in Lima.

In addition to his novel *Mañana, las ratas* (Tomorrow, the rats, 1984), Adolph's science fiction works consist of several short stories contained in different books. None of his short-story collections are exclusively dedicated to science fiction texts. In fact, they cover a wide range of styles (from the fantastic to the realistic) and topics; his science fiction always addresses issues that are of social, historical, political, or religious concern. In *Mañana, las ratas*, for example, the setting is a futurist environment in the year 2034. The author proposes a new sociopolitical order in which, after the disintegration of the geographical boundaries that define countries, the world is divided into two great blocks: the Western and the Asiatic. While the latter is defined as the "Marxist-Confucianist Empire," the former is characterized by free trade carried to an extreme degree of technical development. It is a system of "supercapitalismo tecnotrónico" (technotronic super-capitalism [72]) in which the leaders are executives and whose power makes them "dioses transnacionales" (transnational gods [71]). In this Western block, free trade and drug consumption have been implanted, a new morality reigns in which sexual satisfaction is the end that justifies whatever means, and decisions—of all types, from emotional to political—are controlled by computers. However, this new order is far from perfect. Although wars are assured to be a thing of the past, the Southern Hemisphere continues to suffer from the social problems of yesteryear such as poverty and social injustice. The city of Lima reflects the existing division between the developed world of the North and the underdeveloped one of the South. Lima has been polarized between the executive, or dominant class, and *las ratas* (the rats), a term that equates economic categories (poverty) to racial ones ("cholos negros, indios, zambos, asiáticos" [mixed race, black, indigenous, mulatto, Asian] [70]). The *ratas* are the ones who, guided by a religious leader defined as "catholic-orthodox," will initiate a revolution that will not be limited to the Earth. Rather, it will expand to outer space in their tireless persecution of the dominant elite who seek protection for themselves on satellites that orbit the planet.

In different short stories, Adolph deals with various themes in a way that will also play a role in his novel. Religion, for example, is one of the principal structural devices in two short stories from the volume *El retorno de Aladino* (The return of Aladin, 1968): "Tesis" (Thesis) and "La asunción de Víctor" (Víctor's assumption, reproduced in the anthology *Los monstruos que vendrán* [The monsters to come, 1973]). In "Tesis," a group of students search for the solution to the problem of the floods that will cause a comet to approach a certain planet. This solution—communicated to the head of a monotheistic tribe from an interplanetary ship—consists of the construction of an ark. Similarly, in "La asunción de Víctor," various Biblical motifs like the plague, the cult of Baal Moloch, and the adoration and sacrifice to a new god are interwoven. This short story presents a scenario of time in a state of disorder and chaos. A mysterious virus has been annihilating children and Víctor, the son of the narrator, is one of the few survivors. A mob, infuriated and fanatical, wants to sacrifice the boy—being all too eager to destroy that which they adore.

Several short stories in *Hasta que la muerte* (Until death, 1971) also make use of religious motifs. In "El escondite" (The hiding place), we see a new genesis where the protagonist identifies as much with Adam as with a redeemed Cain. "El viaje" (The voyage) and "Los bromistas" (The jokers) attribute the creation of humanity to other beings. In this last tale, the creator has been confined to an asylum for this actions. In "Los mensajeros" (The messengers), human beings are elevated to the status of gods but later question their status, which hints at loss of faith as an issue to contemplate.

In other short stories, Adolph develops a favorite theme of science fiction: the apocalyptic catastrophe that results in the destruction of the earth (or of a planet similar to it). Such is the case in "Exploración" (Exploration) from *Cuentos del relojero abominable* (Stories of the abominable watchmaker, 1974), "Sodoma y Gomorra" (Sodom and Gomorrah), and "A quien corresponda" (To whom it may concern) from *Mañana fuimos felices* (Tomorrow we were happy, 1975). While in the first two stories, destruction is caused by wars, in the last one an entire race commits collective suicide. "Fin del mensaje" (End of message), from *Invisible para las fieras* (Invisible to beasts, 1972), presents a similar situation with the annihilation of a group of nonconformists in what constitutes a "final solution." A negative vision of humanity is also seen in "¿Quieres una manzana?" (Would you like an apple?) from *El retorno de Aladino*. Here, a group of earthlings encounters some beings whose superior intelligence makes the inhabitants of earth look brutish and ignorant. "Hablando de cocodrillos" (Speaking of crocodiles) and "Artemio y Multical" (Artemio and Multical), both from *Mañana fuimos felices*, suggest the close relationship—carried to emotional and sexual extremes—that can exist between man, machines and computers.

Another theme that Adolph deals with in his short stories is the continuity between the past and future, as made evident, on the one hand, by the contradiction in the title "Mañana fuimos felices," and on the other hand by the short story "Persistencia" (Persistence) from *Cuentos del relojero abominable*. In this story, Christopher Columbus's expedition to what should be America becomes an intergalactic adventure. This short story has been included in German and Swedish anthologies.

The universal theme of death (symbolized in the "abominable watchmaker"), present in the previously mentioned topic of the destruction of the earth, is by contrast related to the theme of immortality. In "Inauguración" (Inauguration, from *Cuentos del relojero abominable*), Adolph parodies official rhetoric by delivering a speech to inaugurate a monument to mortal beings . . . made by immortals. Satire aside, immortality is an attempt to vindicate the human species and place it on the same level as divinity. Immortality is also the central theme of "Nosotros, no" (Not us) and "Hasta que la muerte," stories included in *Hasta que la muerte*. In the former story, the attainment of mortality creates an insurmountable generation gap, although eternal life comes to be considered a punishment. The latter story expands on this last idea: immortality can make everything useless, including love; dying implies separating oneself from a loved one. With this conviction, the character states his beliefs about death: "neither reject, nor seek it. Follow it fighting . . ." (*Hasta que la muerte* [137]).

Despite Adolph's vast, varied, and interesting literary production, criticism on his work is limited to short notes appearing in anthologies. Beleván points out that Adolph is one of the few exponents of Peruvian science fiction literature. Bosco and González Vigil both note the connection between his science fiction and social elements. The latter calls this facet of his work "política-ficción" (political-fiction [214]), while the former maintains that through Adolph "la fantaciencia latinoamericana se tiñe . . . de sentido humano y contenido social" (Latin American science-fantasy is tinged . . . with human meaning and social content" [20]).

Other notes of anecdotal nature were published in magazines and newspapers, for the most part in Lima. These notes appear, in general, at the time the books were published and do not offer a rigorous critical focus. Studies that are exclusively concerned with science fiction texts are virtually nonexistent. It is necessary, then, to fill this void. However, as indicated before, science fiction in Adolph should be studied in relation to social, political, historical, and religious problems. The author himself, in his preface to *Mañana fuimos felices*, points out the importance of the social aspect of his works (12–13). This facet, far from making Adolph a propaganda or pamphlet writer, establishes him as an author concerned about the multiple—social, political, economical—problems that afflict Peru. And although it is not easy to propose solutions—such as the option of self-destruction—Adolph does not choose the evasion or escapism that can accompany a genre like science fiction. (This does not exclude the use of humor, the fantastic, or the magical as a means to counteract the tedium of existence.) In his concern for social and economic issues, Adolph includes all regions of the country—not just the capital—in writing about Peru and, at the same time, situates his country in an international context. In this way, he reveals the multiple existing connections in a world that is more and more dependent on long-distance means of communication and economies that transcends borders.

José Alberto Bravo de Rueda

Works

"La asunción de Víctor." *Los montruos que vendrán*, ed. Rodolfo Alonso. Buenos Aires: Rodolfo Alonso, 1973, 101–8.

Cuentos del relojero abominable. Lima: Universo, 1974.

"El día que saltaron los chinos," in *El cuento peruano 1975–1979*, ed. Ricardo González Vigil. Lima: Ediciones Copé, 1983, 215–20.

"The Falsifier," trans. Andrea Bell, in *Cosmos Latinos: An Anthology of Science Fiction from Latin America and Spain*, ed. Andrea Bell and Yolanda Molina-Gavilán. Middletown, CT: Wesleyan University Press, 2003, 154–57.

Hasta que la muerte. Lima: Moncloa-Campodónico, 1971.

Invisible para las fieras. Lima: Instituto Nacional de Cultura, 1972.

Mañana fuimos felices. Lima: Instituto Nacional de Cultura, 1975.

Mañana, las ratas. Lima: Azul-CEDEP, 1984.

"Los mensajeros," in *Antología del joven relato latinoamericano*. Buenos Aires: Compañía General Fabril Editora, 1972, 208–11.

"Nosotros, no," in *Ciencia ficción: cuentos hispanoamericanos*, ed. José María Ferrero. Buenos Aires: Huemul, 1993, 61–64. Also in, *Antología del joven relato latinoamericano*. Buenos Aires: Compañía General Fabril Editora, 1972, 206–8.

"Persistencia," in *Lo mejor de la ciencia ficción latinoamericana*, ed. Bernard Goorden and R. E. Van Vogt. Buenos Aires: Hyspamérica, 1988, 157–59.

El retorno de Aladino. Lima: Eudeli, 1968.

Criticism

Belevák, Harry. "José B. Adolph," in *Antología del cuento fantástico peruano*, ed. Harry Belevák. Lima: U.N.M.S.M., 1977, 160.

Bosco, María Angélica. "Los temas y los hombres," in *Antología del joven relato latinoamericano*. Buenos Aires: Compañía General Fabril Editora, 1972, 17–20.

González Vigil, Ricardo. "José B. Adolph," in *El cuento peruano 1975–1979*, ed. Ricardo González Vigil. Lima: Ediciones Copé, 1983, 213–14.

Juan Nepomuceno Adorno (1807–1880)

MEXICO

Juan Nepomuceno Adorno was born and died in Mexico City. A philosopher, mechanic, and inventor, he dedicated his energies to the study of the hydrography, meteorology and hygiene, of the Valley of Mexico. He wrote several books on these topics, and also designed a drainage project for the capital. He traveled in Europe between 1848 and 1859 and presented some of his inventions—such as the melograph piano or pianola that when played, recorded music on a roll of paper and then printed it out—at the Paris World's Fair in 1855. He explained the mechanism of this device in his book *Melographie oú nouvelle notation musicale* (Melography or new musical writing, 1855). He also published his *Introduction to the Harmony of the Universe or Principles of Physico-Harmonic Geometry* in London (1851), which he translated into Spanish in a revised and enlarged edition upon his return to Mexico, publishing it as *Armonía del Universo: sobre los principios de la armonía física y matemática* (Harmony of the universe; On the principles of physical and mathematical harmony, 1862). Although his original intention was for his works to be published after his death, only the second volume of his work was published posthumously, in 1882. He was well-known among Mexican intellectual circles of the time. He also lectured in Barcelona on a topic he called his "providential philosophy," which clearly revealed (as is seen in his writing) the influence on his thinking of the utopian and philosophic works of Charles Fourier and Count Saint-Simon.

Adorno had a blind faith in all types of mechanisms, believing that they could make the small- and large-scale ideals of humanity a reality as long as they were in tune with the aims of divine Providence. He lacked confidence in legal reforms that tried to achieve the same things through institutional bureaucracy. He invented and patented all sorts of machines, including a weapon that could fire up to 70 rounds of ammunition per minute, a "rapidinámico" (superdynamic) railway, and devices for manufacturing cigarettes, cigars, and shredded tobacco. He attempted to modify metallurgical procedures and mechanisms and designed a steam mill in Mexico City, earthquake-safe houses, devices for pumping floodwater from dwellings, and three-wheeled antirollover armored vehicles. None of his inventions was actually produced since when his patents where checked by experts the scope of his ingenuousness was revealed. He habitually dismissed the importance of significant technical, financial, or assembly problems that kept his visionary inventions from becoming a reality. During a lecture given in 1873 on social, political, and economic problems in Mexico, he presented 16 new inventions, including a machine that would produce counterfeit-proof documents for the national treasury, but none of them was ever commissioned.

Upon feeling misunderstood by his contemporaries he turned to his writing, and in his providential philosophy foresaw a highly promising future time when his advice would be heeded and people would embrace the reforming and progressive power of machines. He divided history into 12 stages that ranged from the primitive and natural to the constitutional (in which he lived) and through several other stages until reaching the last stage of human evolution. Here, man returns to his natural status, simple and pure yet enriched by all sciences and arts; having conquered all vices and passions, he would fulfill the his destiny as designed by the Creator. According to Adorno, not all societies would reach this stage at the same time, but those arriving first would help all others to attain it. Then, there will be philosophic federations that preach tolerance and embrace the fraternal bond of human societies. Tyrannies with be gradually nullified, international problems will be solved diplomatically, and war would be completely eradicated. As he couldn't, nor did he pretend to, provide a date or any further information about when this stage might be attained, he stated that the only way he had to foresee what will happen was through "intuitive poetry." He thus named a literary genre that now we undoubtedly call "science fiction." And, in fact, in a chapter of his *Armonía del Universo* titled "El remoto porvenir" ("The Distant Future"), he describes, in an ecstatic tone, the spectacle he imagines to behold before him: in the future, humanity will be able to communicate from one end of the world to the other; underwater telegraph lines will encircle the globe, greatly facilitating action and thought; steam, electricity, magnetism, and the earth's own heat will provide man with prodigious force; gas and electricity will turn night into day; huge vessels will traverse the oceans and human flight will take to the skies to complete the potential of human power, men and women will have equal rights, marriages will be programmed, and sexual instinct would be limited to avoid the excess and unnecessary waste of energy—he even speaks of a technique very similar to today's genetic engineering.

Miguel Ángel Fernández Delgado

Works

Armonía del Universo: sobre los principios de la armonía física y matemática. Mexico City, 1862.

"The Distant Future," trans. Andrea Bell, in *Cosmos Latinos: An Anthology of Science Fiction from Latin America and Spain*, ed. Andrea Bell and Yolanda Molina-Gavilán. Middletown, CT: Wesleyan University Press, 2003, 24-35.

Criticism

Fernández Delgado, Miguel Ángel. "Juan Nepomuceno Adorno y la poesía intuitiva o ciencia ficción mexicana del siglo XIX." *Umbrales: Literatura fantástica de México* 41 (1999): 2–21.

González Casanova, Pablo. *Un utopista mexicano.* Mexico City: Secretaría de Educación Pública, Lecturas Mexicanas, 1987. (Includes in the appendix the entire text of "El remoto porvenir.")

Trujillo Muñoz, Gabriel. "Juan Nepomuceno Adorno: el armonizador del universo," in *Biografías del futuro: la ciencia ficción mexicana y sus autores.* Mexicali, Mexico: Universidad Autónoma de Baja California, 2000, 39–48.

José Agustín (b. 1944)

MEXICO

José Agustín was born in Acapulco, Guerrero in 1944. He has lived in Mexico City since he was a youth, where he now works as a journalist both in the print media and television. He became famous as a literary author through being identified with the *literatura de la onda* (new wave or "hip" literature) generation of writers of the 1960s and early 1970s that includes Gustavo Sainz (b. 1940) and many others. In fact, Agustín has come to be considered, with Sainz, as one of the paradigmatic figures of *Onda* writing. Among his most well-known books are the novels *La tumba* (The grave, 1964), *De perfil* (Profile, 1966), *Se está haciendo tarde (final en laguna)* (It's getting late [Lacunal ending], 1973), and the short-story collection *Inventando que sueño* (Inventing that I dream, 1969). Agustín has received grants or scholarships from the Centro Mexicano de Escritores (Mexican writer's center, 1967), the Guggenheim Foundation (1977), and the Fulbright Commission (1978).

In 1986 he published *Cerca del fuego* (Near the fire), which together with *Ciudades desiertas* (Deserted cities, 1984)—the chronicle of a Mexican in the United States during the Reagan era—represent a step forward in his narrative. In *Cerca del fuego*, Agustín creates a novel based on a series of short episodes that narrate the story of Lucio, who has forgotten the last six years of his life. To recoup his memory he goes in search of his brothers and finds a Mexico City that is in a complete state of chaos. He cannot believe the pollution, corruption, violence, and vileness that he encounters. In confronting his past, Lucio must also confront himself through the memories he slowly recovers. He is the alterego of the average Mexican, who sees the country falling apart around him and realizes that only through a process of purification (in this case by fire) can he find redemption both for himself and for a Mexico—again invaded by the United States—that can yet regenerate itself and survive.

Cerca del fuego is Agustín's only science fiction text and it is obvious that he is not a writer of fantasy, but rather a realist. The text may be classified as a "novelized local-color sketch of Mexico situated in the near future, where the circumstances of national life have changed for the worse." In this Mexico, only memory serves to get a grip on reality. Lucio is a man obsessed with recovering six years of his life, but his struggle also involves a recovery on a much larger scale—that of Mexico, his familiar surroundings, his family, friends, pleasures, and habits. He turns to a psychiatrist to help him untangle his mind, but his loss of memories and sensations and fundamental events in his life seem to be always just out of reach, making it impossible for him to return to who he used to be. With *Cerca del fuego*, Agustín has managed to create a science fiction novel based on the collective fears of the national soul, the nightmare of a history that repeats itself—the invasion by the United States in 1846–1848—in a tomorrow where Mexico has a bleak future as an independent nation. In the novel, the president of Mexico, says devotional prayers every morning, prostrate and facing the direction of the United States embassy. At a distance, Agustín's apocalyptic novel is but a pale reflection of today's Mexico; neither utopian dreams nor catastrophic disasters have occurred, which makes this futuristic view of reality particularly unsettling.

Gabriel Trujillo Muñoz

Work

Cerca del fuego. Mexico City: Plaza y Valdés, 1986, reprint 1991.

Criticism

Schaffer, Susan C. "The Process of Individuation in José Agustín's *Cerca del fuego.*" *Mester* 21.1 (1992): 31–40.
Steele, Cynthia. "Patriarchy and Apocalypse in *Cerca del fuego*, by José Agustín." *Studies in Twentieth-Century Literature* 14.1 (1990): 61–80.

~

Eugenio Alarco (1908–?)

PERU

Eugenio Alarco was born in Lima, Peru in 1908. He studied at the Escuela Nacional de Ingenieros (National school of engineers) and graduated as a civil engineer in 1928. Alarco was a learned man in many areas and his vast knowledge enabled him to reflect on diverse aspects of Peruvian culture and reality. He was the author of a comprehensive eight-volume history of Peru, *El hombre peruano en su historia* (Peruvian man in his history, 1971), in which he studies prehispanic culture and the period of the conquest and colonization under Spanish rule. He also wrote a book of essays on the contemporary social, political, and economic situation in Peru titled *La rebelión de los ejecutivos* (The rebellion of the executives, 1989). In this book, Alarco proposes that political power be controlled by business executives, since the modern country is run like a corporation. He is also the author of a three-volume collection of essays titled *Reflexiones desde el Tercer Mundo* (Reflection from the Third World, 1979–1980).

Alarco's contribution to science fiction is his novel *La magia de los mundos* (The magic of the worlds, 1952), and to a lesser extent another novel, *Los mortales* (The mortals, 1966). In the first, a race from the future that has achieved immortality and the capability of space travel finds two inhabitants of Earth, Angel and Néstor, who have survived an accident in their own ship and are adrift in space. This encounter brings to the fore the conflict between opposing forces: the future and the past, and eternal life and death. Néstor and Angel are the last survivors of a world viewed as primitive, dominated by wars and machinations, which ultimately led to its destruction. According to the visitors from the future—who claim to be from a perfect world—the human race was the victim of its own uncontrolled passions. However, the mortals, mainly Angel, see the other race as weak and insensitive due to the easy life it leads: a world where every whim and desire are satisfied makes it, in no uncertain terms, incapable of love. In the end, Angel is condemned to a mortal life, while Néstor, to whom the race offers the gift of eternal life, prefers instead to sacrifice himself.

In spite of its futurist setting, the novel is conceived with a classical style and spirit. In this sense, Alarco's science fiction can be classified as anachronistic, as much of the themes and the rhetoric echo Homeric writing. The influences of Dante Alighieri (1265–1321) and Miguel de Cervantes (1547–1616) are obviously visible, which only serve to produce an imbalance in the narrative. Science fiction becomes a prop to display classical conflicts.

This tendency is more evident in the novel *Los mortales*. Magic, more than science fiction, predominates in the text. Some of the characters are able to fly, and the many scenes include royal courts with hunchbacks, dwarfs, courtesans, and birds with magic properties. The narrative is structured around long monologues in which the characters defend their ideas and points of view, as in classical dialogue.

In sum, Alarco's work is overdetermined by classical models of rhetoric and a reliance on Greco-Latin mythology. This, added to his excessive use of enclitic pronouns and affected vocabulary, makes for tedious reading. His intent, through the vehicle of science fiction, is to condemn the irrational side of humanity, though his style does not adequately correspond to a discourse of denunciation and nonconformity.

José Alberto Bravo de Rueda

Works

La magia de los mundos. Buenos Aires: n.p., 1952.
Los mortales. Buenos Aires: n.p., 1966.

Elena Aldunate (b. 1925)

CHILE

Elena Aldunate Bezanilla, the only daughter of writer Arturo Aldunate Philips, was born in Santiago, Chile, in 1925. She has complemented her work as a writer with contributions to newspapers and magazines and she has also worked as a scriptwriter for radio and television in Chile. Furthermore, she has participated in and directed literary workshops. For Aldunate, writing is an instrument of communication that helps her overcome introversion and explore questions of time through fiction. It is also a means to express her feminine world and articulate her interest in science fiction. Although she began to publish in the early 1950s with her novel *Candia* (Candia, 1950), it was not until the 1960s that she began to write science fiction, a genre she continues to cultivate up to the present. Her readings of authors such as Ray Bradbury, Olaf Stapledon and Isaac Asimov have influenced her own texts.

Rather than relying on a pseudoscientific discourse, Aldunate's is poetic (Droguett 25). She does not try for credibility in her short stories; she accentuates fantasy. Even when she introduces real places and characters, fantastic elements are present in her texts. There are a few recurrent topics in her works; for instance, fear and curiosity aroused by the unknown. The author emphasizes the need of communication among her characters, who break barriers of time, space, and species to achieve it. This desire to communicate is represented at times in a setting where beings from different and distant worlds come into peaceful contact with one another. Communication is the means to overcome the loneliness in which some of her characters live. Sometimes loneliness helps the author create an exhausted image of the future as a period of extinction and Darwinian evolution. Nevertheless, the future is not always viewed in negative terms. It is also seen as the period in which utopia is achieved. With this double vision of the future, Aldunate's science fiction undergoes a change with regard to the type of reader for whom her texts are meant. Even though she began writing science fiction for adults with "Juana y la cibernética" (Juana and cybernetics, 1963), from 1987 onwards she wrote mainly for children and adolescent audiences. The novel *Del cosmos las quieren vírgenes* (The cosmos wants virgins, 1977) is key in marking her change of audience. However, her passion for juvenile literature is present in some stories (not necessarily scientific fantasies) that precede this novel. Despite this passion, Aldunate has written stories of raw imaginative harshness. In "Juana y la cibernética," included in *El señor de las mariposas* (The lord of the butterflies, 1967), the protagonist overcomes her routine and sexual frustration by coming into intimate contact with the machine with which she is working. This contact reaches a degree of masochist paroxysm in which the protagonist, freeing herself from the norms of behavior, wants to feel to the extreme everything that is prohibited—to the point of self-destruction. This text was Aldunate's debut in the genre of science fiction. Although it is a story in which neither the fantastic or the unreal has a place, it presents many of the topics with which the author is obsessed. "Juana y la cibernética" adheres to a real world in which human beings in a machine shop are made aware of their loneliness. There are no scientific or technological advances that place the work in the future. Technological fantasy is introduced not from the narrator's perspective, but from the point of view of the protagonist who falls into a hallucinatory state. The personification of the machines, which happens in the mind of the character, leads to a sadomasochist orgy between the woman and the machine. "Juana y la cibernética" thus relates to those technological fictions in which the human being loses all control under the will of some sort of artificial intelligence (Pierce 95).

Despite the fact that lyricism dominates Aldunate's writings, she carefully explores the dehumanized world of machines. In "El ingenio" (The machine), part of the collection *Angélica y el delfín* (Angelica and the dolphin, 1976), the machine is also a central character in the story. There is a detailed description of a crewless spaceship that visits Mars for the first time, where some creatures await the arrival of man as a messianic event. The tremendous efforts made by the ship in order to photograph the surface of the planet are described with a wealth of detail. This space adventure confirms one of the author's obsessions: that of insisting that man is not alone in the universe.

Space travel is the story line in several of her works; sometimes it is the earthlings who depart for other worlds; other times it is the extraterrestrials who visit the Earth. Like "El ingenio," the stories about space travel show an investigative curiosity toward the unknown and a desire to apprehend the "other." Fear of the unknown and anxiety arise as well. In any case, a pacifist perspective always triumphs, which serves to counteract any possible violence during the encounters between two worlds. "Golo" (Golo, in *El señor de las mariposas*) and "Ela y los terrícolas" (Ela and the earthmen, in *Angélica y el delfín*) respectively narrate a voyage from the Earth to the moon, and from the Earth to Ela, an imaginary planet. "Golo" also touches on the topic of individual isolation, a constant theme in Aldunate's ficiton. Golo, which anticipates the Ur of her children's fiction, is the name of the sole survivor of a highly evolved race that once inhabited the moon. Aldunate does not create hostile extraterrestrials; on the contrary, she humanizes and romanticizes them. Golo represents, despite his highly evolved status, the anguish of loneliness.

"Golo" and "Ela y los terrícolas" advocate a vital understanding between different beings. The earthlings' survival depends on Golo's (and the Ela inhabitants') ability to understand their vital needs. Aldunate obsessively underscores that the instrument to survival is communication, although this is mostly achieved without overtly expressing such through language. Interpreting semiotic codes is the key to communication and survival in both stories. After the extraterrestrials manage to interpret the signs of a dehydrated body, the Elanians figure out the formula for water, an unknown on their planet. A similar communication process is narrated in "Golo," where a dog that has been launched into space survives the lack of oxygen and dehydration thanks to its body language being picked up immediately by Golo, who saves it. Likewise, the discovery of interspecies' nonlinguistic modes of communication is presented in "Angélica y el delfín," a short story that won a prize sponsored by the Club de Ciencia Ficción (Science fiction club) of Madrid in 1975. In this case, the author takes on the topic of dolphin intelligence.

The distress caused by the lack of communication among human beings who are separated by time occupies a prominent place in "La bella durmiente" (Sleeping beauty, in *Angélica y el delfín*). The story belongs to a long intertextual tradition of both children's literature and science fiction because it can be linked to *When the Sleeper Wakes* (1889) by H. G. Wells. In the story, a group of archaeologists, who belong to a highly evolved civilization in the year 2900, finds the fossilized remains of a woman in a primitive state of hibernation. In their quest to study the past, the scientists set out to wake her. Through scientific-like language, the reanimation of each limb, after a millennium of hibernation, is thoroughly described. Aldunate imagines the loneliness of the fossilized woman as both observed and observer. Although the woman awakes in a utopian world in which evil and violent instincts have been abolished, the woman-fossil experiences the terror of feeling alone in the wrong era. In this sense, the representation of a utopian future becomes, paradoxically, a nightmare. The desire to overcome the time barriers that prevent communication between human beings is a clear concern in the text. The story also examines the concept of utopia by questioning the abolition of instincts and the nonexistence of old age, death, and illness as an ideal situation.

This double vision of the future (utopian and nightmarish) marks a difference regarding the reader of Aldunate's texts. The novel *Del cosmos las quieren vírgenes* is typical in this way. The story, like the collection of children's stories in which Ur is the protagonist, narrates how extraterrestrials visit our planet. These stories explore the relationships between beings of different origins that always avoid violence. *Del cosmos las quieren vírgenes* combines a genetic fantasy with a cosmic one. From the union of a few chosen earthlings and certain extraterrestrials, some supermen and superwomen will be born. These new beings will be in charge of counteracting the destructive power characteristic of humanity throughout history. Sometimes in this novel there is an attempt to imitate the discourse of science. The characters live in a scientific environment. The protagonist's husband is an astronomer at the observatory of Mount Tololo. Despite this, the predominant element in the novel is the fantastic one: blue butterflies appear at just the right time to save the characters.

The four stories of the Ur collection, *Ur . . . y Macarena* (Ur and Macarena, 1988), *Ur . . . y Alejandra* (Ur and Alejandra, 1989), *Ur . . . e Isidora* (Ur and Isidora, 1992), and *Ur . . . y Maríaceleste* (Ur and Maríaceleste, 1995), have a similar structure. Ur is a malleable form of energy that comes in contact with some children to teach them about the natural history of the Earth. Furthermore, Ur reveals to them the need to care for and respect the planet. At the same time, Ur wants to learn and experience the sensory wealth of the human body. The author presents, without taboos, topics like sexuality and the psychical/erotic evolution of the teenage body. Aldunate's stories fit a pacifist and ecological tendency. She is worried about violence and about the possible destruction of the planet. This dual interest is obvious in almost all her science fiction work. It is even more obvious in her juvenile science fiction stories, which contain a strong educational focus.

With the exception of a few scattered notes and reviews in newspapers, there has been no critical appraisal of Aldunate's works. Nevertheless, her books offer a variety of interesting prospects for study that range from science fiction to children's literature and feminist studies.

Mercedes Guijarro-Crouch

Works

Angélica y el delfín. Santiago: Aconcagua, 1976.
Del cosmos las quieren vírgenes. Santiago: Zig-Zag, 1977.
El señor de las mariposas. Santiago: Zig-Zag, 1967.
Ur . . . y Alejandra. Santiago: Editorial Universitaria, 1989.
Ur . . . e Isidora. Santiago: Editorial Universitaria, 1992.
Ur . . . y Macarena. Santiago: Editorial Universitaria, 1988.
Ur . . . y Maríaceleste. Santiago: Editorial Universitaria, 1995.

Criticism

Droguett, Alfaro. "Elena Aldunate o la anticipación." *Las últimas noticias* [Santiago] (19 March 1997): 25.
Pierce, John J. *Great Themes of Science Fiction*. Westport, CT: Greenwood Press, 1987.
Szmulewicz, Efraín. *Diccionario de la literatura chilena*, 2nd ed. Santiago: Andrés Bello, 1984.

Enrique Araya Gómez (b. 1912)

CHILE

Enrique Araya, of German and Spanish ancestry, was born in Santiago, Chile on September 28, 1912. He spent his childhood in the capital as well as in Chile's arid north and was educated at the Colegio de los Padres Franceses. He went on to study first at the Universidad Católica and later at the law school of the Universidad de Chile, finishing his degree in 1947 with a thesis on the economic aspects of alcohol legislation.

Araya spent much of his professional life as a civil servant, and in that capacity had ample scope for exercising his natural gifts of observation and analysis. He developed an intimate and lightly humorous way of writing about what he observed in himself and others, which brought him immediate success as a novelist. His first effort, *La luna era mi tierra* (The moon was my earth, 1948), which, in spite of its title, is not a work of science fiction, quickly went through several editions and won the prize for best new novel in a literary contest sponsored by the city of Santiago. Araya cultivated his particular blend of satire, irony, and farce in a dozen subsequent books, many of which build on personal anecdotes and are characterized by a breezy and accessible narrative style through which the sting of a sudden penetrating critique of society can nevertheless be felt. In addition to prose fiction, he wrote numerous plays and published a volume of short stories, *La tarjeta de Dios* (God's calling card, 1974). He was a cultural attaché for the Chilean government in Argentina, Mexico, and Peru, and had been a member of the Playwright's Society, the Writer's Society of Chile, and the Pen Club.

Only one of Araya's literary works can be classified as science fiction, for as was typical of Chilean writers before the 1960s, he did not consider himself as a science fiction author or openly acknowledge the genre's influence on his work. The novel in question, *El caracol y la diosa* (The snail and the goddess, 1950) has as its fictional framework a thesis presented by a student of medical law. The thesis tells the story of a young man—now an inmate in a mental institution—whose mother hid him in a cubbyhole in the chimney of their house so that he would not be drafted to fight in World War III. While confined in the chimney the young man learns to use his mind in order to travel about in the company of X-Z 482, a being from the year 20,912. Many of the novel's chapters recount the pair's disembodied journeys through space and time on a series of observational adventures. Their trips become the basis of lengthy conversations on diverse topics in philosophy and metaphysics. Each adventure closes with the young man's consciousness rejoining the body he left behind in the chimney hideaway, until one day, his mother having died some days ago, the police discover his refuge and haul him off to an asylum.

The protagonist's trips into the future acquaint him with a world both familiar and profoundly strange, a world in which human biology has been altered so radically that fundamental processes such as eating and eliminating have been rendered superfluous. The products of astonishing new technologies permeate society, most of it designed to make life more efficient and pleasurable for the humans, androids, and other beings that populate the future. Technology, however, has failed to impress the snail and the goddess, the book's title characters, and in them we see a strong critique of two aspects of modern life. The goddess is an enormous sentient computer that the young man meets on one of his journeys. She represents the imperfect union of the human and the machine, for though she is an inorganic construct, she is run by a crew of humans. The humans are the spark that brings the goddess to life, for they operate the complex machinery of which she is made. Sphinx-like, the human-computer goddess exists in order to answer all questions put to her, but the imperfection of her fusion with humans becomes evident in her limitations. She can only answer factual questions, is incapable of that particularly human attribute—the appreciation of beauty, and is devoid of true creativity. In her eyes, the human-computer mix is a failure, for those qualities that make humans unique are not transferable to machines. She suffers deeply, "a prisoner in the cage of logic and truth" (120) and feels bitterly toward mankind. In her quest for self-knowledge, she asks whether intelligence—and indeed her own identity—is merely the outcome of throwing switches or if she truly is more than the sum of her parts. But the goddess is plotting her revenge. She will make her creators know her suffering by nursing humanity on "her poisonous milk, science" (121). The warning is clear: slavish devotion to science, to progress and rational thinking, will destroy our appreciation of beauty and rob us of the gift of creativity. The irony implied by the goddess's situation is that, as we chase after factual knowledge and technological progress in the belief that it will make us godlike, we lose that which is godlike in us now. It is a theme that will prove to be among the most cherished by later science fiction authors in Latin America.

The character of the snail plays a much smaller role in the novel, and the criticism he makes of society is a variation on the sentiments expressed by the goddess. Toward the end of the novel, the young man discovers the snail crawling along the wall in his chimney refuge. Their subsequent conversation revolves around the nature of progress, with the snail taking the position that his species is far superior to more evolutionarily advanced ones because the latter live such harried, fast-paced lives that they have no time to be contemplative. Taken with the goddess's comments, the snail's observations further develop an important theme in *El caracol y la diosa*—namely that modern life controls and diminishes us. Araya's novel is both an entertaining, well-told story and the platform for many sophisticated ideas. It is certainly one of the most satisfying examples of early Chilean science fiction, heralding the type of writing that would emerge during Chile's first flowering of science fiction (from about 1959 through the early 1970s).

The only other known work of science fiction Enrique Araya has written is a short story, "Minerva," which can be found in Andrés Rojas Murphy's anthology of Chilean science fiction. The story is about an inventor—a physically unattractive man—who creates the ideal wife: a robot who satisfies his every possible physical, emotional, and intellectual desire. He invites a friend from Santiago to visit them in New York. The visitor falls madly in love with the robot, but all ends happily when the inventor builds a redheaded robot-wife for his friend to enjoy. It is difficult to attribute any deeper themes to the tale, and the writing style is not as accomplished or memorable as that found in other works by Araya. This story, which may strike a modern reader as a product of the male-fantasy school of pulp-era science fiction, implies a cavalier attitude on Araya's part toward the genre—an attitude still shared by many Latin American readers, writers, and publishers. *El caracol y la diosa* is a more stylishly written and intellectually powerful work than "Minerva," but then it was never classified as science fiction and hence is likely to have been treated by the author as a more "worthwhile" project.

                                                                                Andrea Bell

Works

El caracol y la diosa. Santiago: Zig-Zag, 1950.
La luna era mi tierra. Santiago, Distribuidora Literaria,1948. Reprints, Santiago: Zig-Zag, 1949; Santiago: Editorial Andrés Bello, 1982; Santiago: Planeta, 1992.
"Minerva," in *Antología de cuentos chilenos de ciencia ficción y fantasía*, ed. Andrés Rojas Murphy. Santiago: Editorial Andrés Bello, 1988, 36–49.
La tarjeta de Dios. Santiago: Gabriela Mistral,1974.

Criticism

Bell, Andrea, and Moisés Hassón. "Prelude to the Golden Age: Chilean Science Fiction from 1900–1959." *Science Fiction Studies* 66 (1995): 187–97.
Lindo, Hugo. "Enrique Araya, humorista chileno." *Cultura* 4 (1955): 103–6.
Silva Castro, Raúl. *Panorama de la novela chilena (1843–1953).* Mexico City: Fondo de Cultura Económica, 1955.

Juan José Arreola (1918–2001)

MEXICO

Juan José Arreola was born in Zapotlán el Grande (today called Ciudad Guzmán), Jalisco in 1918. He showed an interest in the world of art from early childhood and first began expressing that interest in theater, as an actor. He later turned to literature and at the age of 18 went to Mexico City where he became involved in the literary circle of the most famous writers of the time, Ali Chumacero, Xavier Villaurrutia, and Rodolfo Usigli, among others. He began to publish some of his first stories in 1940. Four years later, he traveled to Paris where he became enthralled by French literature. Upon his return to Mexico, he began working for the Fondo de Cultura Económica in publishing and he also entered the Colegio de México as a student of philosophy.

During the late 1940s and early 1950s Arreola and Juan Rulfo—also from the state of Jalisco—began to transform Mexican literature, taking it in new directions, away from the epic realist narratives of the Revolution and the *novela indigenista* (novels based on the indigenous experience). While Rulfo created an autonomous world in his novel *Pedro Páramo* (1955) where the living and dead coexist, Arreola wrote stories of the fantastic wherein anything can happen. With a concise prose and a flavor for the bizarre his stories reveal not only his mastery of language, but a prodigious and unstoppable imagination. His extraordinary stories are gathered in several collections: *Varia invención* (Varied invention, 1949), *Confabulario* (Confabulario, 1952), *Bestiario* (Bestiary, 1958), and *Palindroma* (Palindrome, 1971). His only novel, *La feria* (The fair), which is really more a collection of stories, appeared in 1963 and earned for the author the Xavier Villaurrutia award. During the early 1960s, Arreola stopped writing fiction and dedicated himself to translating poetry and to promoting culture via television, thus becoming quite a public personality, easily recognizable from his eccentric hats and capes. In addition to the above-mentioned award, he also won the National Award for Journalism (1977), the National Award for Linguistics and Literature (1979), and the UNAM Award (1987).

Although his entire oeuvre can be classified as fantastic literature, only some of his stories may be considered as pertaining to science fiction. Those that do, however, are masterpieces of the genre and can be counted among the very best of science fiction writing not only in Mexico but worldwide. Among such stories are "Flash," "Alarma para el año 2000" (Alarm for the Year 2000), "Interview," "Los monos" (The monkeys), and "Informe de Liberia" (Report from Liberia) from *Varia invención*; and "En verdad os digo" (In truth I tell you), "El guardagujas" (The switchman), "Anuncio" (Announcement), "Baby H.P.," and "Pablo" from *Confabulario*. These texts comprise a body of works that are among the most festive, hilarious, and innovative works of science fiction in Latin America, and can be compared with the works of Argentines Adolfo Bioy Casares and Jorge Luis Borges of the same time period.

In general, Arreola's science fiction stories rely on the technique of proposing what would happen if a normal situation were carried to extreme circumstances. For example, the comforts of modern life taken to the extreme with the invention of the Baby H.P.—the ultimate household appliance–nanny–energy source. In "Anuncio," Arreola pokes fun at the barrage of publicity made possible through the advent of mass media that is used to sell the "ideal woman," who is turned into little more than a product herself by such practices. In other texts, parallel universes appear, as in "El guardagujas," or unborn children wage a crusade against birth, preferring instead to remain where they are. This story predates by almost 20 years a story by Brian W. Aldiss that explores a similar topic. In another story, "En verdad os digo," Arreola presents his character Arpad Niklaus, a wise man who promises all the rich people on the planet the salvation of their souls. He is able to do so because of his scientific invention that enables him to dissemble a camel and make it pass through the eye of a needle in a stream of electrons. A receiver at the other end reassembles the electrons from the molecular level on up until the camel is returned to its original state. In "Pablo" he relates the tale of a being capable of going forward and backward in time to see the most distant things in space and time. He ends up by committing suicide so that the universe can begin anew.

Arreola is, ultimately, a storyteller of the future, and as such he is a moralist who is concerned for human beings and humanity in general. However, his stories of the future do not contain an overt moral. As in the theater, they only provide a space where the voice and image of man are magnified and echoed back to us.

Gabriel Trujillo Muñoz

Works

"Baby H. P.," in *El futuro en llamas: cuentos clásicos de la ciencia ficción mexicana*, ed. Gabriel Trujillo Muñoz. Mexico City: Vid, 1997, 109–11. English version as "Baby H. P.," trans. Andrea Bell, in *Cosmos Latinos: An Anthology of Science Fiction from Latin America and Spain*, ed. Andrea Bell and Yolanda Molina-Gavilán. Middletown, CT: Wesleyan University Press, 2003, 59–60.

Bestiario. Mexico City: Universidad Nacional Autónoma de México, 1958.

Confabulario. Mexico City: Fondo de Cultura Económica, 1952. English version as *Confabulario and Other Inventions*, trans. George D. Schade. Austin: University of Texas Press, 1964.

Confabulario total, 1941–1961. Mexico City: Fondo de Cultura Económica, 1962.

"En verdad os digo," in *Visiones periféricas: antología de la ciencia ficción mexicana*, ed. Miguel Ángel Fernández Delgado. Mexico City: Lumen, 2001, 47–50.

Narrativa completa. Mexico City: Alfaguara, 1997.

Palindroma. Mexico City: Joaquín Mortiz, 1971.

Varia invención. Mexico City: Tezontle, 1949.

Criticism

Acker, Bertie. *El cuento mexicano contemporáneo: Rulfo, Arreola y Fuentes; temas y cosmovisión*. Madrid: Playor, 1984, 59–112.

Bente, Thomas O. "'El guardagujas' de Juan José Arreola: ¿sátira política o indagación metafísica." *Cuadernos americanos* 185 (1972): 205–12.

Burt, John R. "This Is No Way to Run a Railroad: Arreola's Allegorical Railroad and a Possible Source." *Hispania* 71 (1988): 806–11.

Chávarri, Raúl. "Arreola en su varia creación." *Cuadernos hispanoamericanos* 242 (1970): 418–25.

Cluff, Russell M., and L. Howard Quakenbush. "Juan José Arreola," in *Latin American Writers*, 3 vols., ed. Carlos A. Solé and María Isabel Abreu. New York: Scribner's, 1989, 3:1229–36.

Gilgen, Read G. "Absurdist Techniques in the Short Stories of Juan José Arreola." *Journal of Spanish Studies: Twentieth Century* 8 (1980): 67–77.

Glantz, Margo. "Juan José Arreola y los bestiarios," in *Esguince de cintura*. Mexico City: Consejo Nacional para la Cultura y las Artes, 1994, 86–95.

González-Arauzo, Angel. "Ida y vuelta al *Confabulario*." *Revista iberoamericana* 65 (1968): 103–7.

Herz, Theda Mary. "Las fuentes cultas de la sátira del *Confabulario*." *Hispanófila* 72 (1981): 31–49.

Heusinkveld, Paula R. "Juan José Arreola: Allegorist in an Age of Uncertainty." *Chasqui* 13.2–3 (1984): 33–43.

Jaén, Didier T. "Transformación y literatura fantástica: 'El guardagujas' de Juan José Arreola." *Texto crítico* 26–27 (1983): 159–67.

Menton, Seymour. "Juan José Arreola and the Twentieth-Century Short Story." *Hispania* 42 (1959): 295–308.

Ortega, José. "Etica y estética en algunos cuentos de *Confabulario*." *Sin nombre* 13.3 (1983): 52–59.

Ramírez, Arthur, and Fern L. Ramírez. "Hacia una bibliografía de y sobre Juan José Arreola." *Revista iberoamericana* 108–109 (1979): 651–67.

Washburn, Yulan M. *Juan José Arreola*. Boston: Twayne, 1983.

Julio Assman (dates unknown)

CHILE

Julio Assman published the only work that is attributable to him under the pseudonym R. O. Land. The title of his 1927 novel, *Tierra firme* (Terra firma) proclaims its identity through the subtitle *novela futurista* (futuristic novel). Although today a forgotten text that is difficult to find outside of Chile, *Tierra firme* nonetheless played a part in the inception of science fiction in Chile. Assman's novel is one of a modest number of nonrealist fiction works that managed to be published while realism still utterly dominated the national literary scene. It is a futuristic utopian fiction that, like David Perry's *Ovalle: el 21 de abril del año 2031* (Ovalle: April 21, 2031 [1933]), presented Chileans with a vigorously optimistic blueprint for society's moral and material evolution.

Assman wrote his novel during a period when Chileans were experiencing—with a mixture of excitement and trepidation—the social upheavals and technological innovations that had been rapidly transforming other parts of the world during the early decades of the new century. In *Tierra firme*, he extrapolates from the marvelous inventions and radical ideas that were capturing the imagination of young intellectuals in order to forecast the near-future rebirth of Chile into a socially progressive paradise, the product of personal initiative coupled with enlightened governance, structured upon ethical thinking and fueled by great technological advances.

The anecdotal framework of the novel is rather slight, for Assman's project was to communicate ideas rather than tell an engaging story. Narrated in the first person, the story is about an unnamed scientist who unwittingly plays a role in the death of his cousin. Already feeling profoundly disillusioned by life in the 1920s, the scientist suggests an unorthodox sentence to the judge presiding over his case: self-exile in Chile's isolated southern reaches. The judge agrees and sentences another man, Nordsen, who is guilty of fiscal improprieties, to accompany the first gentleman into exile. The narrator then goes on to describe the two men's lives on a southern island. Thanks to their discovery of an important mineral, they are allowed to develop a small mining enterprise in cooperation with the state. This is their chance to implement new models of social organization, and over the years a veritable utopian society blossoms. Though borrowing from some of the theoretical ideals of communism and fascism, this new society is neither the one nor the other; rather, it a postfeudal hybrid of the two, where land and resources are owned by the state but are distributed in perpetuity to individuals who promise to abide by certain principles such as collectivism, equality, and respect for the environment and for others. Civil service is obligatory, but it takes the form of social work rather than conscription into a military.

One day in 1950 the narrator is taken to visit the mainland by his long-lost son. This is his first chance to witness the changes that have taken place in his homeland since he withdrew from it almost 30 years previous. To his delight, he finds that society at large has undergone the same sort of utopian transformation that he had overseen on his island. New laws—the product of an enlightened social philosophy—endeavor to provide all with a better standard of life and to ensure that all will contribute their efforts toward the common good. Moreover, many technological advances have brought about positive changes in the areas of transportation, communication, and the environment. Indeed, the dedication to environmental protection is one of *Tierra firme*'s more remarkable features. In the book, colonies of people leave the cities in order to live in greater commun- ion with nature. Recycling is the norm—newspapers, for example, are printed using disappearing ink, making it much easier to reuse the paper—and the pre- dominant modes of transportation are ones that do not rely on fossil fuels and are only minimally polluting, such as bicycles, zeppelins, and electric trains.

Tierra firme is a decidedly optimistic imagining of Chile's future. In contrast to the violent social upheavals that were redefining Europe and the Americas dur- ing the early nineteen hundreds, it posits a nonviolent revolution grounded in a sort of humane pragmatism and made real through the wonders of science. A responsible government directs a citizenry inspired by the belief that if they do not cooperate, respect one another, and take care of the natural world, they risk losing everything. Assman set his book in the near future—a sign both that he hoped to encourage his fellow Chileans to act quickly, and that he believed in the near-term attainability of his dream.

Andrea Bell

Work

Tierra firme. Santiago: Imprenta y Librería "Cisneros," 1927.

Criticism

Bell, Andrea and Moisés Hassón. "Prelude to the Golden Age: Chilean Science Fiction from 1900–1959." *Science Fiction Studies* 66 (1995): 187–97.

Juan-Jacobo Bajarlía (b. 1914)

ARGENTINA

Juan-Jacobo Bajarlía was born in Buenos Aires, in the bosom of a middle-class family. When he was an infant, his family moved to Santiago, Chile, where he attended primary school. His father, a polyglot, and his mother, an avid reader who bought many books for her young son, organized meetings with writers in their home. Bajarlía graduated with a degree in law from the University of Buenos Aires, where he specialized in criminal law. His vast literary output includes poetry, narrative, drama, and essays. However, his first experience with writing came from journalism. In 1945, he began to participate in the activities of the avant-garde group "Arte Concreto-Invención" (Concrete-invention art) led by Tomás Maldonado. This group of painters, sculptors, and poets essentially followed the tenets of Dadaism and European Surrealism without accepting their automatism and incorporating concepts of image and abstraction. Its intention was to move beyond Surrealism as an artistic expression.

In 1948, he founded and edited the journal *Contemporánea* (Contemporary), a publication that centered on surrealism, dodecaphonism, and European abstract art. In addition, in Buenos Aires Bajarlía was a follower of the so-called *signismo* (signism), a literary movement in which he authored the *Manifiestos signistas* (Signist manifestos). It proposed that linguistic signs were insufficient to address contemporary matters and that they should be replaced by ones produced by mechanical instruments in order to signify an age of disintegration of the human condition. Bajarlía's first book was *Literatura de vanguardia* (Avant-garde literature, 1946). It was followed by a poetry collection, *Estereopoemas* (Stereopoems, 1950), and the essay *Notas sobre el barroco: Undurraga y la poesía chilena. Gongorismo y Surrealismo* (Notes on the Baroque: Undurraga and Chilean poetry. Gongorism and Surrealism, 1953). These early publications reveal his preference for Baroque and symbolic aesthetics.

Bajarlía was also an accomplished playwright whose works include *La esfinge* (The sphinx, 1955), *Pierrot* (1956), and *Las troyanas* (The women of Troy, 1956). His play *Los robots* (The robots, 1955), a science fiction drama in one act, was read during a meeting sponsored by the Buenos Aires Town Hall in 1963, and it was broadcast on National Radio. The author called this work a *tragedia mecánica* (mechanical tragedy). This play was followed by *La billetera del Diablo* (The devil's wallet, 1969) and *Teléfora* (Telesphora, 1972), which was also broadcast on National Radio. In 1962, he published a dramatic monologue called *La confesión de Finnegan* (Finnegan's confession) and a play, *Monteagudo* (Monteagudo), which received several distinguished awards including the Municipal Prize for Best New Play awarded by the National Foundation for the Arts, and the Sash of Honor from the Argentine Society of Writers.

An examination of Bajarlía's works enables one to observe several characteristics of his writing—namely, his utilization of the stylistic and thematic conventions of detective fiction and science fiction and fantasy literature. Moreover, he infuses his writing with many references to classical and erudite sources, giving his texts a characteristic encyclopedic intertextuality that requires an active and well-informed reader. *Historia de monstruos* (History of monsters, 1969) represents Bajarlía's first significant treatment of science fiction prose. It is written in a mature, contemplative tone and includes a series of thought-provoking stories and texts on the origins of science fiction such as "La serie del tiempo" (The series of time), "Dos leyendas sobre el tiempo" (Two legends about time), "Robot contra cyborg" (Robot against cyborg), "La máquina del tiempo" (The time machine), "La literatura fantástica" (Fantastic literature), and "El principio de indeterminación de la ciencia-ficción" (The principle of indetermination in science fiction). As a whole, the volume constitutes a compendium of common science-fiction topics: time travel, extraterrestrial beings, the parodic treatment of mythological figures, interplanetary voyages, extraordinary lost civilizations, fantastic beings, and the future and destiny of man.

His poem *Canto a la destrucción* (A song to destruction, 1968) presents a struggle on Earth between robots, which have overtaken the planet, and cyborgs. The last surviving human being holds the key to salvation for the robots but he refuses to help, since he doesn't want to facilitate their domination of Earth. He prefers, instead, that all be destroyed. As if to offer a thematic complement to this text, Bajarlía wrote *Poema de la creación* (Poem of creation) in 1970, which was only published in 1996. He states in the prologue that, obviously, the cybernetic era in which we live demands a different kind of writing, a knowledge that includes the totality of a universe not ruled by random and mystery. Likewise, in 1970 he published *Fórmula al antimundo* (Formula for an antiworld) with a prologue dated a year prior, in which Bajarlía insists that the characteristic themes of science fiction such as time machines, the plurality of worlds, and mass destruction, define the genre. In addition these stories include artificial life forms and the paranormal. The most representative story from this volume is "Los omicritas y el hombre-pez" (The omicrites and the fish-man).

Another collection of stories that fluctuates between the fantastic and science fiction is *El día cero* (Day zero, 1972). Here, Bajarlía explains that "en lo fantástico la naturaleza pierde sus atributos, y en la ciencia-ficción se multiplican y se reestructuran a través de una conciencia sobre el cambio" (in the fantastic, nature loses its attributes, and in science-fiction they multiply and rebuild themselves through an awareness of change [Prologue, 9–10]). The stories are divided into three sections: "La eternidad" (Eternity), "Los mundos simultáneos" (Simultaneous worlds), and "El gran ignorante" (The great ignoramus). These narratives deal with the motifs of dreams, the golem, the end of the world, the fish-man, life on the moon, magic, and the last man.

Under the pen name John J. Batharly, the author published the detective novel *Los números de la muerte* (The numbers of death, 1972), and in the same year, but using his real name, he published *Nuevos límites del infierno* (New limits of hell), a book of poems written between 1963 and 1969. In this latter book, Bajarlía coins the neologism "robotpoema" (robotpoem), which etimologically implies the "inventive structure proper of the robot." This is to be understood not as a robot that uses electronic language, but as one that exists by itself, having lost the memory of being created by man, which has nothing to do with the human concept of poetry. Bajarlía injects a good deal of humor into his texts because he believes that it "es otra de las formas de la poesía" (is another form of poetry [10]). For example, in the last part of the book, titled "Las máquinas copuladoras (1963–1967)" (The copulating machines [1963–1967]), he includes ironic games that incorporate mathematical language: "Robotpoema 1. Aceleración del futuro" (Robotpoem 1. Acceleration of the future), "Robotpoema 2. Multiplicación" (Multiplication), "Robotpoema 4. Compasivo con el hombre" (Compassionate to man), "Robotpoema 6. Principio de indeterminación" (Principle of Indetermination), and "Robotpoema 7. Protección del amor" (Protection of love).

Another exponent of the mixed genres in his writing is the detective novel *El endemoniado señor Rosetti* (The devilish mister Rosetti, 1977), which consists of an Argentine rewriting of the wolf-man legend. At midnight, the creature preys on newborn babies in order to eat their brains. The wolf-man is the seventh consecutive son born to his mother, to which Bajarlía attributes demonic and paranormal qualities in relation to the astral bodies during the transfiguration. This establishes the possibility of criminal acts through telepathic or paranormal powers, including the ability to move objects. The author also uses the fictional strategy of including himself as a character in the novel, using the name Bajarlía-Lynch, who is a criminologist in Buenos Aires.

Sables, historias y crímenes (Cutlasses, stories and crimes, 1983) is based on Juan Manuel de Rosas's second period of government (1832–1852) and rewrites Argentine history of the period using historical documents in endnotes and by developing an intertextual game. The different narrative instances acquire a distinctive tone in this historical-fiction text, especially when one takes into account Bajarlía's declaration that "la historia es el misterio de los pueblos. Ningún héroe pudo dominarla, y ella ha sabido sobreponerse continuamente a todos los acontecimientos, cercenando cabezas y obliterando el tiempo" (history is the mystery of the people. No hero was able to dominate it, and it has known how to continuously overcome all events, lopping off heads and obliterating time [123]). This kind of gothic aesthetics, so appreciated in the River Plate region, and evident in much of Bajarlía's fiction, also appears in his book-length essays *Drácula, el vampirismo y Bram Stoker* (Dracula, vampirism, and Bram Stoker, 1992) and *H. P. Lovecraft: el horror sobrenatural* (H. P. Lovecraft: Supernatural horror, 1996).

Following the tradition set by Jorge Luis Borges and Enrique Anderson Imbert, Bajarlía creates in his literature a number of textual games that comprise a quest for metaphysical expression. This, in addition to the wide gamut of influences and erudite intertextual references in his writing, contributes to making Bajarlía's literature more fit for the intellectually astute reader than the average fan of science fiction. Nevertheless, his writing has much to offer anyone who attempts the voyage.

María Alejandra Rosarossa

Works

Canto a la destrucción. Buenos Aires: Puma, 1968.

"La civilización perdida," in *Cuentos argentinos de ciencia ficción.* Buenos Aires: Editorial Merlín, 1967, 7–16.

La confesión de Finnegan, in *Teatro de una voz.* Buenos Aires: Cuadernos del Siroco, 1962, 229–37.

Cuentos de crimen y misterio, ed. Juan-Jacobo Bajarlía. Buenos Aires: Jorge Alvarez, 1964.

"Desde la oscuridad," in *Los universos vislumbrados: antología de ciencia-ficción argentina,* ed. Jorge A. Sánchez, intro. by Elvio E. Gandolfo. Buenos Aires: Ediciones Andrómeda, 1995, 125–30. Also in *Cuentos con humanos, androides y robots,* ed. Elena Braceras. Buenos Aires: Colihue, 2000, 59–63.

El día cero. Buenos Aires: Emecé, 1972.

Drácula, el vampirismo y Bram Stoker. Buenos Aires: Almagesto, 1992.

El endemoniado señor Rosetti. Buenos Aires: Emecé, 1977. Reprint with the title *Hombre Lobo: El endemoniado señor Rosetti.* Mexico City: Universo, 1980. Reprint with original title, Buenos Aires: Almagesto, 1994.

Estereopoemas. Buenos Aires: Ediciones los Tres Vientos, 1950.

Fórmula al antimundo. Buenos Aires: Galerna, 1970.

Historia de monstruos. Buenos Aires: Ediciones de la Flor, 1969.

H. P. Lovecraft: el horror sobrenatural. Buenos Aires: Almagesto, 1996.

Monteagudo. Buenos Aires: Talía, 1962.

Notas sobre el barroco: Undurraga y la poesía chilena. Góngora y surrealismo. Buenos Aires: Santiago Rueda, 1950.

Nuevos límites del infierno. Buenos Aires: Master Fer, 1972.

Los números de la muerte. Buenos Aires: Acme Agency, 1972. Reprint, Buenos Aires: Ofra, 1978. Titled as *Vudú, secta asesina.* Mexico City: Universo, 1980.

Poema de la creación. Madrid: Grupo Cero, 1996.

Sables, historias y crímenes. Buenos Aires: Bruguera, 1983.

Sadismo y masoquismo en la conducta criminal. Buenos Aires: Abeledo-Perrot, 1959.

"Los sueños del Innominado," in *La ciencia ficción en la Argentina: antología crítica,* ed. Marcial Souto. Buenos Aires: Editorial Universitaria de Buenos Aires, 1985, 59–67.

"La suma de los signos," in *Ciencia ficción: cuentos hispanoamericanos,* ed. José María Ferrero. Buenos Aires: Huemul, 1993, 85–88. Also in *Los argentinos en la luna,* ed. Eduardo Goligorsky. Buenos Aires: Ediciones de la Flor, 1968, 83–87.

Criticism

Interview with Juan-Jacobo Bajarlía. *Umbral tiempo futuro* [Buenos Aires] 5 (1978): 57–66.

Marechal, Leopoldo. Prologue to *Historia de monstruos.* Buenos Aires: Ediciones de la Flor, 1969, 7–8.

Souto, Marcial. *La ciencia ficción en la Argentina.* Buenos Aires: Eudeba, 1985, 63–67.

Adolfo Bioy Casares (1914–1999)

ARGENTINA

Adolfo Bioy Casares was born in Buenos Aires on 15 September 1914. He was the only child of Adolfo Bioy and Marta Casares and enjoyed all the comforts, privileges, and advantages that his parent's wealth had to offer him. He traveled to Europe when he was ten and to the United States at the age of 15, where he claims to have fallen in love with the coat-check girl at a New York hotel. These and many other details of his youth are included in his "auto-cronología," a biographical chronology of events that detail key moments in his life from birth to 1980 (it is reproduced in Levine's *Guía de Bioy Casares*). He further states that he commenced studies at the University of Buenos Aires in 1933, and studied in several different subjects between 1933 and 1935. He dropped out of the university in 1935 and convinced his father to let him move to the family's country estate and run the ranch. In 1932, he met Jorge Luis Borges at the home of Victoria Ocampo, the influential founder and director the cultural/literary magazine *Sur* (South). Bioy and Borges would become lifelong friends and publish many works in collaboration, including their famous *Seis problemas para don Isidro Parodi* (*Six Problems for Don Isidro Parodi*, 1942). He met Victoria Ocampo's sister Silvina, also an accomplished writer and artist, in 1934. The two married in 1940 and had one daughter together. Bioy led an active literary life and was a prolific writer, producing over 40 books and earning many of the most prestigious literary awards. Most of his major works of fiction have been translated into English as well as many other languages. He died on 8 March 1999.

Although he published several works prior to 1940, it was the publication of *La invención de Morel* (*The Invention of Morel*) that year that established Bioy as a writer. In his prologue to it, Borges called it the perfect novel. It earned him his first major award in 1941, the Municipal Prize for Literature granted by the city of Buenos Aires. Other prizes that followed included the National Literature Prize (1969), the Argentine Society of Writers' Sash of Honor (1975), and the crowning achievement for any writer in the Spanish language, the highly prestigious Cervantes Prize in 1990, 50 years after the publication of *La invención de Morel*. Bioy's novel has become a classic text of Hispanic letters, and while he wrote many subsequent texts of equal caliber, none has attained the status of this seemingly simple tale of a man on a deserted island. The main character is a fugitive, who in his escape from the law ends up on an unidentified island. It is not long before he discovers that he is in fact not alone on the island. However, first appearances are not what they seem and strange occurrences lead the man to discover that the people he sees, and who seem not to notice him, are projected images from a machine whose power or activation is controlled by the tides. The protagonist falls in love with the image of a woman, Faustine, and in a desperate effort to remain with her, he decides to enter the flow of images and become part of this alternate reality. Morel, the scientist who created the machine, does not appear. The protagonist finds his diary and notes, which provide an explanation to the machine. The novel often has been compared, as Borges does in his prologue, to H. G. Wells's *The Island of Dr. Moreau* (1896). Bioy's subsequent novel, *Plan de evasión* (*A Plan for Escape*, 1945) also takes place on an island that serves as a penal colony, one very similar to Devil's Island. And like *La invención de Morel*, it presents a series of events that stretch the limits of reality. The plot in this case is much more sinister, involving experimental surgery on prisoners that is intended to change their perception. Instead of seeing only their cell walls, their reality would be altered so that they would perceive instead paradisiacal visions of island beauty. Suzanne Jill Levine has studied both novels at length, specifically as they relate to science fiction (*Guía de Bioy Casares*). Malva E. Filer has likewise examined Bioy's novel *Dormir al sol* (*Asleep in the Sun*, 1973) as a continuation of the author's appropriation of the Dr. Moreau model. She applies Darko Suvin's characterization of science fiction narrative to the text and concludes, quite convincingly, that *Dormir al sol*, like the previous novels, is an excellent example of classic science fiction. To a somewhat lesser extent, the novella *El gran Serafín* (The great seraph, 1967) and novel *Diario de la guerra del cerdo* (*Diary of the War of the Pig*, 1969) may also be read as science fiction texts—the first in its presentation of the end of the world, the second for the depiction of a society where the young attempt to exterminate the aged.

Bioy Casares also wrote a number of excellent science fiction short stories. His "La trama celeste" (The celestial plot, 1948) is considered a classic of the genre and an excellent, original representation of the theme of parallel realities. "Los afanes" (Desires, 1967) is equally representative of the author's work in the genre; in this case he returns to the theme of scientific experimentation, which goes awry and causes havoc. The story also contains two of Bioy's recurring narrative elements: humor, and the presentation of interpersonal relationships. Humor is one of the main ingredients in "El calamar opta por su tinta" (The squid chooses its ink), a story about an alien who finds itself in a small town in the interior of the country.

Science fiction was but one genre that Bioy Casares experimented with, and like his detective fiction, his texts have become classics. Beginning with *La invención de Morel*, he forged a prominent place in the history of Argentine science fiction by taking the foreign and completely naturalizing it into the landscape of national literature with his unique style.

Darrell B. Lockhart

Works

Los afanes. Buenos Aires: Arte Gaglianone, 1983.

"Los afanes," in *Cuentos argentinos de ciencia ficción*. Buenos Aires: Editorial Merlín, 1967, 17–56. Also in *Cuentos con humanos, androides y robots*, ed. Elena Braceras. Buenos Aires: Colihue, 2000, 35–57.

Diario de la guerra del cerdo. Buenos Aires: Emece, 1969. English version as *Diary of the War of the Pig*, trans. Gregory Woodruff. New York: McGraw Hill, 1972.

Dormir al sol. Buenos Aires: Emecé, 1973. English version as *Asleep in the Sun*, trans. Suzanne Jill Levine. New York: Dutton, 1975.

"Esse est percipi," in *Historias futuras: antología de la ciencia ficción argentina*, ed. Adriana Fernández and Edgardo Pígoli. Buenos Aires: Emecé, 2000, 101–5. (With Jorge Luis Borges.)

El gran Serafín. Buenos Aires: Emecé, 1967.

El héroe de las mujeres. Buenos Aires: Emecé, 1978.

Historias fantásticas. Buenos Aires: Emecé, 1972.

La invención de Morel. Buenos Aires: Losada, 1940. English version as *The Invention of Morel, and Other Stories from "La trama celeste,"* trans. Ruth L. C. Simms. Austin: University of Texas Press, 1964.

La invención de Morel. El gran Serafín, ed. Trinidad Barrera. Madrid: Cátedra, 1984.

La invención y la trama: una antología, ed. Marcelo Pichon Rivière. Mexico City: Fondo de Cultura Económica, 1988.

"Otra esperanza," in *Historias futuras: antología de la ciencia ficción argentina*, ed. Adriana Fernández and Edgardo Pígoli. Buenos Aires: Emecé, 2000, 87–100.

Plan de evasión. Buenos Aires: Emecé, 1945. English version as *A Plan for Escape*, trans. Suzanne Jill Levine. New York: Dutton, 1975.

Selected Stories, trans. Suzanne Jill Levine. New York: New Directions, 1994.

La trama celeste. Buenos Aires: Sur, 1948.

"La trama celeste," in *Los universos vislumbrados: antología de ciencia-ficción argentina*, 2nd ed., ed. Jorge A. Sánchez. Buenos Aires: Ediciones Andrómeda, 1995, 83–113. Also in *El cuento argentino de ciencia ficción: antología*, ed. Pablo Capanna. Buenos Aires: Ediciones Nuevo Siglo, 1995, 44–74.

Criticism

Barrera, Trinidad. Introducción. *La invención de Morel. El gran Serafín* by Bioy Casares. Madrid: Cátedra, 1984, 9–84.

Bejel, Emilio, and Luisa María Getz. "La perfección de *La invención de Morel* de Bioy Casares." *Chasqui: revista de literatura latinoamericana* 7.3 (1978): 5–15.

Block de Behar, Luisa. "Una épica de la invención." *Cuadernos hispanoamericanos* 609 (2001): 57–66.

Camurati, Mireya. "Adolfo Bioy Casares," in *Latin American Writers*, 3 vols., ed. Carlos A. Solé and María Isabel Abreu. New York: Scribner's, 1989, 3:1201–8.

———. *Bioy Casares y el alegre trabajo de la inteligencia*. Buenos Aires: Corregidor, 1990.

Curia, Beatriz. *La concepción del cuento en Adolfo Bioy Casares*. Mendoza: Universidad Nacional del Cuyo, 1986.

Filer, Malva E. "*Dormir al sol* de Adolfo Bioy Casares: fechorías de un discípulo porteño del Dr. Moreau." *Alba de América* 6.10–11 (1988): 109–15.

Gallagher, David. "The Novels and Short Stories of Adolfo Bioy Casares." *Bulletin of Hispanic Studies* 52.3 (1975): 247–66.

García, Mara L. "Lo fantástico y el proceso creativo en *La invención de Morel.*" *Signos literarios y lingüísticos* 2.2 (2000): 123–29.

Giacone, Lidia. *Símbolo y mito en Adolfo Bioy Casares*. Buenos Aires: Agon, 1984.

Kovacci, Ofelia. *Espacio y tiempo en la fantasía de Adolfo Bioy Casares*. Buenos Aires: Universidad de Buenos Aires, 1963.

Levine, Suzanne J. *Guía de Bioy Casares*. Madrid: Fundamentos, 1982.

———. "Parody Island: Two Novels by Bioy Casares." *Hispanic Journal* 4.2 (1983): 43–49.

Mac Adam, Alfred J. "Adolfo Bioy Casares: The Lying Compass," in *Modern Latin American Narratives: The Dreams of Reason*. Chicago: University of Chicago Press, 1977, 37–43.
———. "Adolfo Bioy Casares: Satire and Self-Portrait," in *Modern Latin American Narratives: The Dreams of Reason*. Chicago: University of Chicago Press, 1977, 29–36.
Martino, Daniel. *A-B-C de Adolfo Bioy Casares*. Buenos Aires: Emecé, 1989.
Mocega-González, Esther P. "Aproximación a los planos estructurales de *Diario de la guerra del cerdo*." *Chasqui: revista de literatura latinoamericana* 4.2 (1975): 44–50.
Rogachevesky, Jorge R. "Ficción y realidad en *La invención de Morel*." *Latin American Literary Review* 9.18 (1981): 41–51.
Ryden, Wendy. "Bodies in the Age of Mechanical Reproduction: Competing Discourses of Reality and Representation in Bioy Casares's *The Invention of Morel*." *Atenea* 21.1–2 (2001): 193–207.
Snook, Margaret L. "The Narrator as Creator and Critic in *The Invention of Morel*." *Latin American Literary Review* 7.14 (1979): 45–51.
Suárez Coalla, Francisco. *Lo fantástico en la obra de Adolfo Bioy Casares*. Toluca: Universidad Autónoma del Estado de México, 1994.
Tamargo, María Isabel. "*La invención de Morel*: lectura y lectores." *Revista iberoamericana* 42 (1976): 485–95.
———. "*Plan de evasión*: The Loss of Referentiality." *Hispanic Journal* 4.1 (1982): 105–11.
———. *La narrativa de Bioy Casares: el texto como escritura-lectura*. Madrid: Playor, 1983.
Torres Fierro, Danubio. "Las utopías pesimistas de Adolfo Bioy Casares." *Plural* 55 (1976): 47–53.
Ulla, Noemí. *Aventuras de la imaginación: de la vida y los libros de Adolfo Bioy Casares*. Buenos Aires: Corregidor, 1990.
Villordo, Oscar Hermes. *Genio y figura de Adolfo Bioy Casares*. Buenos Aires: Editorial Universitaria de Buenos Aires, 1983.

Ignácio de Loyola Brandão (b. 1936)

BRAZIL

Ignácio de Loyola Brandão was born in Araraquara, a small city in the interior of the state of São Paulo, in 1936. When he was 20 years old he moved to the capital of the state, São Paulo, where he started to work at the newspaper *Ultima Hora* (Last hour). In the eight years between his arrival in São Paulo and the beginning of the military rule after the coup d'état of 1964, Brandão had the opportunity to familiarize himself very well with the enormous, vibrant city. This knowledge of the geographical idiosyncrasies of the metropolis, of the complex political issues of the day, and of the human face of the city will make his novels—especially *Zero* (1974; English translation as *Zero*, 1983) and *Não verás país nenhum* (1981; *And Still Is the Earth*, 1985)—remarkable both as literary events and documents of a traumatic era in the history of Brazil.

In terms of his position in Brazilian literature, Ignácio de Loyola Brandão has been placed in the "Geração dos 70" (Generation of the 1970s). Others prefer to call this group that appeared mainly during the last military dictatorship in Brazil the "Geração intermediária" (Generation in between). Obviously, it is not clear what it is "in between" of. It is clear that most of the members of this generation, especially Ivan Angelo, Márcio Souza, Roberto Drummond, and Brandão responded to the conditions of the dictatorship and started, in Brandão's words, "to make a literature that documents, that pictures, just like a camera filming the country in order to show it on the screen of the book; later this screen was obscured by censorship" (*O Estado de São Paulo*, July 17, 1997).

Precisely because of censorship, the beginning of Brandao's career was not easy. Although he had published *Bebel que a cidade comeu* (Bebel eaten by the city) in 1968, initially he could not publish *Zero* in Brazil. The novel was written in 1969 but was published only in 1974, in Portugal, where it was a great success. When Zero was translated into Portuguese and published in Brazil it was almost immediately censored. Only in 1981 was *Zero* finally made available in Brazil once again. Since then, the novel has enjoyed several editions and has been translated into several languages. Presently, Brandão is a writer with the newspaper *O Estado de São Paulo* (The state of São Paulo). His last book, *A veia bailarina* (The dancing vein, 1996), reflects on a brain operation he underwent in 1995.

One can say that both *Zero* and *Não verás país nenhum* constitute two of the finest examples of science fiction in Brazilian literature. Of course, neither of these two novels features spaceships, robots, or aliens from outer space. And yet, because of the way Brandão works his material, both novels create (or portray) a world in which science—at the service of dictatorial rule—has taken control of the most intimate aspects of human life and seeks to destroy it from within.

Zero is Brandão's best-known novel. Its experimental nature—parallel columns, different letter fonts, collage of texts from several sources—signals the presence of the chaos that permeates the story itself. Here, as in other of Bran-dão's stories, the main character is overwhelmed by what can be understood as the inhuman forces that control his world. It is not clear, in the end, whether the protagonist José Gonçalvez—a John Doe—is destroyed by the ball of fire. The clearest message, however, is that unless people organize themselves to fight, to defend themselves and their beliefs, they will continue being crucified, just as José's friend Gê was crucified.

Não verás país nenhum is more of a conventional novel, at least in the graphic aspect of the page. Unlike what he does in *Zero*, here Brandão does not split the page or use collages. He does, however, use extensive subtitles. This may well be a reflection of a journalistic intention. The subtitles function as the headlines in a newspaper and can help the hurried reader to get the gist of the story without actually reading it. But of course, the reading of the story is what gives the total flavor of Brandão's construction of a São Paulo after the day that all cars were ordered to stop running. In this apocalyptic city, all individual guarantees are eliminated and human beings revert to some brutal stage in which one can only survive by outwitting the others. And survival is measured by one's ability to obtain even the most basic element, water.

The main character of the story, Souza, is a former history professor who one day wakes up and sees that he has a hole in the palm of his hand. The existence of this hole becomes the starting point of a new consciousness: he starts to question the system that controls his life, that determines the buses he takes, the clothes he buys, and even the bathrooms where he is allowed to urinate. Souza's wife becomes afraid of him and eventually disappears. He does not look for her; instead, he allows his nephew to bring in three strange men whose bodies show several stages of decomposition.

It is with these men that Souza begins to learn about the situation beyond the protected circles around the city. He learns about the destruction of several areas of Brazil, the elimination of people, the transformation of the Amazon into a desert, the selling of a number of Brazil's regions to multinationals, and the ex-pulsion of Brazilians from their homes, their cities, and their states in order to make room for the new, foreign owners. It is also because of his involvement with these men that Souza eventually loses everything: his house, his most cherished memories, his clothes, his name. But he does not lose his humanity—or his hope. In the end of the novel, after having gone through the greatest degradations—hunger, torture—he finds himself under one of the most important works of the regime: the enormous marquee built to protect people from the skin-burning rays of the sun. People stand all day like cattle under the protective shade of this marquee, a Pharaonic work of the "system." If one falls or slips out from under the shade he is immediately killed by the sun. At night, people lie down around the marquee and suffer the bitter cold of the night. Every day there are fewer and fewer people.

It is at this last stop that Souza remembers the meaning of beauty and the power of hope. One of the condemned who stand by his side under the marquee has a pretty object hanging from a necklace. When asked what it is for, he tells Souza that the object has no use whatsoever, but that it is pretty and makes him feel good. Souza, until then blind to the relentless effect of the official propaganda, had forgotten this simple truth: not everything has to have a practical use. At this moment, even though he can barely believe he will be alive the next day, Souza says that he feels the wind. In the destroyed landscape, there is no more wind, just devastating hurricanes. But Souza insists it is wind, a wind that will bring rain—not acid rain, but rain that will wet the soil and make it alive again. He reflects that the rain may be very far away, but that it is headed in their direction. The last words of the novel emphasize the hope of rain and pose a direct question to the reader: "Does anybody know if it is raining over there?"

Of course, the allegorical nature of the novel cannot be denied. For anyone who has experienced life under a dictatorship, Souza's *via dolorosa* is recognizable as the possible life of any citizen. The way Brandão found to express the almost inexpressible horrors some of his generation went through was to place Brazil in an (imperfect) future, which sometimes resembled the very real present. The São Paulo of *Não verás país nenhum* recreated as a nightmarish science-fiction place really existed. But, just as in *Zero*, here too the novel ends on a positive note, in a call to solidarity. The epilogue, a quote from Galileo—"E pur si muove" (However, the Earth moves)—expresses quite well that hope exists and change is inevitable. Of course, these last words of the novel contradict the title of the English version.

Eva Paulino Bueno

Works

Não verás país nenhum. Rio de Janeiro: Codecri, 1981. Reprint, São Paulo: Global, 2000. English version as *And Still Is the Earth*, trans. Ellen Watson. New York: Avon Books, 1985.
Zero. Lisbon: Bertrand, 1974, 1976; Rio de Janeiro: Editora Brasilia, 1975. Reprint, São Paulo: Global, 2001. English version as *Zero*, trans. Ellen Watson. New York: Avon Books, 1983. Reprint, Normal, IL: Dalkey Archive Press, 2003.

Criticism

DiAntonio, Robert E. "The Evolution of Ignácio de Loyola Brandão's Dystopian Fiction: *Zero* and *Não verás país nenhum*," in *Brazilian Fiction: Aspects and Evolution of the Contemporary Narrative*. Fayetteville: University of Arkansas Press, 1989, 138–54.
Monegal, Emir Rodríguez. "Fiction Under the Censor's Eye." *WLT* (Winter 1979): 19–22.

José Alberto Bravo de Rueda (b. 1956)

PERU

José Alberto Bravo de Rueda was born in Lima, Peru in 1956. He received a degree in linguistics and literature at the Universidad Católica. In his country, he worked as an educator at the secondary and university levels. He also contributed to various literary publications. In 1989, he traveled to the United States to pursue graduate studies at the University of Maryland, where he earned Master's and Ph.D. degrees. He has collaborated with several Latino journalism organizations in the Washington, D.C. area and is currently an assistant professor of Spanish at North Carolina A&T State University.

Bravo de Rueda has published the novel *Hacia el Sur* (Southward bound, 1992) and a book of short stories, *El hombre de la máscara y otros cuentos* (The man in the mask and other stories, 1993), for which he received first prize in the Literary Competition of the Peruvian-Japanese Association in 1993. In addition, he has published the poetry collection *Intento de ala* (Winged purpose, 1983). Two of the author's short stories, "Sangre de familia" ("Family blood") and "Arakné," received honorable mentions in the Premio Copé competition in 1994 and 1987, respectively.

Bravo de Rueda came to literature via Gabriel García Márquez and Julio Cortázar. Likewise, writers such as Edgar Allan Poe, Jorge Luis Borges, Guy de Maupassant, Horacio Quiroga, and Franz Kafka among others, shaped his narrative technique and contributed to his formation as a writer. His writing is concerned with violence as well as the problems of racism, social inequality, and sexual and religious intolerance. A constant fear emerges from his science fiction: that humankind has not learned to coexist peacefully and is therefore headed towards its own destruction.

Bravo de Rueda turns to science fiction in the novel *Hacia el Sur* and in the short stories "Sobreviviente" (The survivor, in *El hombre de la máscara*) and "Arakné." Although the novel deals with concrete problems in Peru during the 1980s—the confrontation between the military and the leftist group "Shining Path"—science fiction is a key element in the text. *Hacia el Sur* consists of a novelistic kaleidoscope. The novel's plot is condensed in the narration of two parallel but temporally separated trips. In the first, the protagonist, history student Pablo Ernesto, is heading to the south of Peru to carry out a research project. He has left his fiancée behind in Lima where she becomes involved in religious fanaticism and subsequently is abducted by the army. This kidnapping motivates Pablo Ernesto, who does not have strong political beliefs, to affiliate himself with a terrorist group. Placed in charge of carrying out an attack on a military club, he is captured and subjected to behavior-modification treatments and brain surgery that transforms him into a type of robot, a living emblem of the ideology and rhetoric of the army. The Frankenstein-like transformation performed by Doctor

Longaño changes Pablo Ernesto into the "Triturador" (shredder). His fiancée, upon seeing him, is not deceived by the transformation and together they embark on a journey of recovery and flight.

Through the treatments the protagonist receives and the pseudoscientific discourse, the text grotesquely links medical power and the military. The alliance between medicine and the army results in the creation of an apparatus of total power that is able to transform individuals according to the parameters of the dominant ideology. The individuals transformed on Doctor Longaño's operating table are changed into apathetic monsters without memory, the spokespersons of fascism and machismo.

The scientific apparatus that controls and transforms individuals in order to place them under the will of those in power is reminiscent of the plot in the film *A Clockwork Orange* (1971), based on the novel by Anthony Burgess. However, the treatment received by the characters in the novel is not only psychological, as in the movie, but surgical as well. Likewise, the science–power dichotomy situated within a science fiction tradition that, like *Brave New World* (1932) by Aldous Huxley, denounces scientific power as a dehumanized instrument of control and manipulation. Nevertheless, *Hacia el Sur* does not look to the future in order to raise this topic. Scenes of a real Latin American country are sufficient to drive home the point of the excess of military power. Likewise, the alliance between medicine and the military also serves as an ironic warning of the abyss between the basic social necessities of Peru and the scientific experiments carried out by the military. Thanks to the army, Doctor Longaño can dedicate herself to her experiments on delinquents and other outcasts. This power relation is mocked in the novel; for example, the doctor designs an infallible serum that cures the venereal illness within the military body.

Science fiction is also present in the novel through a metafictional strategy. The protagonists attend a showing of a movie that reflects the novel with its double plot of love and violence. The film, on the one hand, presents an interplanetary love story and, on the other, it offers up yet another *Star Wars*-like adventure. An atomic war changes the protagonist of the movie into a monstrous being. If the Frankenstein-like transformation of Pablo Ernesto into the Shredder is an inversion of the romantic theme of beauty and the beast, in the movie, the sexual roles of the legend are upended. Despite the mutations of the extraterrestrial, the film culminates in Hollywood style, with happiness ever after for the interplanetary couple. In this layered construction (the film within the novel), the former is used as a device for commentary, since it serves to launch criticism about the function of commercial and evasive art as a form of social proselytism. The happy ending of the interplanetary love story serves as counterpoint to the novel.

The theme of destruction by atomic radiation is the starting point for the story "Sobreviviente." Two principal motives converge in this short story: the danger of a nuclear catastrophe, and jealousy. The character survives a nuclear explosion, but ends up being a victim of his own impulses. The vision of humanity proposed in "Sobreviviente" is entirely a negative one. The story postulates that human beings are wont to destroy the slightest possibility of achieving happiness. The character in "Sobreviviente" is unable to control his emotions, signaling the irrational aspect of humankind. The story echoes apocalyptic movies such as *Planet of the Apes* (1968) and *The Day After* (1983). As in *Hacia el Sur*, it shows concern that the arrogance and ignorance of the military elite or heads of state can destroy the world.

"Arakné" is also a story where science is confronted with irrationality and where jealous impulses triumph. The story narrates the tale of an entomologist on the verge of achieving the creation of artificial spider silk that would revolutionize the world. In order to successfully complete his experiment, he needs an exotic specimen that can only be obtained in Kenya. His trip complicates the relationship with his fiancée, and the conflict between science and passion is resolved tragically. The ending is foreshadowed throughout the story through a series of premonitions. In this way, the story opens with a detailed description of a spider's behavior while stalking its prey. Likewise, from the perspective of other characters, there is an analogy between the physique of the protagonist and that of the arachnids. The female protagonist also sees herself as a poisonous arachnid, thus accentuating in her the feminine stereotype of destruction.

Bravo de Rueda's works so far have garnered scattered reviews that are largely impressionistic. However, the author's texts lend themselves to a variety of critical approaches. For example, a feminist analysis of "Arakné" would prove to be quite interesting. Despite the fact that his texts manage to confront machismo and violence, various feminine stereotypes appear in the texts. Likewise, in *Hacia el Sur*—a complex text due to the heterogeneity of discourses and perspectives—a masculine point of view paradoxically predominates. One may ask if the denunciation of machismo is successful, since it is done with sexist language and through the perspective of a machista character. This type of analysis, which would open up numerous debates, would also be useful for "Sobreviviente." On the other hand, studies that examine the intertextual relationships between cinema and literature would readily lend themselves to analyses of Bravo de Rueda's narrative. In particular, *Hacia el Sur* would benefit in this regard. The novel's kaleidoscopic nature requires the participation of an active reader. Analyses that range from postmodern and postcolonial positions to Bakhtinian readings would find fertile ground in the social, political, and historical representations implied in the text. Analyzing the intersections between fiction and history as well as studying fiction as a critical commentary on history are possible avenues of future exploration of the novel.

                                                        Mercedes Guijarro-Crouch

Works

"Arakné," in *"Cide Hamete Benengeli coautor del Quijote" y los cuentos ganadores del Premio Copé*. Lima: Copé, 1987, 49–64.

Hacia el Sur. La Yapa Editores, 1992.

El hombre de la máscara y otros cuentos. Lima: Concurso de Creación Literaria, Premio Asociación Peruano Japonés, 1993.

Criticism

Betanzos, Juan. "*Hacia el sur* de José Alberto Bravo de Rueda." *Caretas* [Lima] 18 February 1993: 85.

Escobar, A. "El hombre de la máscara." *Expreso: Página abierta. El suplemento dominical* [Lima] 2 April 1995: 8.

Santiváñez, Roger. "Novela brava." *Oiga* [Lima] 19 April 1993: 64.

Ruth Bueno (date unknown)

BRAZIL

Ruth Bueno (Ruth Maria Barbosa Goulart) was born in Juiz de Fora, Minas Gerais, Brazil. Her parents were Sylvio Goulart Bueno and Carmen Barbosa Goulart Bueno. In 1946, she began to study law at the Faculdade Nacional de Direito (National Faculty of Law) in Rio de Janeiro. She became known as a lawyer, a professor, and a feminist. In 1970, she wrote *Regime jurídico da mulher casada* (Juridic regime of the married woman), a legal work on the rights of Brazilian women. She represented her country on several occasions in Europe and United States, participating in United Nations programs and conferences on human rights.

Bueno, primarily known as a writer, published her first work of fiction, *Diário das máscaras* (Diary of masks) in 1966. Like her narratives—mostly novels—that followed, it is characterized by its carefully structured, lyrical prose. The novel *Asilo nas torres* (Asylum in the towers, 1979) is the author's contribution to science fiction. Time in *Asilo nas torres* is unspecified—it may occur in the present or future—but the setting is defined by sophisticated technology. The narrator doesn't establish *when* the action takes place but does establish *where*. The world of the towers is located on Saturn, a much different scene and atmosphere than that to which we are accustomed. A complete and colorful rainbow appears every sundown in the Saturn sky, as a backdrop for the towers. There are three towers described as equal but of different height, one of them rising into the infinite. Social life in the towers is not only described in terms of its fantastic existence, but it is also an allegorical world characterized by its hierarchical system, individualism, and anomie. The ruling society presented by Bueno resembles Aldous Huxley's *Brave New World* (1932) as well as the oppressive climate of Franz Kafka's bureaucratic works adapted to Third World realities. In the towers, there is a king who, like all kings, lives in isolation from the masses. Bueno uses this earthly social hierarchy of class divisions to communicate her message of social criticism. The represented reality is that of the modern world, thinly disguised as technology-based capitalism. Bueno utilizes science fiction as a way to demonstrate that issues of human suffering and anguish are universal and atemporal. She also makes use of diverse Biblical verses at the end of some of the vignettes that comprise the book.

In the novel, anomie is represented through the use of initials for the characters' names: L, X, M may be anyone and no one in particular. The only characters represented as individuals are the king and his immediate circle of friends, along with two women whose names are Salomé and Assunta. On the allegorical level, Salomé and Assunta symbolize opposite values. Salomé (another Biblical reference) represents death and destruction, while Assunta is a symbol of the simplicity and carnality of Brazilian life. In the novel, the two are opposing forces that clash in battle. Ultimately, hope rises from the warm blood of Assunta, symbolizing the triumph of life. Salomé is a fantastic character who owns the winds, can transform her appearance and the weather, and is always surrounded by her

harpies. This relation to Greek mythology opens up the novel to another symbolic field. Like the king, Salomé is part of the establishment. She is a cruel and
outrageous mother figure whose power is used against the common people in the
towers and makes their lives obviously more miserable.

The title of the novel refers to the most marginal population within the towers,
the *asilados*, or those aged and retired from work. When they are no longer able to
work, earn a salary, and produce, they are forced to live a humiliated existence—in
the shadows, coming to the tower only for food or company. The *asilados* occupy
the lowest level of the hieratic society and thus complete Bueno's allegory of the
towers as a capitalist machine where ironically, as David W. Foster states, "individuals clamor for admission but which inexorably annihilates their human qualities"
(141). The *asilados* and workers suffer the low artificial temperature necessary for
the efficient operation of machines. However, the king enjoys the cold air and
Salomé helps him to the rooms kept freezing cold. Bueno does not explain—nor
does she feel the need to—how Saturn came to be populated. Only the grim life of
anonymous men and women in a virtual space serves as a point of reflection for
Bueno's *Asilo*. There is a clear parallel in the novel between the fictional city created
on Saturn and the historic foundation of the modern city of Brasilia, the new capital of Brazil, constructed during the 1960s in the middle of the jungle.

Asilo nas torres follows a classical model of science fiction that consists of the
exaggeration and criticism of contemporary social tendencies and the creation of
an absurd and nightmarish world. Yet the novel is clearly adapted to a Brazilian
context, which helps to make it one of the best examples of science fiction to be
written in Brazil.

Cristina Guzzo

Works

Asilo nas torres. São Paulo: Atica, 1979.
Diario das máscaras. Rio de Janeiro: Tempo Brasileiro, 1966.

Criticism

Duarte, José Afrânio Moreira. "Ruth Bueno," in *A Dictionary of Contemporary Brazilian
    Authors*, ed. David W. Foster and Roberto Reis. Tempe: Arizona State University, Cen-
    ter of Latin American Studies, 1982, 22.
Foster, David William. *Alternate Voices in the Contemporary Latin American Narrative.*
    Columbia: University of Missouri Press, 1985, 140–43.
Leonardo, Stella. "Conversa com Ruth Bueno." *Minas Gerais Suplemento Literario* [Minas
    Gerais, Brazil] 14.779–80 (September 5–12, 1981): 10–11. (Interview.)
Lindstrom, Naomi. "Innovation in the Novel's Popular Subgenres: Two Brazilian Exam-
    ples." *Luso-Brazilian Review* 24.1 (1987): 47–57.
———. "The Recent Work of Ruth Bueno: An Esthetic of Insubstantiality." *Dactylus* 9
    (1988–89): 37–40.

Ilda Cádiz Ávila (b. 1911)

CHILE

Ilda Cádiz Ávila was born in Talcahuano, Chile, in 1911. She studied pedagogy in English at the Universidad de la Concepción and worked in Santiago as a bilingual secretary until she retired. She was also an employee for the Dutch airline KLM. In her youth, Cádiz Ávila contributed to the magazine *Don Fausto*. Later, she wrote for the magazine *Margarita*, which was geared towards a female audience. At that time, she used the pseudonym "Dolores Espina." The publication of *La Tierra dormida y otros cuentos* (The sleeping earth and other stories) in 1969 marks the first time that the author used her own name to sign her works.

Having worked for KLM for 11 years afforded Cádiz Ávila the opportunity to travel throughout the world. During a stay in London, the author spent time in the British Museum doing research on the life and works of Lawrence of Arabia, about whom she wrote various articles. One of these essays won first prize in the *Concurso de la Municipalidad de Santiago* (Municipal competition of Santiago) in 1975. Her extensive travel experience inspired many writings that still have not been compiled or published into book form. Some of these appeared in the Santiago newspaper *El Mercurio* (Mercury). In her writing she reveals a feminist outlook. The author tried to bring the female characters of the Bible out of anonymity by doing research on several of them (Maack 13). Likewise, her book *La pequeña Quintrala de Joaquín Toesca* (Joaquin Toesca's little Quintrala, 1993) is the result of her investigative spirit as well as her feminist concerns.

Historical research was not the only motivation of the works of Cádiz Ávila. The author has also felt a great affinity for science fiction. Ray Bradbury and Isaac Asimov are her favorite writers of this genre. After reading Bradbury she began to write fantastic short stories, though being also influenced by Arthur C. Clark and Fred Hoyle. Her science-fiction stories are collected in *La Tierra dormida y otros cuentos* and *La casa junto al mar y otros cuentos* (The house by the sea and other short stories, 1984). Despite the 15 year span between the two publications, the common denominator in both texts is the questioning of reality.

"La imagen" (The image, in *La Tierra dormida*) contains many of the constants that mark the narrative of the author. It is the story of an aficionado of astronomy who discovers an extraordinary object through his telescope near the Centaurus constellation. The discovery of this object places this narrative within the cosmic fiction of space. The object, which steadily increases in size, takes on the appearance of the Earth. The telescopic lens seems to turn into a mirror that reproduces an object mimicking the world of the protagonist, who sees himself engaged in the act of looking into space. The fascinating unfolding of reality—which lends the text a certain Cortázar–like quality—is a common theme in the work of Cádiz Ávila. The end of the story is left open since there is no reasonable explanation for the phenomenon. As with many of the author's stories, it concludes with vacillation and the protagonist's doubt. The blurring of reality, the imposition of doubt as a narrative solution, duality, and the scientific atmosphere and theme of space presented in "La imagen" are common themes found in both collections. Another point in common is that each anthology contains both science fiction and detective stories.

The narratives with a detective story line are fewer in number than the stories with science fiction plots. In the former, the author almost always creates a mysterious atmosphere where the enigma is generally unsolvable. Sometimes the lack of a solution, as seen in "La balanza" (The scale, in *La Tierra dormida*) makes the stories border on the parapsychological. In "La balanza," 20 years separate the narrations of two murders. In the first, it is the woman who tries to kill her lover by pointing at him with her index finger. The black glove on the woman's hand seems to transform her index finger into a revolver. In the second murder, the male lover is presumed to be the killer. Inexplicably, these two murderers are linked by the changing of the facts in the written accounts of the victim and assassin as well as the medical circumstances of the deaths. The bodies don't show even the slightest injury, but the hearts have been torn to pieces. The detective himself emphasizes the unexplainable nature of the event and the unsolvable cases.

In "La casa junto al mar," the voices of the two narrators tell the story. While one presents a discourse emphasizing the superstitious, the other puts forth a scientifically based hypothesis. If the narrator's desire, as well as the reader's, is to connect the text to the detective-story model, other aspects of the work liken it to science fiction. As in gothic science fiction, the house is immersed in an atmosphere of mystery. The owner of the house, who is rather insane, has some features in common with Captain Nemo, Jules Verne's character. The hypothesis of one of the narrators involves evolutionary theories and adaptation to the environment. The obsessive attraction that the owner of the house feels for the sea has slowly managed to change him into an amphibian that has gradually adapted to aquatic life.

The scientific theme of adaptation to the environment is broached in several of the stories in *La Tierra dormida*. In "Final de un sueño" (End of a dream), RS, a scientist of another species, is obsessed with adapting to his sterile means of life living cells that can be collected after the explosion of the Earth. The story is markedly pessimistic. RS's desire to adapt the cells to the planetoid he inhabits frustrates him. The pieces of the Earth that he manages to collect only contain petrified cells, since the planet was just as sterile as the planetoid. The inevitable destruction of the planet is forecasted in "Una pequeña muestra" (A little sample), "Nostalgia," "La Tierra dormida," and "Los seres de los Andes" (The beings from the Andes). The first two stories are set in a distant future that provides a melancholic look at the life of a lost planet. The past becomes an obsession for the protagonists of these stories, much like the curiosity of science and archaeology for the beings of other worlds in "Una pequeña muestra" and rebellious temptation in "Nostalgia."

The stories "La Tierra dormida"—from which the book takes its title—and "Los seres de los Andes" open and close the anthology. They announce the return of a glacial era in which life disappears from the planet until the heat from the deepest stratospheres of the Earth bursts in a volcanic eruption. In contrast to the radical pessimism of "Final de un sueño," these two stories warn of a cycle of destruction and revitalization of the planet. These narrations attempt to provide an explanation of the hecatomb that is a cross between pseudoscience fiction and fantasy. In "La Tierra dormida," the narrative action is secondary to the treatment of catastrophe. The description of the process of a meteorologist freezing to death is told with great detail. The story explores the timeless consciousness of feeling alive. "Los seres de los Andes" has a certain intertextual relationship with the Biblical account of the flood. With the arrival of a new glacial era, humans and animals are forced to take refuge in Andean caves to survive. Through the succeeding generations, these beings begin to adapt to the cold and cave life until they evolve into quadrupeds with extremely gifted intellects. The survivors of "Nostalgia" depend on other strategies to escape the destruction of the planet. These human beings do not hide out in caves; rather, they flee to a satellite city sustained by oxygen towers. As with the stories of Aldous Huxley, an individual's liberty is put face-to-face with the totalitarianism of the state that programs its citizens for predetermined tasks. Through these means, the past is installed in the minds of the characters as a time of utopia.

Cádiz Ávila revisits this confrontation between the state and the individual in "Bil Tu" (Bill Two, in *La casa junto al mar*). In addition to the control the state exercises over the reproduction of its citizens, the story is also about an android fantasy. Bil Tu is a robot, a younger, perfected version of Bil Uan (Bill One)—the husband of the protagonist. The author takes advantage of English homophones to mark the doubling. Later on, Bil Tu is replaced by an identical Bil Zri (Bill Three). Due to Bil Tu's human appearance, he could be considered an android. Nevertheless, Asimov's idea of presenting a robot as the ideal servant prevails (Pierce 82). The android/robot reaches such a level of perfection that the protagonist sees him as a way to satisfy her sexual frustrations and uses him as a substitute for her husband. The android is the pretext for exposing human problems. The story explores jealousy and how time deteriorates a couple's relationship. The examination of human relationships is also presented through the theme of space travel: on the one hand, "Misterio en el espacio" (Mystery in space, in *La Tierra dormida*) looks at the antagonisms between the sexes and on the other, the story articulates the possibility of love triangles in outer space.

The degradation of old age as well as the attitude of human beings about failure are presented in "Aquí Cóndor CC-X10" (Here Condor CC-X10, in *La Tierra dormida*). The story is set in an era in which the energy of the human mind is powerful enough to move a capsule telepathically. Nevertheless, the telepathic advances have limitations, since the power of mental concentration can become weak due to a loss of consciousness, a dream state, or fatigue. While elderly persons are experts in concentration during their youth, they now become exhausted when trying to exercise these tantalizing mental feats. The author elaborates with irony on the themes of failure and frustration in the stories "La célula perdida" (The lost cell) and "Cuenta regresiva" (Countdown), both from *La Tierra dormida*. Science never succeeds in imitating the natural process of human gestation. "Cuenta regresiva" could be read as a scientific version of "Viaje a la semilla" (Voyage to the seed) by Cuban author Alejo Carpentier. As with Carpentier's text, the narration inverts the lineal chronology of the development of life. The story reinvents the Faustian myth of eternal youth. In "La célula perdida," the tradition of the mechanical doll found in E. T. A. Hoffmann is incorporated, along with that of *Frankenstein* by Mary Shelley. Cádiz Ávila is interested in the ethical problem of the creator and the created. The author explores the reaction of a human being in a laboratory upon being given an identity and in turn trying to reconstruct the past.

Ilda Cádiz Ávila's works have not yet received the critical attention they deserve. This silence should be rectified by analyzing her texts and compiling her dispersed materials—the nonpublished and the scattered published magazine and newspaper articles alike. It would be fitting to question why an author so concerned with history did not touch upon the problematic history of Chile in her time. When she introduces the conflict between the individual and the totalitarian state, she does not do it in present time but instead in a fantastic future. By the same token, one would have to question her almost complete absence of a female narrative voice, which seems to contradict the author's feminist interest. The theories related to textual liberation and the fantastic or uncanny provide a relevant critical basis from which to examine the author's work. In sum, the possible methods for studying the texts of Cádiz Ávila are mulitple.

Mercedes Guijarro-Crouch

Works

La casa junto al mar y otros cuentos. Santiago: Editorial Universitaria, 1984.
"Nostalgia," in *Antología de cuentos chilenos de ciencia ficción y fantasía*, ed. Andrés Rojas-Murphy. Santiago: Editorial Andrés Bello, 1988.
La Tierra dormida y otros cuentos. Santiago: Talleres de Arancibia Hnos, 1969.

Criticism

Maack, A. "Ilda Cádiz Avila, autora de cuentos de ciencia ficción." *Revista Cauce* 182 (1988): 13.
Pierce, John J. *Great Themes of Science Fiction*. Westport, CT: Greenwood, 1987.

Diego Cañedo (pseudonym of Guillermo Zárraga) (1892–1978)

MEXICO

Guillermo Zárraga was a Mexican architect about whom little biographical information is available. Although he is best-known for his short stories and novels of the fantastic, Cañedo is also the author of two important science fiction novels. The first, *El réferi cuenta nueve* (The referee counts nine, 1943) begins in San Miguel de Allende during the Second World War, where a diary manuscript is found wrapped in a Mexico City newspaper dated 1961. The Nazi invasion of the country in a parallel universe is described in the newspaper, revealing the existence of concentration camps in several states of the republic. Likewise, there is an account of the confiscation and subsequent incineration of any and all books that recall Anglo-Saxon, particularly American, influence on Mexican culture. The first stage of the invasion consisted of Germany attempting to invade the United States. In this work, Cañedo shows his concern for Mexican society's general acceptance of Nazi propaganda during the Second World War, which, according to Ross Larson, places him among the few Latin American authors who preferred the United States' cultural influence over that of Germany. Aside from this consideration, this impressive novel is one of the most important works in the history of Mexican science fiction.

His second novel, *Palamás, Echevete y yo, o el lago asfaltado* (Palamás, Echevete and I, or the asphalt lake, 1945), relates the incidence of time travel in Mexican science fiction, an obvious homage to H. G. Wells, to whom Cañedo offers an apology at the beginning of his novel. The novel relates the story of a Mexican man's journey into the past in a time machine accompanied by Professor Palamás, who comes from a future where freedom is oppressed. Their purpose is to study in detail the first years of Spanish colonization as well as particulars about the human sacrifices performed by the Aztecs. Perhaps in an effort to change the image of malinchismo (associated with a traitor) that *El réferi cuenta nueve* brought upon him, this novel contains several nationalist elements and ideas, as its subtitle suggests. The "asphalt lake" refers to the now-dry lake Texcoco, where the remains of the ancient city of Tenochtitlán survive in the middle of modern, urban Mexico City.

Miguel Ángel Fernández Delgado

Works

Palamás, Echevete y yo, o el lago asfaltado. Mexico City: Stylo, 1945.
El réferi cuenta nueve. Mexico City: Cultura, 1943.

Criticism

Larson, Ross. *Fantasy and Imagination in the Mexican Narrative.* Tempe: Arizona State University, Center for Latin American Studies, 1977.

Ramírez Pimienta, Juan Carlos. "Diego Cañedo: ciencia ficción y crítica social en tres novelas mexicanas de los años cuarenta." *Revista de crítica literaria latinoamericana* 28.55 (2002): 207–20.

Trujillo Muñoz, Gabriel. "Diego Cañedo (Guillermo Zárraga): el arquitecto clarividente," in *Biografías del futuro: la ciencia ficción mexicana y sus autores.* Mexicali, Mexico: Universidad Autónoma de Baja California, 2000, 81–90.

Alfredo Cardona Peña (1917–1995)

MEXICO

A Central American by birth, a Mexican by choice, and a citizen of the world by right of the imagination, Alfredo Cardona Peña—born in San José, Costa Rica in 1917—is a singular figure in the history of Mexican science fiction. He studied in Costa Rica and El Salvador, where he began his career as a journalist. In 1938, at 21 years of age, he arrived in Mexico where he began working for the newspaper *Novedades* (News). In 1945, he began teaching Spanish American literature during the summer at the Universidad Nacional Autónoma de México (National Autonomous University of Mexico). During the early stages of his career as a literary author he published both poetry and prose. His books of poetry include *Los jardines amantes* (The lover gardens, 1952), *Poemas numerales* (Numeral poems, 1959), and *Cosecha mayor* (Main harvest, 1964). Of his early prose works one can mention *El secreto de la reina Amaranta* (The secret of queen Amaranta, 1946). In addition, he wrote several works related to his job as a journalist: *Semblanzas mexicanas. Artistas y escritores del México actual* (Mexican portraits. Artists and writers of contemporary mexico, 1955) and *El monstruo en su laberinto. Conversaciones con Diego Rivera 1949–1950* (The monster in his labyrinth. Conversations with Diego Rivera, 1969). Cardona Peña died on 31 January 1995 at the age of 77. By the end of his life, he had accumulated a variety of distinctions that includes the Premio Centroamericano (Central American Award, 1948), the Continental Prize (Washington, D.C., 1951), and he twice received the National Literary Prize from Costa Rica (1961, 1981). Between 1969 and 1980, he was the director of the Mexican comics division for the publisher Novaro, where he pushed for the creation of Mexican comics that displayed greater originality and social conscience. In 1997, Cardona Peña was honored as a pioneer of Mexican science fiction at the Third National Convention of the Asociación Mexicana de Ciencia Ficción y Fantasía (Mexican association of science fiction and fantasy), presided over by Gonzalo Martré.

Cardona Peña's participation in science fiction began during the 1960s. His contribution to the genre is significant, beginning with the publication of his book *Cuentos de magia, misterio y horror* (Stories of magic, mystery and horror, 1966), which contains several science fiction stories. Of particular resonance is his poem "Recreo sobre la ciencia ficción" (A diversion on science fiction), a rather long epic text that praises the virtues of the genre and names its principal authors in a kind of poetic homage. The poem was published in the prestigious journal *Cuadernos americanos* (American notebook, 1967), and that same year it appeared in the Venezuelan journal *Zona franca* (Free zone). It was later published by the Spanish science-fiction magazine *Nueva dimensión* (New dimension) and led to Cardona Peña being known as the "science fiction poet." As a poet, he joined and became part of a poetic science-fiction tradition that has few but significant antecedents, such as *Oh hada cibernética* (Oh cybernetic fairy, 1963) by the Peruvian Carlos Germán Belli, *Canto a la destrucción* (Song to destruction, 1968) by the Argentine Juan-Jacobo Bajarlía, and *La ciudad muerta de Korad* (The dead city of Korad, 1964) by the Cuban Oscar Hurtado.

The author also continued to publish short stories in several books: *Fábula contada* (Told fable, 1972), *Los ojos del cíclope* (The eyes of the cyclops, 1980), and *Los mejores cuentos de magia y misterio* (The best magic and mystery stories, 1990). His stories are characterized by their rapid development and resolution as well as by their intensity and polished irony. His texts explore such diverse futuristic themes as love between robots and women, an android population explosion, and the creation of artificial worlds where life exists in test tubes. Many of Cardona Peña's stories may be classified as pertaining to hard science fiction, like one of his most well-known, "La niña de Cambridge" (The girl from Cambridge), where the humanization of a computer serves as a fable that warns of the inherent dangers in misusing science and technology. Other stories present not only the topic of artificial intelligence but also contact with alien civilizations, future apocalypses, and ingenious mechanical devices of the twenty-first century. In all his texts, Cardona Peña knew how to reveal—as his story "Enero, 2040" (January, 2040) shows—the joy of discovery and the possibility of finding millions of living mysteries.

Gabriel Trujillo Muñoz

Works

Cuentos de magia, misterio y horror. Mexico City: Novaro, 1966; 2nd ed., 1980.
Fábula contada. San José, Costa Rica: Editorial Universitaria Centroamericana, 1972.
"Juegos florales electrónicos," in *Visiones periféricas: antología de la ciencia ficción mexicana*, ed. Miguel Ángel Fernández Delgado. Mexico City: Lumen, 2001, 97–99.
Los mejores cuentos de magia y misterio. Mexico City: Diana, 1990.
"La niña de Cambridge," in *Todos los caminos del universo*, ed. Oliva Rodríguez Lobato. Mexico City: Promotora de Ediciones y Publicaciones, 1974.
Los ojos del cíclope. Mexico City: Diana, 1980.
"Recreo sobre la ciencia ficción." *Cuadernos americanos* 150.1 (1967): 189–95.

Pedro Castera (1846–1906)

MEXICO

Pedro Castera was born and died in Mexico City. Most sources cite his birth year as being 1938, but this is incorrect. He was trained and worked as a mine engineer and fought against French intervention and the empire of Maximilian of Hapsburg. With military victory and the restoration of the republic, he became a delegate to congress and wrote journalism and literature. Castera is best known for his novel *Carmen: memorias de un corazón* (Carmen: memoirs of a heart, 1887), styled after Jorge Isaacs's *María* (1967) and other similar nineteenth-century romantic novels. His short story "Un viaje celeste" (A celestial voyage) was first published in the periodical *El Domingo, Semanario de Literatura, Ciencias y Mejoras Materiales* (Sunday weekly of literature, sciences and material improvements) on December 1, 1872. It has been recently recovered and published in the science fiction anthology *El futuro en llamas* (The future in flames), edited by Gabriel Trujillo Muñoz. It begins with a verse by Camille Flammarion in which he declares that man is a citizen of heaven. Castera then begins his story by mixing Auguste Comte's positivist philosophy—which was adopted by the Mexican government for its educational programs—with his religious beliefs, making for a mental voyage from the micro- to the macrocosmos in the style of a Christian Olaf Stapledon. He begins with a contemplation of particle matter and atoms, discovering that they are populated by minute living creatures governed by the omnipotent energy of life and love. Before jumping to the macrocosmos, he says a prayer, and at the speed of thought is transported to a place among the stars. He mentally controls the velocity of his voyage as he observes and describes a multitude of spheres, some of them enormous and engulfed in fire, others somewhat flattened at the poles. They were entire planetary systems, with their stars wholly populated by men and angels, for which he renewed his gratitude to God for His supreme omnipotence. Upon sighting Jupiter, he distinguishes multicolored birds and a multitude of cities spread over its surface—a true paradise where pain is unknown. On Saturn, he observes beings surrounded by a luminous aureole of indescribable beauty, until a comet jolts him from his contemplation. Wrapped in its tail, he is taken to a purple and gold star, and from there to other worlds where life also thrives, all the while praising divine goodness and offering prayers. He traveled so far that he quickly crossed stellar abysses and forgot the way back. He had no choice but to ask God for help, hoping He would forgive his mad pride and show him the way back. It was in this predicament that a friend found him and shook him from his rapture or sidereal voyage thus returning him to his body. When he recovered from his ordeal, he took a walk with his friend now more convinced than ever that the universe is the homeland of humanity and man is its citizen.

Castera published a few other texts that may be considered to be early early examples of Mexican science fiction. His story "Rosas y fresas" (Roses and strawberries), included in the short-story collection *Dramas en un corazón* (Dramas in a heart, 1890), narrates the tale of a young mining engineer who marries a beautiful young woman who used to sell flowers and fruit in a market (thus the title). The couple lives happily on a large hacienda, near where the engineer also owns and operates a mine. He is the inventor of a series of mechanical devices—most of them unknown at the time, which lends the text its futuristic quality. The main narrative vein, however, revolves around the love affair between the engineer's young wife and one of his colleagues. Castera's novel *Querens* (1890) is his attempt to reconcile faith and reason (*fides quarens intellectus*), wherein the figure of woman represents faith while that of the man represents reason. In the end, the reconciliation fails. The unnamed protagonist of the novel (who seems closely modeled after the author himself) is a hypochondriac who, following the advice of his doctor, moves to the small town of Tlalpan. Once there, he meets an unusual, self-taught scientist who dabbles in experiments with the human mind and the protagonist is soon employed as his assistant. The scientist, whose work is similar to that of Franz Anton Mesmer's with hypnotism, concludes that the best way to transfer thoughts and sensations by brain-power is by harnessing man's volition or will. In order to prove such hypotheses, they use a sick girl, who only acts as a human when under hypnosis. The protagonist falls in love with the girl and when he confesses his love to the scientist, they attempt to hyponotize the girl with the intent of giving her the emotional capability to reciprocate the protagonist's feelings. There is ample material in the text to support the claim that *Querens* is the first Mexican novel of science fiction.

Miguel Ángel Fernández Delgado

Works

Dramas en un corazón. Mexico City: Tip. de E. Dublán, 1890.

Impresiones y recuerdos; Las minas y los mineros; Los maduros; Dramas en un corazón; Querens, ed. Luis Mario Schneider. Mexico City: Editorial Patria, 1987.

Querens. Mexico City: Imp. Escalerillas, 1890. Reprint, El Paso, TX: Talleres Linotipográficos "La Patria," 1923.

"Un viaje celeste," in *El Domingo, Semanario de Literatura, Ciencias y Mejoras Materiales,* December 1, 1872. Also in *El futuro en llamas: cuentos clásicos de la ciencia ficción mexicana,* ed. Gabriel Trujillo Muñoz. Mexico City: Grupo Editorial Vid, 1997, 45–54.

Criticism

Trujillo Muñoz, Gabriel. *La ciencia ficción: literatura y conocimiento.* Mexicali: Instituto de Cultura de Baja California, 1991, 307–9.

———. *Los confines: crónica de la ciencia ficción mexicana.* Mexico City: Vid, 1999, 47–57.

———. "Pedro Castera: el viajero estelar," in *Biografías del futuro: la ciencia ficción mexicana y sus autores.* Mexicali, Mexico: Universidad Autónoma de Baja California, 2000, 49–54.

Fósforos Cerillos (pseudonym of Sebastián Camacho y Zulueta) (1820?–1915)

MEXICO

Sebastián Camacho y Zulueta was a Mexican politician and businessman, born in Jalapa, Veracruz, who wrote scientific articles and one science fiction story during his youth. He received a degree in engineering from the Escuela de Minas (School of mines) in Jalapa. He came to have important investments and held managerial positions with the railroads. He was city councilman in Mexico City and a senator until his death.

In 1840, El Ateneo Mexicano (The Mexican athenaeum), a literary and scientific association, was created in Mexico City. The group began publishing a magazine under the same title in 1844 with the purpose of providing useful knowledge on a variety of subjects. It was especially intended for the needy and less-educated people and included moral lessons disguised in vestments of fables. Sebastián Camacho y Zulueta contributed to the first issue of *El ateneo mexicano* with an article on the daguerreotype—which had first arrived in Mexico at the end of 1839—and another about aerostatic balloons. In the same issue of the magazine, *Camacho*, using the pen name Fósforos Cerillos, wrote the short story "México en el año 1970" (Mexico in the year 1970) in which he speculated on the future application and usefulness of the two inventions he had written about. The author presents a dialogue between two men, Próspero and his nephew Ruperto, in which they comment on the most recent news, talking about new studies, costumes, politics, and inventions that already were a part of daily life. The death of the governor of California is discussed, and in spite of being very far from the mother country, the news arrived in Mexico City the same morning it happened. The president ordered that troops from Mexico, Puebla, Veracruz, Jalisco, and three other northern places be transported in a flotilla of aerostatic balloons to attend the funeral. Próspero explains to his nephew that because of his advanced age, a balloon voyage would do him harm. However, this was not a reason to miss the event entirely, since it was possible to take a couple of large photomurals (daguerreotypes of eight-by-six meters in size) of the funeral procession, leaving one at the California palace and bringing another to Mexico City. They also comment on the elopement of two young lovers by means of the most common method of transport—again the aerostatic balloon. They are able to escape her uncle, who also happens to be the minister of commerce, by deflating his balloon before fleeing. The girl's uncle also fell into disgrace, since he was found guilty of a betrayal of confidence—he had been transporting himself by aerostat to New Orleans every week to attend French theater shows. His was also accused of illicit gains, which was—as the author states—an isolated case, since it had been years since there was a corrupt official in Mexico. Being a public officer, he was sure to receive the death penalty. At the end of the story, Camacho provides some future statistical data. Mexico City's population will be 800,000 in 1970 and it will have 22 theaters, 43 libraries, 164 secondary and preparatory schools, and 32 hospitals. Mexico City's good health and social tranquillity and freedom will make it the most beautiful city in America.

Miguel Ángel Fernández Delgado

Work

"México en el año 1970," in *El ateneo mexicano* 1 (1844): 347–48. Also in *El futuro en llamas*, ed. Gabriel Trujillo Muñoz. Mexico City: Vid, 1997, 37–44.

Criticism

Staples, Anne. "Una primitiva ciencia ficción en México." *Ciencia y desarrollo* [Mexico] 73 (March–April 1987): 145–52. (The complete short story is also published here.)

Daína Chaviano (b. 1960)

CUBA

Daína Chaviano Díaz is the most internationally recognized Cuban author of fantasy and science fiction (SF). She studied English philology at the University of Havana and worked for Cuban public radio and television—hosting, writing scripts, and directing the broadcasting of local and foreign productions of fantasy and SF. Chaviano was also very much involved with the SF literary movement of Havana, finally becoming the literary advisor of the Oscar Hurtado Workshop during the 1980s—probably the most important SF workshop of the time in Cuba—to which many of the most important contemporary Cuban SF writers belonged.

In the late 1970s, the Cuban government sponsored the creation of a SF literature award, the now-prestigious *Premio David* (David prize). It was Daína Chaviano who was its first recipient in 1979 with her collection of short stories *Los mundos que amo* (The worlds I love), in which she followed a more traditional, almost hard-core, SF style, with aliens, alien worlds, and spacecrafts. Also included was a long story with a more realistic style that gives its name to the entire collection. In fact, the story "Los mundos que amo" became so popular that it inspired different radio, film, and even photo-romance adaptations in Cuba.

After the publication of *Los mundos que amo* in 1980, Chaviano published three other collections of short stories and novellas: in 1983, *Amoroso planeta* (Loving planet); in 1986 *Historias de hadas para adultos* (Fairy tales for adults); and in 1990, *El abrevadero de los dinosarios* (The dinosaurs' watering hole). Although the three collections contain stories with very different plots and scenery, all of Chaviano's stories contain an important component of magic and eroticism, and they place fantasy at the core of each work. It is precisely this latter quality that has triggered most of the criticism of her writing. Her work became so important on the Caribbean island that it produced an open debate within the Cuban SF movement. Some fans and fellow authors rejected her oeuvre for being too soft and too new-wave, while others rallied in defense of her texts and narrative style. Probably the most significant point of contention in this debate came with the publication of *Fábulas de una abuela extraterrestre* (Fables of an extraterrestrial grandmother) in 1988. The novel, almost 500 pages long, was the first and only book the author published in Cuba. It tells the story of a boy whose destiny has endowed him with the power to re-open the borders that separate the different realities that exist in the universe. *Fábulas de una abuela extraterrestre* became a Cuban bestseller, but its fame produced even more controversy. The novel openly defied the conventions of fantasy and SF literature—even the words in the title are defiant ("fable," "extraterrestrial"). However, Chaviano did not delve into the debate between science and magic on her own. The novel opens with two quotes, one of them from *The Golden Bough: A Study in Magic and*

Religion by Sir James George Frazer, who defends the idea that magic is a fruitless science. Chaviano will incorporate Frazer's ideas into the plot when one of the main characters, the grandmother, explains to her grandson Ijje that "La magia es una ciencia plagada de preguntas; la ciencia es una magia que ha encontrado respuestas" (magic is a science plagued by questions, science is a magic that has found answers [280]).

Controversies aside, *Fábulas de una abuela extraterrestre* is an excellent literary work and a masterpiece of Latin American science fiction. It is also one of the author's most well-crafted novels, with a highly complicated plot involving three different universes that increasingly connect as the plot develops, and a language that accommodates each one of the realities described. Some critics have understood these three universes with their three corresponding characters to represent the same, unique entity as an allegory of the deconstruction of the modern socialist man that the Cuban regime defended during the 1970s and 1980s. Chaviano also achieved international recognition with *Fábulas de una abuela extraterrestre* when it won the Anna Seghers International Prize from the Academy of Arts in Berlin in November 1990. With this honor, she became the first Cuban fantasy and SF writer to win an international award.

However, her fame as a writer has become even more relevant since she moved to Miami and won the Spanish Azorín award for her novel *El hombre, la hembra y el hambre* (Man, female, hunger) in 1998. Ever since she left the island, Chaviano appears to have stopped writing SF to move into a more mainstream literature. In recent years, she has published three novels of a series titled *The Occult Side of Havana*, of which *El hombre, la hembra y el hambre* has been the most popular. But then, in 2001, Chaviano published *País de dragones* (Land of dragons), a collection of short stories for children originally written in Cuba but never published due to political reasons, for which she won the *La Edad de Oro* award, a national prize for children's and young adult literature sponsored by Editorial Nueva Gente (New people publishing house). That publication seemed to indicate her return to the fantasy and SF genres, proof of which was the re-release of *Fábulas de una abuela extraterrestre* in Mexico in March of 2003.

Juan C. Toledano

Works

El abrevadero de los dinosaurios. Havana: Letras Cubanas, 1990.

Amoroso planeta. Havana: Letras Cubanas, 1983.

La anunciación. Havana: Ediciones Universidad de La Habana, 1990. (Film script with Tomás Piard.)

"The Annunciation," trans. Juan Carlos Toledano, in *Cosmos Latinos: An Anthology of Science Fiction from Latin America and Spain*, ed. Andrea Bell and Yolanda Molina-Gavilán. Middletown, CT: Wesleyan University Press, 2003, 202–7.

Fábulas de una abuela extraterrestre. Havana: Letras Cubanas, 1988; Mexico City: Océano, 2003.

Historias de hadas para adultos. Havana: Letras Cubanas. 1986.

Los mundos que amo. Havana: Ediciones Unión, 1980.

País de dragones. Madrid: Espasa Calpe, 2001 (with a limited edition published in Venezuela [Caracas: Editorial Rondalera, 1994]).

"Para una bibliografía de la ciencia-ficción cubana." *Letras cubanas* 6 (1987): 273–78.

Criticism

Molina-Gavilán, Yolanda. *Ciencia-ficción en español: una mitología moderna ante el cambio*. Lewiston, NY: Edwin Mellen Press, 2002.

Toledano Redondo, Juan Carlos. *Ciencia-ficción cubana: el proyecto nacional del hombre nuevo socialista*. Dissertation, University of Miami, 2002.

Carlos Chernov (b. 1953)

ARGENTINA

Carlos Chernov was born in Buenos Aires in 1953. After receiving a degree in medicine in 1977, he dedicated his career to psychiatry and psychoanalysis. Although from an early age he developed his writing as an activity parallel to his professional work—his first book of poems was written while he was as a youth, *Movimientos en el agua* (Movements in the water, unpublished)—his participation in literary circles came relatively late in life, given that his first work was published in 1992. Nevertheless, in this brief time, Chernov has been able to develop his own distinct style within the panorama of Argentine literature. To date, he has published three books: the short-story collection *Amores brutales* (Brutal love; 1992), which won the Premio Quinto Centenario; the novel *Anatomía humana* (Human anatomy, 1993), which won the Premio Planeta; and a second novel, *La conspiración china* (The Chinese conspiracy, 1997). His writing reveals what could be called a "unique Chernovian style" characterized by certain recurring obsessions: the idea of love as an illusion that masks the biological and reproductive drives of the human body; the belief that identity is an illusion, and that we are only objects (biological and sexual) that view ourselves as individual subjects; the possibility that sex is consequently little more than a mechanical/anatomical activity regulated by the imperatives of the species; and a pessimistic treatment of reality tinged with a strongly negative utopian tone in the tradition of the novels *1984, Brave New World,* or *We,* accompanied by the sarcastic use of humor and by a certain compassion towards human beings and their laughable attempts to feel like individuals.

For the most part, these obsessions have to do with Chernov's personal history, which he claims to have been permanently marked by the experience of working with cadavers when he was a young medical student. Moreover, he states that "la muerte es el momento en que nos transformamos de nuevo en cosa" (death is the moment in which we are transformed again into a thing ["Después de las palabras" 12]). Chernov has held this reductionist view of the human body as purely biological since his adolescence and combined it with his interest in science fiction and anti-utopian literature. This may explain, at least in part, why his narratives occupy a nebulous territory among allegory, the fantastic, and science fiction, in which the human body and sexuality are the objects of all types of mutations and scientific experiments. Although, in a strict sense, only the novels could be classified as science fiction, select short stories from *Amores brutales* inspired one critic to declare Chernov's style as that of "un Sade desapasionado y costumbrista cruzado con un científico que alucina" (A dispassionate Sade and local-color writer crossed with a scientist who hallucinates [from the back cover of book]). These short stories pose a question regarding the excesses that erotic obsession can lead to. Likewise, they present an image of the human body as a series of organic processes and anatomical mechanisms, and a vision of sexuality from a purely biological and animal-like dimension that dismantles all romantic and idealized notions of love. In one story, an immensely obese man is only able to reach an orgasm by contemplating the agony of his guests, who he kills by forcing them to ingest food until they literally burst from gorging themselves. In another, a pornographic film actor, famous for the unusually large size of his genitals, goes mad believing that he is being attacked by an ancient Chinese illness in which the penis retracts into the abdomen like a dagger that ends up piercing and killing the affected person. In yet another short story, an autistic young woman who is raped and later dies as the result of a botched abortion ends up being turned into a doll secretly loved by the anatomist who embalms her. In a final story, a secret society of doctors, gravediggers, pathologists, and other people equally fascinated by the mysteries of the human body organize weekend competitions in which the participants must find and identify the hidden remains of a dead body in order to reconstruct through narration the possible cause of death. As the title of the collection indicates, these are fantastic and "brutal" love stories that underscore the fine line between eroticism as a psychological drive and the biological materiality of the human body that sustains it.

Chernov's first novel, *Anatomía humana*, is without doubt his most successful work and the one that is generally more in line with the apocalyptic science-fiction tradition. Although perhaps it would be more appropriate to call it "sex fiction," since the novel revolves around the speculation on the different forms that human sexuality might be able to adopt should social structures be radically altered. The novel narrates the misfortunes of a man who survives an unexplainable natural catastrophe in Buenos Aires that virtually kills all the men on the planet while the women remain alive and well. With this masculine fantasy made real—to have all the women in the world for oneself—as a point of departure, Chernov produces a disturbing anti-utopia that, among other things, questions certain contemporary debates about gender and sexuality.

Following the initial surprise and short-lived satisfaction of being sought after by every woman, the protagonist soon understands the horror of his new situation, and with great dread is witness to the establishment of new standards of social organization designed to ensure the survival of the species. Upon the death of the male half of humanity, existing social structures quickly collapse, and armed bands of women appear that compete ferociously to claim possession of the few surviving men. When the protagonist is finally captured by one of the clans into which the female population has been divided, he finds himself subjected to cruel medical experiments designed to maximize his semen production and artificially inseminate the greatest possible number of women. At the same time, some desperate or visionary women attempt anatomical modifications to the female body such as the significant enlargement of the uterus and vagina, in order to make copulation with horses possible. Through innumerable incidents with various groups of women—sects that are looking to connect with the spirits of dead men, mystics who believe in the benefits of sexual relations with the trees in the forest, prostitutes who dress as men in order to sell a simulacrum of masculine love—the protagonist ends up joining a clan that adores him as a man-god and bring him their adolescent daughters for him to inseminate. An entourage of female lovers now satisfies his every whim and desire. However, and in one final paradox, the protagonist discovers that not even in this does the utopia he was looking for exist. In turn, he dedicates himself to inner contemplation and asceticism. The novel ends with the protagonist insisting, "No, no quiero nada" (No, I don't want anything) in response to the attentive care of adoring women. The implicit question in the novel is: What would happen if the material conditions of reproduction were to change? And furthermore, how much of sexual/gender roles is cultural and how much is biological? If only a few men were to remain as the sole semen producers in a universe of women, would man be transformed into a mere object of sexual reproduction, just as women were considered for centuries? Chernov casts a merciless gaze on certain notions—romantic love, individuality, sexual desire, gender as a cultural construct—in order to dismantle them, affirming that the ultimate driving force of all human activity is the biological imperative of reproduction, and showing that the body—as an anatomical mechanism made-up of muscles, nerves, and fluids—is the only real and tangible thing about human existence.

Chernov's second novel, *La conspiración china*, begins as a detective mystery about a communist conspiracy that could have pushed Marilyn Monroe to commit suicide. In a plot that includes 1960s radicals, beatnik poets, CIA agents, geneticists, and Marilyn herself, the novel describes the events that culminate in the death of the star. She is the victim of an ancient, esoteric Chinese sect—the Silent Ones, men able to slowly kill beautiful women by their gaze—operated during the Cold War by the Chinese government in order to undermine the power of Hollywood as an apparatus of propaganda and capitalist indoctrination. On the one hand, the novel is an allegory of the combination of the feminine desire to possess eternal physical beauty (exemplified by Marilyn, the sexual object par excellence created by the film industry's dream-machine), and the masculine desire to trap feminine beauty by means of the voyeuristic gaze. The Silent Ones, with their ability to kill women with their penetrating stare, are the ultimate symbol of erotic masculine desire and Chernov's tentative answer to the inverted classic Freudian question (*What do men want?* Instead of, *What do women want?*). On the other hand, the novel delves into Chernov's concern for the biological and anatomical components of sexuality. In order for the Silent Ones to surreptitiously infiltrate the United States and thus be able to kill leading movie stars, the Chinese secret service sets in motion an improbable plan created by a blind, homosexual American poet, who sympathizes with the Maoist cause known as "Project Chimpansex." The original project consists of the false claim that Chinese laboratories are on the verge of achieving the sexual union between man and chimpanzees in order to procreate a new race of super-workers and are going to invite the American government to collaborate on the research. Later, with the ruse that the Silent Ones are genetically predisposed for successful genetic-crossing with animals, they will be shipped to the United States where they will carry out the destruction of Hollywood through their secret plan. However, what the mastermind behind Project Chimpansex does not foresee is that the Chinese authorities end up actually believing in the possibility of procreating the Great Worker—a combination of man and monkey—which leads to all types of genetic experiments in the novel's more outrageous chapters. After a failed first attempt to inseminate animals with the sperm of volunteers—the 23 human chromosomes do not coincide with the 24 in the ova of the female monkeys, an old gardener who is an expert in botanical grafting is placed in charge of the following experiment: the grafting of monkeys' testicles onto the testicles of prisoners in order to produce a genetic cross and achieve the creation of human spermatozoids with 24 chromosomes. The prisoners die due to infections caused by the graft, which leads to a subsequent experiment with victims of a priapism epidemic in a remote Chinese province. The men, who all share the same chromosomal aberrations, are affected with a constant erection that drives them mad and compels them to compulsive sexual activity in which they do not distinguish between men and women or between people and animals. They then lock them up with female monkeys, with the hope that one of them will manage to impregnate an animal in their frenzied sexual behavior. Although the desired result is apparently not achieved, a secret document found at the end of the novel reveals that a female monkey in the hands of the CIA is pregnant after having been raped by one of the priapic men. Intelligence agents impatiently await the birth of the creature in order to verify if this is the first *Mono Sapiens* in history.

Chernov's texts are excellent, if not often disturbing, narratives that combine science fiction and futuristic literature with his training as a psychiatrist to produce fascinating tales that both entertain and cause one to question the nature of humanity.

Fernando Reati

Works

Amores brutales. Buenos Aires: Sudamericana, 1992.

Anatomía humana. Buenos Aires: Planeta Biblioteca del Sur, 1993.

"El apocalipsis de las utopías," in *La Nación. Sección Cultura* (13 November 1994): 3.

La conspiración china. Buenos Aires: Perfil, 1997.

"Después de las palabras," in *Clarín. Sección Cultura y Nación* (17 November 1994): 12.

"La enfermedad china," in *El nuevo relato argentino*, ed. Héctor Libertella. Caracas: Monte Avila, 1996, 11–26.

"La guerra de los sexos," in *Clarín. Sección Cultura y Nación* (12 August 1993): 12.

"Los ojos cerrados de Marilyn Monroe," in *Clarín. Sección Cultura y Nación* (30 October 1997): 4.

Criticism

Chiaravalli, Verónica. "Marilyn, la bomba ideológica." *La Nación. Sección Cultura* (26 October 1997): 3. (Interview.)

Moncalvillo, Mona. "Carlos Chernov," in *Entrelíneas: confesiones y opiniones de once escritores en diálogo con Mona Moncalvillo*. Buenos Aires: Planeta, 1993, 33–47. (Interview.)

Reati, Fernando. "Mujer y posfeminismo: 'sexo-ficción' en Anatomía humana de Carlos Chernov," in *Memorias de JALLA Tucumán 1995 II*, ed. Ricardo J. Kalimán. Tucumán, Argentina: Universidad Nacional de Tucumán, 1997, 512–20.

Miguel Collazo (b. 1936)

CUBA

Miguel Collazo has had an arduous and difficult life. He studied in various public and private schools in addition to having been in Cuba's National Academy of Fine Arts. He is a multifaceted artist who as a painter has participated in numerous collective expositions, and has also worked as a textile illustrator, a television scriptwriter, and a newspaper and magazine columnist.

His science-fiction works include *El libro fantástico de Oaj* (The fantastic life of Oaj, 1966) and *El viaje* (The voyage, 1968). In the former, Collazo develops a parallel story between a Cuban writer named Juan, who narrates the arrival of the Saturnians to Earth, and the Saturnian author named Oaj who is writing a science fiction novel about the Earth. The narrations of these two science fiction writers are interwoven with news stories and the dialogue of Earth inhabitants that inform the reader of the appearance of flying saucers and cold, red-skinned, translucent Saturnians. Collazo presents us with an unimaginable topic, patiently dismantled and reconstructed in such a way that he is able to make it perfectly compatible with the everyday world of Havana. One of Collazo's projections in this work is the exploration of space in a peaceful manner with the curiosity of a writer who, in his ongoing research, discovers universes and dimensions that he shares with his readers.

In *El viaje*, Collazo creates a planet, Ambar, whose inhabitants live a life that is circular and without meaning. The future is of no importance—only the past is, which began with the character Nur B. At the beginning of the novel, the Ambarians live in two areas: the valley and the desert, and there are no existing cities, only ruins. Gigantic flowers grow in the desert, whose emanations irritate the inhabitants of the planet so that they settled between the two areas to avoid being affected by them. With the birth of the first Ambarian able to tolerate the flower's toxic effect came the possibility of venturing beyond the area to which the inhabitants were confined. This Ambarian opened his mind and created illusions that the others could see as holograms, and from this point on the inhabitants of this strange planet were able to do the same, and thereby hope emerged. A leader rose who convinced the Ambarians to unite the strength of their thoughts and cross the chaotic zone of the planet to arrive at "the mountain," where they would achieve the fullness of their destiny. This union of thoughts caused pain and anguish to take control of the population and hence cities emerged. Through this image, Collazo presents the search for higher forms of social coexistence, thus expressing an encouraging message to Cubans, Latin Americans, and all peoples of the Earth. The achievement of a better way of life is not without suffering or anguish, and is only attained when all individuals unite in search of the common good.

The universe created by Collazo en *El viaje* indeed pertains to the science fiction genre and not that of fantasy. Ambar is governed by the planet's own physical laws; for example, its laws of gravity and cycles of rotation and movement are unique. If it were fantasy, the characters would violate these physical laws. Collazo does not describe complex extraterrestrial spaceships or futuristic technology, instead, he offers ideas, exotic information, and suggests the possibility of a future society that works diligently to achieve the social ideal he proposes. His works may be described as pertaining to "soft science fiction" that, as opposed to "hard science fiction," is concentrated in the social and anthropological sciences instead of technology. The language, the description of the characters and the Ambarian geography, the holographic creations, and the imaginative resources turn this work into a voyage through the multiple possibilities of science fiction.

Heidi Ann García

Works

El libro fantástico de Oaj. Havana: Ediciones Unión, 1966.
El viaje. Havana: Instituto del Libro, 1968.

~

Gerardo Cornejo (b. 1937)

MEXICO

Gerardo Cornejo was born in Tarachi, Sonora in 1937. At the age of 17 he left his native land in the north to travel through the southern regions of Mexico in search of the indigenous, ancestral roots of the country. He lived in other parts of Latin America and Europe while working for national and international organizations. In 1982, he returned home to live in Sonora where he founded the Colegio de Sonora (College of Sonora), an institute of higher learning dedicated to research on the history, economics, politics, and social issues of northeastern Mexico. As rector of the college, he is an active participant in the cultural activity of this region of the country.

His first works reflect his interest in the local culture, specifically that of indigenous populations of the Mexican desert. It is here that he situates his collection of short stories *El solar de los silencios* (The lineage of silences, 1983) and his novel *La sierra y el viento* (The sierra and the wind, 1977). His prose belongs to a wider body of work by Sonoran authors that collectively can be characterized as both realist and contestatory while at the same time exhibiting strong elements of the fantastic. Cornejo's work is also highly influenced by the sociocultural and economic realities of life in the U.S.–Mexican border region. From his vision of this region, especially of the United States as a threat to a way of life experienced in northern Mexico, comes his only science fiction work, *Al norte del milenio* (North of the millennium, 1989). The novel follows a tendency in the contemporary Mexican narrative to fictionalize current political circumstances. In this sense, it is a predecessor of work like *El dedo de oro* (The golden finger, 1996) by Guillermo Sheridan or *La destrucción de todas las cosas* (The destruction of all things, 1992) by Hugo Hiriart.

Cornejo's novel speaks to the author's fear of losing Mexico, of the fading of the country's cultural and spiritual identity before a trilogy of forces that, according to him, again have plotted to sell the northern part of the country to the highest bidder. This trilogy is comprised of the political clergy, the local bourgeoisie, and a conservative party that together make for his worst nightmare come to life. The novel is a warning call, a sounding of the alarm against a perceived cunning invasion taking control of the region. One of the North American politicians in the novel declares that a military invasion is not even necessary, since that portion of the country already belongs to them politically, economically, and culturally. A prophetic novel of the near future, *Al norte del milenio* can be seen as a northern version of *Cerca del fuego* (Near the fire, 1986) by José Agustín. The Mexico of the early twenty-first century is presented as being dangerously perched between independence and submission to foreign control. Horror is followed by hope, and after the national debacle comes collective redemption.

Ultimately, Cornejo's science fiction work is a utopia whose threshold consists of disaster and social indifference. As in Dante's *Inferno*, to arrive at paradise, one must first pass through hell and purgatory. It will be the same for the future of northern Mexico if we do not wake up in time. But as in many other works of science fiction, reality is much faster than fiction. Cornejo's future Mexico is but a pale shadow of the real Mexico. As the writer Federico Campbell has pointed out, the tijuanization of the country is complete, General Jack-in-the-Box and Colonel Wal-Mart have won the final battle without firing a single shot.

Gabriel Trujillo Muñoz

Work

Al norte del milenio. Mexico City: Leega/Programa Cultural de las Fronteras, 1989.

~

Jorge Cubría (b. 1950)

MEXICO

Jorge Cubría was born in Mexico City on 4 August 1950. He holds two degrees in Hispanic literature, the first earned in 1975 at the Universidad Iberoamericana, followed years later by a Master's degree from the Universidad Nacional Autónoma de México (UNAM), awarded in 1996. For over 20 years Cubría has taught literature classes at the Universidad Iberoamericana. Among the courses he regularly teaches is one on the "science" in science fiction, which he recently expanded to include considerations of fantasy and the supernatural. For awhile, Cubría also pursued an indirectly related career in veterinary medicine. He cites Isaac Asimov as the inspiration behind this, for Asimov's books on science, which Cubría discovered in his mid-twenties and proceeded to consume voraciously, awoke in him an interest in the formal study of science. While still teaching his literature classes, he earned a degree in veterinary medicine at the UNAM in 1982 and worked as a researcher in its virology laboratory until 1985. Although he has not worked as a veterinary technician since 1986, he still maintains a strong liking for Asimov.

Cubría is an active supporter of his country's science fiction community. He was elected secretary, and later treasurer, of the Mexican Association of Science Fiction and Fantasy. Over the years, he has served as a discussant and literary guest on a variety of local television programs about science and science fiction, and he organizes a weekly science-fiction film series at the UNAM's science museum, which features discussion sessions with invited scientists, film specialists, and the general public. Cubría is also a frequent contributor to the Mexican edition of *Asimov's*, which has published almost a dozen articles by him on various aspects of the late author's work. As a writer of science fiction and fantasy, Cubría has so far worked exclusively with short fiction. *Venus en blue jeans* (Venus in blue jeans, 1997)—named after a Neil Sedaka song—is his first book. It is a collection of 21 short (and some very short) stories, 11 of which Cubría classifies as either science fiction or fantasy. Many of these texts were previously published in magazines and fanzines such as *El cuento*, *Umbrales*, and *Punto Cero* and have done well in literary competitions: two of the stories were awarded honorable mentions, three were finalists, and one, "El tesoro de la reina de Rapapolvo" (The queen of Rapapolvo's treasure), won first prize in the España 1992 fiction contest. His story "Pastillas de felicidad" (Happiness pills) was selected for inclusion in volume two of Federico Schaffler's *Más allá de lo imaginado*, a three-part anthology of Mexican science fiction.

Venus en blue jeans has the feel of a personal album about it, for interspersed among the short works of fiction are numerous illustrations ranging from artwork borrowed from outside sources to Cubría's own whimsical drawings and photographs of his relations. The stories that make up the collection showcase the author's idiosyncratic yet unadorned writing style and his playfully ironic world-view. He believes that the social and physiological evolution of humankind destines us to such things as collective consciousness, immortality, the eradication of poverty and human manual labor, the instantaneous electronic absorption of knowledge, and the complete control of one's emotions through technological means. Many of these ideas are explored in the stories in *Venus*, often revealing problematic, bizarre, or threatening ramifications of our possible future.

A good example of this is the story "Pastillas de felicidad," which describes a society in which the citizenry is kept manageable and content by means of an obligatory weekly dose of happiness pills. One day, a woman announces to her husband and neighbors that, for the first time in her life, she has refused to take her pill. Although depression, worry, and an emerging social conscience are more painful to her than anything she had ever imagined, she insists that she would rather endure authentic emotions than abdicate them to governmental control and manufactured serenity. Her husband and neighbors admit to a certain curiosity about the range of feelings the woman is experiencing, but they are steadfast in their conviction that life before happiness pills was an endless nightmare of misery and barbarism, often caused by ill-conceived notions (such as Hitler's and the United States') of what was good for the world. The pills take away any desire to strive for change, and since the entire population enjoys complete contentment, all different types of people can get along together. Even the introduction of genetic engineering—which creates a more efficient working class by giving humans gills or monkey tails—is greeted with smiles, for after all, the new hybrid workers have their happiness pills too, so no one suffers. Eventually, and "for her own good," the woman is brought back from her dangerous flirtation with independence, and with unmistakeable irony, the husband, watching his wife dance upside-down on a kitchen table, celebrates with relief her return to sanity.

The simplicity and directness of the narration in "Pastillas de felicidad" heighten the sense of absurdity and unperceived chaos that are so fundamental to the story. The dialogue, even the discourse of government agents, mimics the speech of children, and the characters' witless behavior is made to seem quite rational in the context of the future world Cubría describes. The author is able to communicate a faint undercurrent of mockery through his text the voice of some implied off-stage manipulators—the creators of the happiness pills—who in their hubris are ridiculing their own flawed creations.

Cubría's science fiction stories do not take as their project the serious, near-term extrapolation of twentieth-century attitudes or technologies. Instead, the author—part editorial cartoonist and part prankster—caricatures the future as a distortion of modern society in which a few select trends have been subjected to exaggeration and critique. This can be seen to effect in "Relaciones sexuales del siglo XXII" (Sexual relations in the twenty-second century: Samuel, on the day he turns 20, must take a series of math and chess-playing tests through which the number of sexual relations (if any) he will be entitled to have in his life will be determined. Because he has studied very hard, he does quite well: he is allotted three sexual relations. He and the three young women who are matched to him (and who have also passed the aptitude test) are then ushered into a large building where they live out the paramount moment of their lives—watching robots on a conveyor belt inseminate the girls' eggs with Samuel's sperm (using their own detached sex organs, which were removed at birth and stored). The laboratory lives of his children thus begun, Samuel ecstatically reflects on how great sex with three women is—a rather pathetic declaration given his ignorance and circumstances.

The possibility of highly selective human breeding that scientific breakthroughs now afford us is taken to an extreme in this story. One's worth to society is derived by test scores, and love, sex, and procreation—distilled to their biological essence—are consigned to a laboratory procedure as sterile as an assembly line and as paradoxically abstract and pragmatic as mathematics. Once unfettered by the artificial construct of class, sex and reproduction are now the privilege of an educated elite. "Relaciones sexuales" does not elaborate on the social context in which the story takes place, hence making it difficult to know what the motivations and consequences of selective breeding in this future society are. One warning that can be inferred, however, is that humanity, in pursuit of a misguided concept of perfection, is surrendering itself to formulas and mechanization and learning to be satisfied with what is only a vicarious experiencing of life.

Cubría's stories are characterized by a rather capricious unfolding of plot and an intentionally unsophisticated treatment of characterization and language—qualities that can be effective when combined with irony in stories like "Cine pornográfico" (Porn theater) or when used to develop themes of evolution and compartmentalization in his lighthearted Asimov tribute, "Fundación y robots" (Foundation and robots). This latter story pokes fun at Asimov's prodigious literary output by positing an army of robots, each programmed on the basis of one aspect of the great author's personality, that cranks out a new Asimov book every day. The childlike part of Asimov, for example, is programmed into the robot corps that writes "his" juvenile books. The robots—with names like Hari Seldon, Susan Calvin, and the Mule—celebrate the fact that Asimov, by becoming a foundation of robots, is now "more Asimov" than ever before. The anecdote suffers when the initial amusing premise is subordinated to a debate about the worth (or lack thereof) of humans in the world of *homo cibernéticus*, although some points in the arguments about the laws of robotics are rather clever. Cubría sent this story to Asimov and then enjoyed a last laugh by reproducing the author's polite, handwritten reply on the final page of his story. Asimov's note reads, "Thank you for your nice letter and best wishes in your sf writing but don't write about me" (57).

Cubría's writing constitutes a singular voice in Mexican science fiction. The science fiction and fantasy texts in *Venus en blue jeans* are distinctive for their spirited sense of humor and almost frivolous attitude toward plot. The narrative voice, always direct, can be wickedly ironic at times and outrageous (though never histrionic) at others. Collectively, the stories convey an attitude of delight in speculating on extremes. Some of the stories are perhaps too insubstantial to be more than the flash of a passing thought, but others infuse the fanciful with intriguing images and ideas and thereby leave a more lasting impression.

Andrea Bell

Works

"Pastillas de felicidad," in *Más allá de lo imaginado II: antología de ciencia ficción mexicana*, ed. and intro. Federico Schaffler González. Mexico City: Consejo Nacional para la Cultura y las Artes, 1991, 91–101.

Venus en blue jeans y otros cuentos de chicle. Mexico City: Edamex, S.A., 1997.

Santiago Dabove (1889–1952)

ARGENTINA

Santiago Dabove was one of the best writers of the fantastic short story in Argentina. According to Jorge Luis Borges, he did not receive the recognition he deserved. This may be due, in part, to his well-known reluctance, even refusal, to publish his stories in book form. In fact, his only book, *La muerte y su traje* (Death and its suit), was published posthumously by friends in 1961. Dabove was born in 1889 in Morón, Buenos Aires, where he also died in 1952. He lived with his brother Julio César, a physician, in the family home in Morón and belonged to a group of friends whose Friday meetings are part of the literary mythology of Buenos Aires. The group, lead by Macedonio Fernández met for their weekly *tertulias* (literary circle) at "La Perla," a popular *confitería* or café on the corner of Jujuy and Rivadavia in the Buenos Aires neighborhood of El Once. Regulars of the meetings included Borges, Raúl Scalabrini Ortiz, Xul Solar, and Leopoldo Marechal, among others.

Dabove's friends have portrayed him as having a personality marked by resentment and reclusiveness, his refusal of prominence, and his piercing eyes. He worked in a bank for a brief period of time when he was young and later worked at the horse track in Palermo for just a few hours a week, which allowed him to spend the rest of his time reading and chatting with friends. He also spent his time translating texts by classic French authors—an exercise, he explained, that helped him to more comfortably read them. His lack of success with women, his walks in the neighborhood, his love for *mate criollo* (Argentine herb tea), and a certain preoccupation with his own death due to his cirrhosis are often anecdotally mentioned as aspects of his life.

The topic of death was a recurring intellectual concern of his. In his personal life, this can be linked to the suicide of his brother Darío. All his short stories deal in some way with the topic of death in an up-close, familiar way as if they were a rehearsal for his own. His first short story was published in September 1933 with the title "La muerte y su traje" in *Revista multicolor* (Multicolor magazine), which was created by Jorge Luis Borges as a weekly supplement to the newspaper *Crítica* (Critique). The same story later appeared with the title "La muerte y sus máscaras" (Death and its masks) in *La muerte y su traje*. Subsequent stories began to appear in this and other like periodicals up to 1946.

"Ser polvo" (Being dust) is his most frequently anthologized story. It is undoubtedly inspired by Kafka and narrates the metamorphosis of a man into a plant and then into dust. With its exquisite narrative tension, "Ser polvo" is a story of just a few pages in length in which the entire destiny of human existence is traced with extraordinary precision. The adaptation of the genre to the local ambience also entails a certain humorous overtone. A *paisano* (typical rural inhabitant) falls from his horse in front of a cemetery after suffering a stroke. Unable to get up, he digs a hole in which he begins to make himself comfortable and he also starts to eat dirt to feed himself. He eventually turns into a cactus, suffers blows from an axe, and in time disintegrates into the earth. In Dabove's stories, the first person is always present. While in the fantastic genre the sensation of a sinister presence is produced through the effect of uncertainty or the confrontation with an unexpected reality, in Dabove it becomes markedly more emphatic through first-person narration. His stories are structured around an "I" narrator, similar to what we find in the stories of *Las fuerzas extrañas* (Strange forces, 1906) by Leopoldo Lugones. In *La muerte y su traje*, the narrator expresses his unequivocal and bitter rebellion against both death and life. This rebellion manages to both incorporate and parody the rigorous rules of the fantastic genre. In "Finis," for example, Dabove gives the classic theme of salvation through eternal love when faced with apocalypse or another turn of the screw: the lover, mad with jealousy, kills his beloved because he suspects she betrayed him. Here, we could compare Dabove to Roberto Arlt—who did not write fantastic stories except for "Luna roja" (Red moon)—since we find in both writers the same existential exasperation and sense of ignominy as the most secret and menacing pain of the conscience. Each of Dabove's stories synthesizes not only a question about death, but also a preoccupied attitude toward existence. In "La cuenta" (The bill) the protagonist creates his own false wake so that he can commit suicide publicly. The story sarcastically presents the intimate human desire to control one's own end. To be the owner of one's own death is Dabove's constant concern.

Despite his unique treatment of the genre, Dabove works with many of the themes typical of literature of the fantastic: "Ser polvo" describes a metamorphosis; "Finis," a universal catastrophe; "Tren" (Train) is a game or temporal extrapolation within a dreamlike reality; "El espantapájaros y la melodía" (The scarecrow and the melody) is a ghost story based on the fraud purported by a medium who in reality is a ventriloquist. Several of Dabove's stories deal with the supernatural but are motivated by realism. We find this in "Tratamiento mágico" (Magic treatment), "La muerte y sus máscaras," and even "Ser polvo," where the fantastic can be interpreted as a nightmare induced by drugs: peyote as medication in "Tratamiento mágico," opium pills as sedatives in "Ser polvo," and just the simple excess of wine and hard liquor in "La muerte y sus máscaras." "Tratamiento mágico," despite its apparent scientific motivation, develops the topic of the alter ego according to the traditional formula: when the alter ego dies, one also dies with it but without suffering. "El experimento de Varinsky" (Varinsky's experiment)—influenced by Poe's "The Case of M. Valdemar," according to critics—has several themes typical of the fantastic such as resurrection and traveling to the past through reincarnation in another soul. Its motivation, though, is scientific or pseudoscientific according to the parameters established by the modernists. Without really fully attaining the characteristics of science fiction, these stories can be considered precursors to the genre. The same can be said of "Presciencia" (Prescience) where the experience of the sinister comes from immersion in a mirror and the subsequent galvanization of the protagonist's hand. But in this story, Dabove also tries to explain this phenomenon in a realistic way: he presents it by means of the protagonist's drunken state and an imminent earthquake, since the strange occurrence takes place in the seismically active city of Mendoza. "Monsieur Trépassé," in contrast, is a story about ghosts and ghostly appearances as can be traced to popular mythology. The dead man, a zombie-like figure, arises to walk about fully dressed; finding someone to carry back to his grave with him is a common popular motif.

Given the limited body of his work and its poor distribution, Dabove's writings have become rarely read material among specialists and readers in general. This may be considered more a lamentable void than an undeserved lack of attention. Nevertheless, his stories, like those of Lugones, are deserving of a critical re-evaluation, particularly for their pseudoscientific elements that may be seen as early samples of the science fiction that blossomed in Argentina during subsequent generations of writers.

Cristina Guzzo

Works

"Finis," in *Los universos vislumbrados: antología de ciencia-ficción argentina*, 2nd ed., ed. Jorge A. Sánchez. Buenos Aires: Ediciones Andrómeda, 1995, 67–80.
La muerte y su traje. Buenos Aires: Alcándara, 1961. Reprints, Buenos Aires: Calicanto, 1976; Madrid: Ediciones Libertarias, 1998.

Criticism

Borges, Jorge L. "Prólogo." *La muerte y su traje* by Santiago Dabove. Buenos Aires: Calicanto, 1976.
———. "Selección y prólogos," in *Cuentistas y pintores argentinos*. Buenos Aires: Ediciones de Arte Gaglianone, 1985.
Cócaro, Nicolás. *Cuentos fantásticos argentinos*. Buenos Aires: Emecé, 1976.
Fernández Latour, Enrique. *Macedonio Fernández candidato a Presidente y otros escritos*. Buenos Aires: Ediciones Agon, 1980.
Rivas, José Andrés. "Dabove y sus máscaras." *Mundi* 1.2 (1987): 88–102.

Michel Doezis (pseudonym of Rolando Sánchez) (date unknown)

CHILE

Visión de un sueño milenario (Vision of a millennial dream, 1950), would appear to be the only published work of fiction by a man who is much better known for his thesaurus and his many books on stenographic history and technique. This one novel, while in some ways conventional to the point of being stereotypical, in other respects is a remarkably unusual and imaginative text that is one of the few examples of science fiction published in Chile before that country's best-known modern science fiction writer, Hugo Correa, began his literary career in 1959. *Visión de un sueño milenario* is a "first-contact" story that narrates the adventures of a crew of Chileans who are the first people to voyage to the dark side of the moon. There, they come upon a matriarchal Selenite society that turns out to be an imperfect mirror-image of terrestrial society. From the start, the Chilean crew and Selenite leaders consider each other with open-minded curiosity and good-will, and they herald the encounter as the beginning of a new age of cooperation and growth for the two worlds. Certain experiences on the moon, however, alarm the Chileans about their hosts' values and powers, and after one of their companions is banished and another is brainwashed, they pack their bags and hasten back to Earth.

Visión de un sueño milenario belongs to that tradition of science fiction narratives that create an alien civilization for the chief objective of using it to critique our own. What is perhaps most interesting about Doezis's project is that the comparisons he sets forth are at times surprisingly complex and ambiguous. For example, the Selenites seem at first to have achieved a utopian existence. They have risen up against the frenzied culture of consumerism and self-serving politics that was corrupting them and replaced it with a culture that values philosophical contemplation, beauty, and peace. Selenites, though ostensibly humanoid, enjoy such evolutionary advances as telepathy and telekinesis. Men and women coexist in ordered harmony in obedience to well-understood gender roles. However, in the course of the narrative, Doezis reveals the flaws in this seemingly ideal world. "Obedience" is maintained at the cost of personal liberty, and those who do not conform are excised from the community. Half of society—the men—are oppressed, but their attempts to organize and rebel are not countenanced by the female authorities. The Selenites' world is neither utopia nor dystopia; Chilean society, against which it is tacitly and explicitly compared, is neither a paragon nor a complete failure. Both cultures have strengths and weaknesses, unique gifts and dangers, and it is this understanding that, in the novel, must inform the new age brought on by contact and that, by extension, must guide Chile's policies and objectives in the future.

Chile during the 1940s was being buffeted by massive labor strikes, by bitterly divisive party politics, and by the repercussions of the Second World War. Doezis constructed his cast of characters in *Visión* to represent—positively and nega-tively—the social, economic, and political mix of his day. The crew of the rocket ship is a hodgepodge of social archetypes who furnish the reader with a general profile of middle-class Chilean society. The significance of their roles, and the fate that befalls them individually and collectively, can be read as a pronouncement on where Chile should look for leadership in the postwar period. The leader of the lunar expedition (and the novel's hero) is the rocket-ship's inventor; he, along with the ship's doctor and pilot/mechanic, are the standard-bearers of science; they symbolize the promise that technology holds for a secure, prosperous future. Indeed, science wins out over religion, commerce, and politics, all of which are represented quite unflatteringly in the novel: religion is personified by a narrow-minded and shrilly dogmatic priest; a woefully racist caricature of a Jewish banker represents commerce; and politics is embodied by a pompous Marxist senator.

In spite of their depiction as buffoons, boors, or bad guys, however, the priest, businessman, and politician are important to Chile's future, even if their contri-butions end in martyrdom. For in the final analysis, *Visión de un sueño milenario* is nothing if not a panegyric to Chile's potential: in the novel, after all, Chileans beat out the rest of the world in inventing a rocket ship and flying it to the moon and back. Millions of people from much more prosperous countries monitor the voyage with amazement and newfound humility. Chileans are triumphant; they are the heroes, the center of the world's attention, the ones who will lead human-ity into the future. And for Doezis, the crew he assembles for his fictional voyage into a new era—the scientists, the actor, the priest, the banker, the factotum and the senator—represents the key components of Chilean society, and the attrib-utes they personify—creativity, knowledge, hard work, leadership, and faith, along with their shortcomings—are his country's best hope for future greatness.

Andrea Bell

Work

Visión de un sueño milenario. Santiago: Imprenta Nascimento, 1950.

Criticism

Bell, Andrea, and Moisés Hassón. "Prelude to the Golden Age: Chilean Science Fiction from 1900–1959." *Science Fiction Studies* 66 (1995): 187–97.

Edmundo Domínguez Aragonés (b. 1938)

MEXICO

Edmundo Domínguez Aragonés was born in Spain in 1938. His parents arrived in Mexico with a wave of Spanish immigrants who fled Francisco Franco's fascist Spain in 1939. He studied philosophy and literature at the University of Guadalajara, and by 1961 he was the editor of the Sunday cultural supplement for the newspaper *La opinión* (Opinion). His career in journalism took him to Mexico City where he contributed to periodicals such as *El universal* (The universal), *El sol de México* (The sun of Mexico), and *Excélsior*. Some of his first reporting was on the Vietnam War. In addition, he did commentaries on a variety of radio and television programs. As an author, he has written around a dozen books, including *Argón 18 inicia* (Argon 18 initiates, 1971), *Donde el agua es blanca como el gis* (Where the water is white like chalk, 1973), *El ladrido del cuervo* (The crow's bark, 1976), and *La fiera de piel pintada* (The beast with painted skin, 1986). The latter won a national prize for detective fiction awarded by the publisher Plaza y Janés.

His science fiction novel, *Argón 18 inicia* revolves around three main characters: Librarius Erectus Hernández, Milagros Leiva, and Pepe Nava. The three develop a political theory—the author's own—on the meaning of time and the reverberations of different autonomous universes that overlap. It is a game of mirrors and different moments in history: 1575 (the conquest), 1968 (the massacre of Tlatelolco), and the future. The shadow of Tlatelolco is especially present in the narration through a significant dose of violence and bloodshed, repression and chaos. The structure of the novel is modeled after a Moebius strip, and the action of the entire text takes place in 30 minutes.

In subsequent years Domínguez Aragonés did not return to science fiction writing, although he did periodically publish newspaper articles or reviews on the subject. Nevertheless, his short story "Árbol de vida" (Tree of life), published in the journal *Comunidad Conacyt* (Conacyt community) in 1981, can be considered a classic story of Latin American science fiction. In a masterful combination of action and reflection, the author presents a first-class ecological story. It narrates the pilgrimage of an average family of the future to see a living tree—a museum relic preserved as testimony of a better and happier past when flora covered the Earth and was not artificial. This story, along with *Argón 18 inicia*, seek to explore various concepts of the human experience such as sexuality, politics, the media, and environmental issues in a world where all problems of all times should be of concern to us.

Gabriel Trujillo Muñoz

Works

"Árbol de vida," in *El futuro en llamas: cuentos clásicos de la ciencia ficción mexicana*, ed. Gabriel Trujillo Muñoz. Mexico City: Vid, 1997, 169–81. Also in *Comunidad Conacyt* (August–September 1981).
Argón 18 inicia. Mexico City: Diógenes, 1971.

Manú Dornbierer (b. 1936)

MEXICO

Born in Mexico City in 1936, Manú Dornbierer has earned a reputation as a nationally known journalist. Her writing has appeared in the magazine *Siempre* (Always) and the newspapers *Novedades* (News) and *Excélsior*. She became famous through the latter publication with her column "Satiricosas" (Satirithings). She later became one of the most respected journalists during the transition to a true and effective democracy in the country. Along with Miguel Ángel Granados Chapa and Carlos Ramírez, her direct style has placed her at the center of discussion in Mexican politics.

Before earning recognition as a journalist, Dornbierer was a gifted fiction writer with a talent for describing the troubled future that awaits us. She is the first woman writer in Mexico whose science fiction works received immediate national attention. She does not write science fiction exclusively, and the majority of her stories have only appeared in book form: *Después de Samarkanda* (After Samarkanda, 1970), *La grieta y otros cuentos* (The crack and other stories, 1978), and *Sonrío, luego existo* (I smile, therefore I exist, 1983). Nevertheless, many of her science fiction texts were first published in a variety of magazines during the 1960s, including the famous Spanish science fiction magazine *Nuevas dimensiones* (New dimensions). Her writing must be situated in that decade that was prodigious not only for Mexican culture—evidenced in the explosion of formal and experimental artistic expression—but for science fiction as well, which reached unprecedented heights. The many texts from this period cover a range of different genres, from the fantastic to fairy tales and the gothic, and from tales of terror and death to the appearance of mythological beings such as the centaur. In terms of science fiction, her story "La grieta" is perhaps the best example of the depth and impact of the genre on a national level in that decade. Her works from the 1980s include *El bien y el mal* (Good and evil, 1986) and *Los indignos* (The unworthy, 1988).

The impact of Dornbierer's narrative is due in large part to her strong female protagonists who are intelligent and independent or are striving for independence in spite of the oppressive circumstances in the magic or future worlds they inhabit. In "La grieta," the move from one reality to another upends the daily domestic routine of an ordinary housewife and transports her to a world where the attitudes and taboos are much different and technology is more advanced. Another essential element that permeates the author's science fiction writing is the psychological perception used in presenting the conflicts her characters must face. Instead of a simple story that goes from one adventure to the next to keep the average reader's interest, Dornbierer's text requires a deeper understanding of the internal workings of the human psyche, the labyrinths of the ego and superego where her heroines struggle in search of identity. Not until the appearance of

José Zaidenweber's work *Festín de los egos* (Feast of the egos, 1988) does Mexican science fiction reach such psychoanalytical heights again.

Manú Dornbierer has earned a special place in the history of Latin American science fiction. Together with the Argentine writer Angélica Gorodischer, she represents a body of literature that is less affected by the culture of comics and the myths of the 1960s: counterculture, drugs, youthful rebellion, the revolutionary dreams of students. Her narrative springs from an intellectual space that is more rigorous in its political postulates, more mature in its conception of the human condition, and less Manichean regarding the possibilities and disasters of contemporary global civilization. For example, in "La verdadera historia de la muerte de un planeta" (The true story of the death of a planet) the author more closely resembles Carlos Fuentes than her science fiction contemporaries Carlos Olvera or Narciso Genovese. Indeed, Manú Dornbierer stands apart from the crowd, as her volume of collected science fiction and fantastic works, *En otras dimensiones* (In other dimensions, 1996), clearly demonstrates. This science fiction author of works from the 1960s and 1970s is a cornerstone of the genre in Mexico and one of the country's most accomplished short-story writers. Dornbierer's writing reveals an author capable of seeing the cracks in the future and the deep abysses of the human conscience in an unstable and absurd tomorrow.

Gabriel Trujillo Muñoz

Works

El bien y el mal. Mexico City: Océano, 1986.
Después de Samarkanda. Mexico City: L. Boro Editor, 1970.
En otras dimensiones. Mexico City: Grijalbo, 1996.
La grieta y otros cuentos. Mexico City: Diana, 1978.
Los indignos. Mexico City: Diana, 1988.
"Pastelería vienesa," in *Visiones periféricas: antología de la ciencia ficción mexicana*, ed. Miguel Ángel Fernández Delgado. Mexico City: Lumen, 2001, 49–56.
Sonrío, luego existo. Mexico City: Diana, 1983.

Bernardo Fernández Brigada (b. 1972)

MEXICO

"Bef," as Bernardo Fernández is largely known, was born in Mexico City on May 11, 1972. He studied graphic design at the Universidad Iberoamericana, developing skills that he would later put to use in his work as an illustrator and magazine editor. His early work was as a writer, artist, and editor for a variety of comics, the most important of these being *Molotov*, which he produced with a group of professional illustrators who financed the first issue with money earned by designing cartoon mascots for a line of french fries. Although his graphic-design work has taken him away from comics, Fernández remains dedicated to them, and in tribute to the genre he signed his first published science fiction story with the name Bruno Díaz—Bruce Wayne's name in the Mexican version of *Batman*.

Fernández's extensive work as collaborator and editorial board member spans many different science fiction, fantasy, and horror publications. In addition to *Molotov*, which appeared intermittently between 1993 and 1997, he worked on the fanzines *Hemofilia* (Hemophilia) from 1990 to 1993, *La sombra del Gólem* (The Golem's shadow, 1992), *Tripodología Felina* (Feline tripodology, 1993), and *Número X* (Number X, 1994). Many of the people who worked on these magazines were, like Fernández, professional designers and illustrators committed to creating a space for genres that continue to be marginalized in Mexico. The experience he gained through working on these publications led him to co-found, with Pepe Rojo and Joselo Rangel, the fanzine *Sub* (1996 to present), whose secondary title identifies it as a forum for "subgenres of subterranean subliterature." Currently, Fernández divides his professional energies between *Sub* and *Complot internacional*, where he works as the director of art and design. *Complot* is a monthly magazine whose individual issues focus on a different theme. He was a leading force behind the September 1997 issue, which was devoted to science fiction.

In addition to his editorial and design work, he has met with success as a published science fiction author, beginning in 1993 with the story "Texto hallado entre la basura de un motel de paso" (Text found among the trash at a no-tell motel). A few years later, his story "Combinaciones posibles" (Possible combinations) won by unanimous vote the 1996 Premio Virtual, awarded by the electronic fanzine *La langosta se ha posado* (The lobster has landed). In 1997, he won third prize for "Error de programación" (Programming error)—a children's science fiction story featuring a robotic incarnation of Scheherazade. This award is particularly noteworthy because it was won in a contest open to writers from all genres, not just science fiction. Although Fernández continues to publish self-standing short stories, he has also contributed two story-chapters (one under the pen name Marisol Guardarrama) to a collaborative science fiction novel that he designed for the magazine *Complot internacional*.

Thus far in his career, Fernández has shown a clear predilection for stories that are thematically or stylistically experimental. Several texts, though not quite cyberpunk, nonetheless show the influence of that subgenre in their characterizations and mood. Even when dealing with conventional plot devices, Fernández's best stories are made special by his feel for rhythm and imagery and his skillful evocation of atmosphere. "Ya no hay lugar libre" (No space left) is a good example of the highly sensory quality of Fernández's writing. The main character exists in a desolate, hostile, rain-drenched world where life is a continuous cycle of drugs and violence. The revelation that the character has merely been playing a game in a video arcade may be a fairly unoriginal twist in contemporary science fiction, but Fernández then adds a nice touch by sending his character out of the arcade and into the streets where, unaware of the irony, he initiates the same cycle of drugs and violence in an ambience of desolation, hostility, and rain.

"Ya no hay lugar libre" contains almost no punctuation or word-beginning capital letters and is written as a series of short, staccato phrases separated by blank spaces and periodically interrupted by onomatopoeic phrases like "POM POM POM" (representing the character's heartbeat) and "BIP BIP BIP" (the sound of the video game), printed in full caps and bold type. The text's physical look thus underscores the rain motif that runs throughout the story, amplifying the pulsating, insistent rhythm of the work and echoing the repetitive clamor associated with video arcades. By narrating the story in the second-person singular, Fernández gives "Ya no hay lugar libre" an almost claustrophobic immediacy. It is a very short story, and its brevity and style hurl the reader into the contained chaos of the text just as a pinball is catapulted into the buffeting world of the video game. The work demonstrates Fernández's talent at getting all parts of his text to work in conjunction, and nicely showcases his talents as both a graphic and prose artist.

"Wonderama" (Wonderama), which was a finalist for the Kalpa science fiction award and has been reprinted in several magazines, is another strongly visual story. It takes place in a bizarre fantasy world clearly evoked by Fernández's graphic prose. The first-person narrator keeps a diary of his life in a world that is like a house-of-mirrors distortion of childhood fantasies: it is a brightly colored, singsong place where his parents lavish him with gifts, his diet consists exclusively of junk food, and he spends his days riding around in his go-cart and playing in places with names like Toy-O-Rama and Cookie-Rama. But disturbing *1984*-like messages keep popping up, flashing him cryptic warnings about the deceptive nature of reality. We eventually learn that the character is a political prisoner being subjected to neural cleansing, and his memories are being systematically replaced with the pleasant hallucinations of life in Wonderama that he records in his diary. Wonderama is a prison disguised as a custom-made paradise. An avatar sent into cyberspace to rescue the narrator gives him a white mask to use as protection from neural control, but the prisoner proves unable, or unwilling, to use it and sinks back into his seductive, artificial world of wish-fulfillment.

"Wonderama" reflects a fairly prevalent attitude in contemporary Mexican science fiction about the modern computer age—that is, that for all its benefits, digital technology represents a beguiling, insidious threat to personal identity, security, and agency. Furthermore, resisting it is useless and dangerous, for it is a menace of our own making that ensnares us in accordance with our desires. The diary entries suggest an unsettling hybrid of the child and adult, speaking in a voice that is superficial, infantile, and complacent until destabilized by the narrator's awakening to the short-lived nightmare of truth and resistance. Fernández's decision to co-opt the language and imagery of childhood for his story was especially inspired, for it is an ironic reminder that these days, computers—arguably one of the most powerful devices in society—are touted as child's play.

Fernández's other published science fiction works cover a range of themes and styles. "Rojo" (Red) is a straghtforward, lightly humorous space-buddies tale about cultural differences; "Sólo se recuerda el primero" (You only remember the first one) and "El trozo más grande" (The biggest piece) are about the survival of the fittest in a world of corruption, anarchy, drugs, and violence. While they are all competent stories, it is not difficult to see why one of his more experimental texts, "Combinaciones posibles," won over the jury of the Premio Virtual contest: it is a cleverly self-referential story about writing a story for a literary contest. The twenty-first-century writer in the story may use different tools—direct interface with the internet, virtual reality goggles, a holographic screen—but he is plagued with the age-old writerly problem of dreaming up a good story and figuring out how best to tell it. Fernández manifests this theme by constructing "Combinaciones posibles" out of some four or five fragments of the fictitious author's creative efforts: one story begins, is broken off and discarded by the dissatisfied "author" after a few paragraphs (he is obsessed with second-guessing the contest judges); he starts up a new story and discards it a few paragraphs later, and so on. Like Fernández's own writings, the story fragments in "Combinaciones posibles" exhibit a diversity of styles, one of them formally experimental like his own "Ya no hay lugar libre," another is about gangs and assassins like "Sólo se recuerda el primero" and "El trozo más grande," and one is told in the form of a diary like "Wonderama." It is a multilayered and orginal text that calls attention to boundaries and challenges convention, as does most of Fernández's best work.

Andrea Bell

Works

¡¡Bzzzzzzt!! Ciudad Interface. Mexico City: Times Editores, 1998.

Combinaciones posibles. Mexico City: Molotov, 1996. (Anthology—out of print.)

"Combinaciones posibles." *Umbrales* 25 (1997): n.p.; *Complot internacional* 8 (1997): n.p.

"Crononáuticas." *Charrobot* 1 (1997): n.p.

"(e)," in *Visiones periféricas: antología de la ciencia ficción mexicana,* ed. Miguel Ángel Fernández Delgado. Mexico City: Lumen, 2001,173–86.

Error de progamación. Mexico City: Ediciones Corunda, 1998.

"Mar eléctrico." *Complot internacional* 16 (1998).

"Nanometronaúticas." *Sub* 1 (1996): n.p.

"Texto hallado entre la basura de un motel de paso." *El lumpen ilustrado* 3 (1993): n.p.

"El trozo más grande," in *Silicio en la memoria: antología cyberpunk*, ed. Gerardo Horacio
    Porcayo. Mexico: Ramón Llaca Editores, 1997.

"El último hacker." *Complot internacional* 16 (1998).

"Wonderama." *Sub* 1 (1996): n.p.

"Ya no hay lugar libre." *Complot internacional* 8 (1997).

~

Henrique Villibor Flory (b. 1968)

BRAZIL

Henrique Flory is one of the most prolific contemporary science fiction writers in Brazil. First published at the age of 19, Flory has thus far dedicated his writing to the genre, in contrast to many writers who merely experiment with science fiction and then return to other forms of expression. He is the author of four books: the short-story collections *So sei que não vou por aí!* (I only know I'm not going there, 1989) and *A pedra que canta* (The singing stone, 1991; this is a reprint of the previous volume with five added texts), and the novels *Projeto evolução* (Project evolution, 1990) and *Cristoferus* (1992).

Flory's short stories present a variety of topics and situations; most deal with some kind of loss (from a simple pleasure or comfort to the destruction of the environment) and an attempt to recuperate or replace it. Many of the stories have a sexual or erotic theme and there seems to be an underlying preoccupation with AIDS—from being a rampant destructive force to having been completely cured. In the story "So sei que não vou por aí," a 190-year-old man seeks to recover a younger body. Due to a medical device called a CAI (Cérebro Auxiliar Inorgânico) or Inorganic Auxiliar Brain that is implanted in the abdomen, people can live much longer, since it continually regenerates tissue and cells. Because of his desire to recover simple pleasures, like having an alcoholic beverage, and a more meaningful quality of life, Mathias Boskovitch rejects his CAI. He seeks an operation that will remove it, restore his youth, and allow him to die, young and happy. In "O Long-Dong" (The long dong), a man unhappy with the size and performance of his penis opts for a surgical procedure (made possible by the medical advances of the future) that will enhance both. In a rather shocking final twist (literally), the man dies from being penetrated by his own giant, malfunctioning member. "Big Ben" narrates the story of illegal drug use at the Olympic games in Seoul, Korea in 2088 by an athlete named Ben-Hur, who is a member of the American Union basketball team. Athletes in the Olympics of the future don't just come from different countries, they come from different planets. Several stories describe the planet as an ecological nightmare, completely destroyed by man's carelessness and greed. In "Ícaro," the myth of Icarus is retold in the figure of a young man whose only desire is to fly—free. Flory describes a world where people are forced to live underground because solar radiation is too intense above ground in his story "Cataclisma do Ozônio" (Ozone cataclysm).

In the novel *Projeto evolução*, Flory presents an Earth in imminent danger of destruction from the formation of a black hole. This situation, however, merely serves as the backdrop for the author to expand on his overriding concern with the topic of AIDS. As a new pandemic of the virus spreads, anyone infected with it is viciously persecuted under a system of control that recalls witch hunts, concentration camps, and a new Inquisition. This atmosphere leads to a war between the Gay Liberation Army and the "macartinistas," or supporters of a Senator Joseph Macartney. Additionally, the novel describes the effort to build spaceships that will allow people to escape the disaster. The novel is a dark allegory of a present world in danger of losing its humanity.

Flory's *Cristoferus* recreates the age of voyage and discovery in a historical science-fiction novel where the past becomes the future all over again. Written by following, rather faithfully, the chronicles of discovery (especially those of Christopher Columbus), the author rewrites history by placing his story in the fifteenth century of the Nova Época, or New Age. While most science fiction appropriates the future to speak of the present, here Flory uses the future to reevaluate the past with surprisingly effective results.

Darrell B. Lockhart

Works

Cristoferus. São Paulo: Edições GRD, 1992.
A pedra que canta. São Paulo: Edições GRD, 1991. (Contains all the stories from *So sei que não vou por aí!* plus five more.)
Projeto evolução. São Paulo: HVF Representações, 1990.
So sei que não vou por aí! São Paulo: Edições GRD, 1989.

Carlos Gardini (b. 1948)

ARGENTINA

Carlos Gardini was born in Buenos Aires in 1948. He is one of the most active and productive science fiction writers in Argentina. In contrast with many authors whose work does not represent a concentrated focus on science fiction, the majority of his works pertain to the genre. Gardini is also a professional translator, having translated into Spanish many classic works by authors as diverse as William Shakespeare, Henry James, and Cordwainer Smith. His many translations of science fiction have brought to the Spanish-reading public a wide variety of works by English-language authors. He began his own career as a writer in 1982 when his story "Primera línea" (Front line) received the Premio Círculo de Lectores (Writer's circle first prize)—on the judges' panel were Jorge Luis Borges and José Donoso. This timely story—written just after the Falkland/Malvinas War—is a chilling, surreal tale of soldiers on the battlefield. It has been anthologized in at least two collections of science fiction literature, as well as Gardini's own *Primera línea* (1983), which includes 17 tales in addition to the title story. This marked the beginning of a prolific career as a writer who since has won numerous other awards and accolades.

Gardini published two books in the famous Minotauro series of science fiction in Argentina: the short-story collection *Mi cerebro animal* (My animal brain, 1983), and the novel *Juegos malabares* (Juggling act, 1984). Both books clearly established the author as a major figure in Argentine science fiction. *Juegos malabares* presents the strange world of an amusement park where each interrelated chapter narrates the story of a character or attraction, each more odd than the previous one: from the stupid space alien, the talking dead man, and the smallest woman in the world to the ghost train, the sphinx, and the house of mirrors. The book is a wild ride through a nightmarish carnival atmosphere. His novel *El Libro de la Tierra Negra* (The book of the black earth) was published in 1993, although it appeared in electronic form in 1991. It is considered to be not only his best novel, but also one of the best science fiction novels from Argentina. It is the first in a series in which the protagonist is a book that narrates itself, placing the focus of the narrative on the power of language and words as a creative and/or destructive force. Likewise, the text *El Libro de las Voces* (The book of voices, 2001) is constructed around a kind of oral book that records the speech—revelations, sayings, and so on—of a priest-like class of people known as the *dómines*. Gardini's book won first prize in the Premio UPC science fiction contest (2001)—an international award and one of the most prestigious. It was the second time he won this top award, the previous time for his *Los ojos de un dios en celo* (The eyes of a god in heat, 1996). His book *El Libro de la Tribu* (The book of the tribe, 2001) represents a change in direction, since it is a vampire story. In *Vórtice* (Vortex, 2002), Gardini tends much more toward fantasy than science fiction in a somewhat complicated story of a woman reporter who is raped by eight men, converted into a prophet who then preaches to the men who assaulted her, and eventually dies and is resurrected a thousand years later.

While not all of Gardini's tales collected in his several volumes of short stories are science fiction in nature, many of them do fit the category. As a whole, his works represent one of the most prominent voices in Latin American literature. While many Argentine writers who once concentrated on the genre and have now abandoned it (Angélica Gorodischer, for example), Gardini continues to write and promote science fiction in Spanish. Unfortunately, despite the author's extensive corpus of works, there is no significant critical appraisal of his writing.

Darrell B. Lockhart

Works

"Cesarán las lluvias," in *Cuentos con humanos, androides y robots*, ed. Elena Braceras. Buenos Aires: Colihue, 2000, 117–23.

"La era de Acuario," in *Historia de la fragua y otros inventos*, ed. Marcial Souto. Buenos Aires: Ultramar Editores, 1988, 49–86.

Mi cerebro animal. Buenos Aires: Minotauro, 1983.

Juegos malabares. Buenos Aires: Minotauro, 1984.

El Libro de la Tierra Negra. Buenos Aires: Letra Buena, 1993.

El Libro de la Tribu. Barcelona: El Aleph, 2001.

El Libro de las Voces, in *Premio UPC. Novela corta de ciencia ficción*, ed. Miquel Barceló. Barcelona: Ediciones B, 2001.

Los ojos de un dios en celo, in *Premio UPC 1996. Novela corta de ciencia ficción*, Carlos Gardini et al. Barcelona: Ediciones B, 1997.

Primera línea. Buenos Aires: Sudamericana, 1983.

"Primera línea," in *El cuento argentino de ciencia ficción: antología*, ed. Pablo Capanna. Buenos Aires: Nuevo Siglo, 1995, 176–92. Also in *Latinoamérica fantástica*, ed. Augusto Uribe. Barcelona: Ultramar Editores, 1985, 39–55.

Sinfonía cero. Buenos Aires: Riesa, 1984.

"Sinfonía cero," in *La ciencia ficción en la Argentina: antología crítica*, ed. Marcial Souto. Buenos Aires: Editorial Universitaria de Buenos Aires, 1985, 157–220.

Vórtice. Barcelona: Sirius, 2002.

Sergio Gaut vel Hartman (b. 1947)

ARGENTINA

Sergio Gaut vel Hartman was born in Buenos Aires in 1947. He is the son of Jewish immigrants from Poland and Russia. From the very beginning, he has been an active reader and writer of science fiction. His first story, written in collaboration with Graciela Parini in 1970, was published in the Spanish science fiction journal *Nueva dimensión* (New dimension). In 1982, he began to work for *Péndulo* (Pendulum), one of the leading science fiction publications in Argentina, which he used as a platform to bring together science fiction fans from throughout the country with the section called "Cartas" (Letters). Gaut vel Hartman founded the Círculo Argentino de la Ciencia Ficción y Fantasía (Argentine science fiction and fantasy club). At around this same, time he also founded two well-known science fiction magazines, *Sinergía* (Sinergy, 1983) and *Parsec* (1984).

In 1983, the journal *Minotauro* (Minotaur) launched the first series of science fiction and fantasy books written in Spanish. Gaut vel Hartman's book *Cuerpos descartables* (Disposable bodies, 1985) was published in this collection. Other authors published in the *Minotauro* series include Carlos Gardini, Mario Levrero, Angélica Gorodischer, Ana María Shua, and Rogelio Ramos Signes. *Cuerpos descartables* won the *Más Allá* (Great beyond) award for best book of the year and it has been translated into Italian. His short stories have been anthologized in numerous collections; he is the editor of *Fase uno* (Phase one, 1987), a volume of science fiction short stories.

Gaut vel Hartman's fiction is characterized by an interest in the coexistence of tangential realities or parallel dimensions. The author speculates on the entropic degradation of the quotidian and the capacity of human beings to adapt to atypical conditions. Furthermore, he utilizes chess as a narrative device, a type of labyrinth and thematic superstructure for metaphysical exploration. In the short story "Carteles" (Signs, in *La ciencia ficción en la Argentina* [1985]), the author replaces daily reality with a sense of remoteness, discomfort, and strangeness. The story presents a reality reflected in signs that define the immediate surroundings of the individual. The signs describe the weather, the temperature, and even the man himself. The author, through a first-person narrator, invites the reader to enter a zone outside the limits of the "human" and the "real." Gaut vel Hartman uses the signs to create tension between the symbolic and imaginary. He allows the reader to imagine the need for far-reaching cultural transformations upon the dissolution or destruction of the line separating the real from the imaginary.

The story "Cuerpos a la deriva" (Bodies adrift, in *Fase uno*) explores tangential reality through cloning or creation of the disposable body. In this story, the body becomes an ideological concept that is produced as the representation of a concrete reality: bodies are bought and sold, worn out and exchanged. With these transferable bodies, the author problematizes the representation of a social reality—or better said, a human reality—which seeks to transcend the limits of a centered "I," socially defined and subject to time.

In "Los contaminados" (The contaminated, in *Cuerpos descartables*), Gaut vel Hartman utilizes all the resources of science fiction to create a terrifying world in which nature has been obliterated. The story presents an ecological nightmare that projects the fears of humanity. Although smog, darkness, and gaseous winds are unable to extinguish the hope of recovering life, the author reveals the dissatisfaction with what the future holds in store. He exaggerates and distorts nature to create a world in which the relationship of the real and unreal is questioned.

Gaut vel Hartman's texts offer the reader an obstinate rejection of the prevailing definitions of the "real" and "possible," a rejection that at times turns into violent opposition. His texts subvert and undermine cultural stability to shatter the fundamental barrier that separates "real life" from the "unreal." His science fiction presents the undefined and the indefinable so as to create a reaction against the "real" transporting the reader to a place where everything is possible, even the real.

Marcelo Willcham

Works

"Caramelos," in *Cuentos con humanos, androides y robots*, ed. Elena Braceras. Buenos Aires: Colihue, 2000, 101–16.

"Carteles," in *La ciencia ficción en la Argentina: antología crítica*. Buenos Aires: Editorial Universitaria de Buenos Aires, 1985, 231–35. (Interview on pages 236–40.)

"Cuerpos a la deriva," in *Fase uno*. Buenos Aires: Sinergia, 1987, 183–94.

Cuerpos descartables. Buenos Aires: Minotauro, 1985.

"En el depósito." *Minotauro* 10 (1985): 71–76.

Fase uno, ed. Sergio Gaut vel Hartman. Buenos Aires: Sinergia, 1987.

"Lapso de reflexión," in *Ciencia ficción: cuentos hispanoamericanos*, ed. José María Ferrero. Buenos Aires: Huemul, 1993, 103–8.

"Náufrago de si mismo," in *El cuento argentino de ciencia ficción: antología*, ed. Pablo Capanna. Buenos Aires: Ediciones Nuevo Siglo, 1995, 214–26.

"Los trepadores," in *Latinoamérica fantástica*, ed. Augusto Uribe. *Ciencia Ficción*, 18. Barcelona: Ultramar Editores, 1985, 15–30.

Narciso Genovese (1911–1982)

MEXICO

Narciso Genovese was born in Turin, Italy in 1911. He immigrated to El Salvador and eventually ended up in Mexico. After moving from one place to another, he ultimately settled down in Tijuana. In the mid-1950s, he began to publish books that mixed philosophical speculation with secret wisdom that, according to the author, had been communicated to him by extraterrestrials from Mars. His most important books are *Yo he estado en Marte* (I've been to Mars, 1958) and *La nueva Aurora* (The new aurora, 1970).

In 1965, Genovese joined the Asociación de Escritores de Baja California (Baja California association of writers) founded by Rubén Vizcaíno Valencia, which helped him to have greater contact with the literary community that up until then had ignored him. In the first edition of *Yo he estado en Marte*, the author claimed that it was a fantasy and a work of science fiction. However, in the 1966 re-edition, he declared frankly and in all seriousness that the novel was in fact based upon his personal experience. Regardless of the author's declarations, one need only read the novel and consider its futurist proposals to determine if it can be classified as science fiction. What stands out in the text, aside from the fabulous affirmations that the trip to Mars really occurred, is that the novel truly is a work of hard science fiction. If the science is questionable, it is due to the fact that the knowledge is anachronic. Like Isaac Asimov who wrote of Venus as a planet covered by oceans and jungles, Genovese imagined an unreal, fictitious Mars but nevertheless an appropriated setting for his optimistic view of Martians. His extraterrestrials are kind beings that want humanity to abandon its violence and egoism and replace them with a scientific–religious utopia, where Christianity and technology live side-by-side. His Martians are true teachers bent on teaching humanity the path to progress and fraternal bliss that will liberate us from the problem of wars and self-destructive conflicts that we have engaged in since the dawn of time.

Yo he estado en Marte is the best and most successful Latin American work of science fiction of the 1950s. One should point out that Genovese wrote it during the Cold War. Science in the author's Martian utopia is used for the benefit of life, not to cause death; moreover, technology serves the common good, not the exploitation of many by few. This may be seen as an update of Jules Verne's adventure fiction—along with his style, which doesn't cease to be nineteenth century, parsimonious, and repetitive in its concepts and vision. Nonetheless, *Yo he estado en Marte* did appear at just the right moment—the initial stages of the space race between the United States and Soviet Union, which led to its becoming a bestseller in Europe and making the author fairly famous. He was asked to participate on television and radio programs and gave numerous lectures.

Genovese died in Tijuana in 1982. Today, he is considered to be a pioneer of

Latin American science fiction, an author who lived modestly while he wrote of a Martian utopia whose sole purpose was to make our world less insensitive and cruel in order for it to be a more inhabitable place. With *Yo he estado en Marte* and *La nueva Aurora*—which was a kind of fictional essay on the future of humanity as citizens of the cosmos—Narciso Genovese added his part to create a science fiction that is contradictorily rational, believable, visionary, and well thought out. In a Mexico of the 1950s, caught between two ideologies at the war's doorstep and with the uncertainty of a better future, Genovese strove to advocate a more livable, sane, and kind future that would never be realized.

Gabriel Trujillo Muñoz

Works

La nueva Aurora. Mexico City: B. Costa-Amic, 1970.
Yo he estado en Marte. Mexico City: Posada, 1977 (copyright © 1958).

Criticism

Trujillo Muñoz, Gabriel. *Los confines: crónica de la ciencia ficción mexicana*. Mexico City: Grupo Editorial Vid, 1999, 113–19.

Eduardo Goligorsky (b. 1931)

ARGENTINA

Born in Buenos Aires, Goligorsky has worked as an English translator, journalist, and editor. His journalistic work focuses on contemporary social and political topics. He published several detective novels under the pseudonym James Alistair and other Anglo-Saxon pseudonyms to which he has not yet admitted. Goligorsky's science-fiction production is limited to a handful of short stories, most of them published in anthologies co-authored with Alberto Vanasco and collected in *A la sombra de los bárbaros* (In the shadow of the barbarians, 1977). The fictional element is accompanied by a series of theoretical reflections on the nature of the genre, which demonstrate a thorough familiarity with the major international and Argentine works of the genre. It is within this national and international framework that he situates his own work, exploring its connections and influences as well as its (not always evident) Argentine characteristics.

Aside from brief prologues, this critical and theoretical vein of Goligorsky's work is mainly represented in *Ciencia-ficción: Realidad y psicoanálisis* (Science-fiction: reality and psychoanalysis, 1969), co-written with Marie Langer. Here, he develops the basis for the humanistic concept of science fiction, which he explores in the stories themselves. The human being is the central preoccupation, comprising the struggle for the preservation of freedom of thought when faced by the repression generated by the misuse of technical advances and the alienation that tends to come as a consequence of mechanical perfection. By "science" he understands not only technology but also economics and politics, and it is this broad understanding that gives his fictional work its depth and variety and links it to contemporary Latin American preoccupations with dictatorship, repression, and underdevelopment. Fear and desire are the most recurrent themes in his work, explored and reflected through utopia, dystopia, or any form of fantasy. The political–humanistic agenda of his stories is based on his tenet that science fiction is inevitably an allegory of society and an exploration of the possibilities of the human mind. He upholds science fiction and fantasy as the best ways to express the ideals of the new humanism and to break the restrictions of the creative imagination.

A la sombra de los bárbaros, which collects most of Goligorsky's science fiction short stories written between 1965 and 1972, has the nineteenth-century Argentine tradition of "civilization and barbarism" as its organizing principle. He reverses the meanings given to these two concepts by Domingo Faustino Sarmiento, that depicts societies where "civilization" is understood as the idealization of the noble savage and of a utopian past that has been led to isolation by outside influences, loss of freedom, and ultimately, total regression and the erasure of all the achievements of humankind. In "Historia de familia" (Family history), for example, humans go through all the stages of development in reverse, until they become monkeys. Foreign countries and their scientific advancements are seen by those in power as the "barbarians" leading toward total apocalypse and moral decay, while they impose a dystopian, totalitarian antimaterialism that passes for civilization. Here, Goligorsky uses science fiction mainly to explore the consequences of the political, economic, and ideological isolation of Latin American regimes from the rest of the world. The book as a whole thus becomes a chronicle of underdevelopment that is still too close in time for Latin American nations, and presents a series of dystopian societies in which the most natural human emotions and their expressions are forbidden: singing and laughter in "Y en sus alas me llevará" (And on his wings he will carry me); writing and the desire to travel and transcend boundaries in "A la sombra de los bárbaros" and "Historia de familia"; and the desire for peace and beauty in "Aclimatación" (Acclimatization). Unsurprisingly, the fascination with space travel does not come from the technological advancement that it represents, but from its potential as a means of escape and of facilitating the human need for global interaction. Spaceships are most often romantically depicted as lights that crisscross the night sky rather than masses of metal and machinery. In "En el último reducto" (In the last refuge, 1967), the spaceship is presented as the only hope for salvation from the stifling heat that will ultimately kill the protagonist. The stories often include a protagonist-messiah who defies the arbitrary laws of the stifling political regimes, who possesses an inner instinct that leads him or her to defy them, and who ultimately represents society's only hope through his or her contact with beings from other worlds. Although in some of Goligorsky's earlier stories, such as "Los verdes" (The green ones, 1967) and "Ellos" (Them, 1967) extraterrestrials are depicted as cruel outsiders seeking to infiltrate and destroy human society, in his later works they tend to become a way of embodying goodness not only in the form of technological progress but also in beauty and human emotion, all of which are forbidden to the isolated societies.

It is not difficult to see the stifling political conditions of Argentina during the 1960s and 1970s as the starting point for Goligorsky's science fiction stories. He admitted as much in his prologue to *Los argentinos en la luna* (Argentines on the moon, 1968), where he sought out responses to censorship and selected materials where fiction predominates over the scientific elements. For him, science fiction is an allegory of the author's own society and therefore he does not consider Argentine science fiction an imitation, but rather a genre that is on the same level as with the rest of the world. He considers the themes of alienation, fanaticism, intolerance, and dehumanization, which characterize much of Argentine science fiction (including his own), as expressions of the sociological and psychological themes that predominate in the genre throughout the world. Although he sees a deep connection between each author and his society, he also believes in the universality of these themes. His own contribution to this anthology (*Los argentinos en la luna*), "El vigía" (The sentinel, 1968), points toward this universality through the use of Biblical mythology, and is linked to other stories in which he has used similar imagery. It depicts a dystopian society where the suppression of eroticism, as a way in which a minority imposes its moral principles upon society, is countered with the sexual pleasure experienced by the killer in charge of upholding those same principles. The story is told on two planes: one describing the sentinel's own feelings while carrying out his deadly mission; and the other moralizing and explanatory, culminating in the escape of a family reminiscent of Mary, Joseph, and Jesus fleeing Herod's massacre. The Biblical theme is also explored in "Un mundo espera" (A world awaits, 1966), where the character of Jesus Christ is reworked as the representative of an extraterrestrial pacifist society seeking a society that they can infiltrate and begin to transform according to their values. Once again, a Christ-like figure is upheld as the hope of rebirth for a human society destroyed by outside forces. The same theme recurs in "El elegido" (The chosen one, 1966), though less obviously and more pessimistically, since the protagonist ends up being destroyed and taking with him all hope for the future.

Although the sociological aspects of science fiction predominate in Goligorsky's work, the psychological elements are also one of his main preoccupations. Human fantasies and dehumanization are explored in "Los divanes paralelos" (The parallel sofas, 1966)—a satirical allegory of how television technology is taking over reality and human contact, and in "Olaf y las explosiones" (Olaf and the explosions, 1966), where men become robotic technicians with programmed brains and without feelings, and women become the rebels through whose rebellion the hope of the end of technological tyranny is expressed. "La cicatriz de Venus" (Venus's scar, 1967) breaks through the boundaries of human life by exploring male pregnancy as a result of sexual relations with a Venusian. If this story expresses how the human body can stretch boundaries, "La cola de la serpiente" (The snake's tail, 1967) does the same for the mind, which is capable of providing at least the illusion of comfort and realizing a man's most urgent desires at the moment of his dying. The power of the human mind in most of Goligorsky's stories is at play with the reader's expectations, often providing surprising final twists that upset conventional and linear ways of thinking and offer a literary experience that is both entertaining and thought-provoking.

Beatriz Urraca

Works

"Aclimatación," in *Cuentos argentinos de ciencia ficción*. Buenos Aires: Editorial Merlín, 1967, 75–87.

Adiós al mañana (with Alberto Vanasco). Buenos Aires: Minotauro, 1967.

A la sombra de los bárbaros. Barcelona: Ediciones Acervo, 1977. Reprint, Barcelona: Ediciones Orbis, 1985.

"Un aroma de flores lascivas," in *Lo mejor de la ciencia ficción latinoamericana*, ed. Bernard Goorden and R. E. Van Vogt. Buenos Aires: Hyspamérica, 1988, 63–76.

Ciencia-ficción: Realidad y psicoanálisis (with Marie Langer). Buenos Aires: Paidós, 1969.

"Cuando los pájaros mueran," in *Ciencia ficción argentina: antología de cuentos*, ed. Pablo
    Capanna. Buenos Aires: Aude Ediciones, 1990, 33–51.
"El elegido," in *El cuento argentino de ciencia ficción: antología*, ed. Pablo Capanna. Buenos
    Aires: Ediciones Nuevo Siglo, 1995, 80–91.
"En el último reducto," in *La ciencia ficción en la Argentina: antología crítica*, ed. Marcial
    Souto. Buenos Aires: EUDEBA, 1985, 43–57. Also in *Historias futuras: antología de la
    ciencia ficción argentina*, ed. Adriana Fernández and Edgardo Pígoli. Buenos Aires:
    Emecé, 2000, 117–26. English translation as "The Last Refuge," trans. Andrea Bell, in
    Cosmos Latinos: An Anthology of Science Fiction from Latin America and Spain, ed. An-
    drea Bell and Yolanda Molina-Gavilán. Middletown, CT: Wesleyan University Press,
    2003, 110–15.
Memorias del futuro (with Alberto Vanasco). Buenos Aires: Minotauro, 1966.
"El vigía," in *Los argentinos en la luna*, ed. Eduardo Goligorsky. Buenos Aires: Ediciones de
    la Flor, 1968, 65–74.

Criticism

Molina-Gavilán, Yolanda. "Mitos posholocáusticos: 'Post-Bombum' de Alberto Vanasco y
    'Cuando los pájaros mueran' de Eduardo Goligorsky," in *Ciencia ficción en español: una
    mitología moderna ante el cambio*. Lewiston, NY: Edwin Mellen Press, 2002, 91–97.

Angélica Gorodischer (b. 1928)

ARGENTINA

The narrative of Angélica Beatriz Arcal de Gorodischer traverses many genres. Principal among these are science fiction and the literature of the fantastic, but she has also produced detective and mystery fiction. Additionally, in her nonfiction writing, she has dealt extensively with women's issues and literary theory.

Gorodischer published her first short story, a detective-thriller titled "En verano, a la siesta y con Martina" (In summer, napping and with Martina), in 1964, followed a year later by her first collection of short stories, *Cuentos con soldados* (Stories with soldiers, 1965). These early works are primarily realist pieces, a trend that ends abruptly with the publication in 1967 of her first novel, *Opus dos* (Opus Two), a work which signals the entry of Gorodischer into the arena of science fiction. The publication of *Las pelucas* (The wigs) in 1968 marks another important signpost on Gorodischer's literary journey. In the 11 stories assembled in this anthology, Gorodischer experiments with a variety of narrative approaches, from dark gothic pieces to whodunits, and even briefly ventures into a sort of narrative poetry.

During the following years she returns to science fiction with the publication of *Bajo las jubeas en flor* (Under the yubayas in bloom, 1973) and *Casta luna electrónica* (Electronic caste moon, 1977). In this latter work she introduces perhaps her most famous character, and certainly one of the most well-known in Argentine science fiction, Trafalgar Medrano. Not only is the introduction of the humorous intergalactic millionaire from Rosario a milestone in Gorodischer's literary trajectory, but so too is the world to which he travels, Veroboar, a world in which the women have replaced the men with machines. The situations described on Veroboar illustrate an important and recurrent theme in Gorodischer's work: her concern with the relations among man, woman, and technological society. With the publication of *Trafalgar* in 1979, both the protagonist's and Gorodischer's place in science fiction are sealed.

While *Trafalgar* marks the end of the first phase of Gorodischer's literary career, the publication of *Kalpa imperial. Libro I: La casa del poder* (Imperial Kalpa. Book I: The house of power, 1983) and *Kalpa imperial. Libro II: El imperio más vasto* (Imperial Kalpa. Book II: The grandest empire, 1984) opens a new period. *Kalpa* is the story (actually a series of stories) of an imaginary empire and the human desires that drive its history. While the manifest fictional world in *Kalpa* pertains to the fantastic, the latent narrative subject is the very real world of human society and social relations.

The propensity for social commentary seen in *Kalpa* becomes explicit in *Mala noche y parir hembra* (Bad night and birth of a female child, 1983), Gorodischer's first unreservedly feminist text. The social criticism found in the 12 stories that comprise the collection is not restricted to the patriarchy but also parodies various dominant social discourses, among them moral instruction, the rules of etiquette, and the conventions of the scientific essay.

Two years later, with the publication of her best-selling novel *Floreros de alabastro, alfombras de Bokhara* (Alabaster flower vases, Bokhara carpets, 1985) Gorodischer returns to the detective-thriller format she used in the first story she published, but this time she employs a feminist twist. The central character is a middle-aged female detective, the first of her kind in Hispanic letters. She is followed by a similar female protagonist in Gorodischer's next novel, another detective-thriller titled *Jugo de mango* (Mango juice, 1988).

In her succeeding literary effort, *Las Repúblicas* (The republics, 1991), Gorodischer returns to science fiction, combining this genre with elements of the fantastic. This collection of five stories also retains her now-characteristic feminist imprint, which in *Las Repúblicas* includes a transsexual character and a concomitant questioning of received sex/gender roles. Additionally, ecological concerns about natural-resource depletion and environmental destruction are posited in this volume.

In 1994, Gorodischer published the novel *Prodigios* (Prodigies), which marks yet another phase in her literary evolution in that it employs experimental narrative techniques. The novel has no plot *per se*, but instead relies upon linguistic manipulation to explore the profundity and ambivalence of language itself. In the absence of a traditional linear plot, the background or setting of the novel—the house through which fragments of lives are glimpsed—becomes the kalidoscopic lense by means of which the reader views the overdetermined discursive space presented. In spite of these stylistic experiments, her concern with human relationships remains constant.

Finally, her 1996 novel *La noche del inocente* (The night of the innocent), can best be described as a critique of contemporary morality loosely veiled as a historical novel. Although the action takes place in a medieval monastery, the immoral atmosphere of corruption and debauchery that permeates the fictional world of the novel seems quite similar to the atmosphere surrounding the current world of Argentine politics. Simultaneously, the novel explores the role of the Church in perpetrating the established relations of power, and the sinners who abuse this power.

Jerry Hoeg

Works

"Acerca de ciudades que crecen descontroladamente," in *Latinoamérica fantástica*, ed. Agusto Uribe. Barcelona: Ultramar, 1985, 259–93.

"A la luz de la casta luna electrónica," in *Historias futuras: antología de la ciencia ficción argentina*, ed. Adriana Fernández and Edgardo Pígoli. Buenos Aires: Emecé, 2000, 127–45.

Bajo las jubeas en flor. Buenos Aires: Ediciones de La Flor, 1973. Reprint, Barcelona: Ultramar, 1987.

"Bajo las jubeas en flor," in *La ciencia ficción en la Argentina*, ed. Marcial Souto. Buenos Aires: EUDEBA, 1985, 69–98.

Casta luna electrónica. Buenos Aires: Andrómeda, 1977.

Cuentos con soldados. Santa Fe, Argentina: Club del Orden, 1965.

"Los embriones del violeta," in *Los universos vislumbrados*, ed. Jorge Sánchez. Buenos Aires: Andrómeda, 1995, 149–93. Also in *Lo mejor de la ciencia ficción latinoamericana*, ed. Bernard Gooden, and A. E. Van Vogt. Buenos Aires: Hyspamérica, 1988, 122–56. English version as "The Violet's Embryos," trans. Sara Irausquin, in *Cosmos Latinos: An Anthology of Science Fiction from Latin America and Spain*, ed. Andrea Bell and Yolanda Molina-Gavilán. Middletown, CT: Wesleyan University Press, 2003, 159–93.

"En el confín," in *Cuentos con humanos, androides y robots*. Buenos Aires: Colihue, 2000, 83–91.

"Epílogo. Carta de Angélica Gorodischer a Marcial Souto," in *Latinoamérica fantástica*, ed. A. Uribe. Barcelona: Ultramar, 1985, 295–98.

Fábula de la virgen y el bombero. Buenos Aires: Ediciones de La Flor, 1993.

Floreros de alabastro, alfombras de Bokhara. Buenos Aires: Emecé, 1985.

Jugo de mango. Buenos Aires: Emecé, 1988.

Kalpa imperial. Buenos Aires: Emecé, 2001. (Both Kalpa books published together.)

Kalpa imperial. Libro I: La casa del poder. Buenos Aires: Minotauro, 1983. Reprint, Barcelona: Martínez Roca, 1990.

Kalpa imperial. Libro II: El imperio más vasto. Buenos Aires: Minotauro, 1984.

"La lucha de la familia González por un mundo mejor," in *El cuento argentino de ciencia ficción: antología*, ed. Pablo Capanna. Buenos Aires: Nuevo Siglo, 1995, 92–120. Also in *Cuentos fantásticos de América Latina*. Buenos Aires: Centro Editor de América Latina, 1983.

Mala noche y parir hembra. Buenos Aires: La Campana, 1983.

"Man's Dwelling Place," trans. Alberto Manguel, in *Other Fires, Stories of Women of Latin America*, ed. Alberto Manguel. New York: Clarkson N. Potter, 1986, 88–94.

"La morada del hombre," in *Los argentinos en la luna*, ed. Eduardo Goligorsky. Buenos Aires: Ediciones de la Flor, 1968, 75–82.

"Narrativa fantástica y narrativa de ciencia-ficción." *Plural: revista cultural de Excélsior* 188 (1987): 48–50.

La noche del inocente. Buenos Aires: Emecé, 1996.

Opus dos. Buenos Aires: Minotauro, 1967. Reprint, Barcelona: Ultramar, 1990.

Las pelucas. Buenos Aires: Sudamericana, 1968.

"La pera irremediable" (with Guillermo Boido), in *Historia de la fragua y otros inventos*, ed. Marcial Souto. Buenos Aires: Ultramar, 1988, 17–27.

"The Perfect Married Woman," "Letters from an English Lady," "Under the Flowering Juleps," "Resurrection of the Flesh," in *Secret Weavers, Stories of the Fantastic by Women of Argentina and Chile*, ed. Marjorie Agostín. New York: White Pine Press, 1992, 243–83.

Prodigios. Barcelona: Lumen, 1994.

"Própositos matinales bajo las frondas," in *Cuentos fantásticos inquietantes*. Buenos Aires: Grupo Editor de Buenos Aires, 1980.

Las Repúblicas. Buenos Aires: Ediciones de la Flor, 1991.

"La resurrección de la carne," in *Ciencia ficción: cuentos hispanoamericanos*, ed. José María Ferrero. Buenos Aires: Huemul, 1993, 121–25.

Trafalgar. Buenos Aires: El Cid, 1979. Reprint, Rosario: Ediciones El Peregrino, 1984. Reprint, Barcelona: Orbis, 1986.

"Under the Yubayas in Bloom," in *Beyond the Border: A New Age in Latin American*

Women's Fiction, ed. Nora Erro-Peralta and Caridad Silva. Pittsburgh: Cleis Press, 1991. New revised ed., Gainesville: University Press of Florida, 2000.

Criticism

Balboa Echeverría, Miriam. "Poder, fabulación y memoria en tres novelas de Angélica Gorodischer," in *Actas Irvine-92. II: La mujer y su representación en las literaturas hispánicas*, ed. Juan Villegas. Irvine: Asociación Internacional de Hispanistas, 1994, 196–204.

Balboa Echeverría, Miriam, and Ester Gimbernat González, eds. *Boca de Dama: La narrativa de Angélica Gorodischer*. Buenos Aires: Feminaria, 1995.

Burgos, Fernando. "Retratos de la historia en el cuento posmoderno hispanoamericano: Luis Arturo Ramos y Angelica Gorodischer." *La palabra y el hombre: Revista de la Universidad Veracruzana* 92 (1994): 143–55.

Dellepiane, Angela. "Contar = mester de fantasía o la narrativa de Angélica Gorodischer." *Revista iberoamericana* 51.132–33 (1985): 627–40.

———. "*Mala noche y parir hembra* de Angélica Gorodischer," in *The Latin American Short Story: Essays on the 25th Anniversary of Seymore Menton's* El cuento hispanoamericano, ed. Kemy Oyarzún. Riverside: University of California. LASP No. 9, 1989, 48–61.

———. "Dos heroínas improbables en sendas novelas argentinas: *Floreros de alabastro, alfombras de Bokhara* y *Jugo de mango* de Angélica Gorodischer," in *Actas del X Congreso de la Asociación Internacional de Hispanistas*, vol. III. Barcelona: Promociones y Publicaciones Universitarias, 1992, 573–83.

Eberle-McCarthy, Karen. "Worlds within Argentine Women," in *Actas de la décimotercera conferencia anual de literatura hispánica en Indiana University of Pennsylvania*. Miami: Miami Universal, 1990, 237–42.

Espulgas, Celia. "Con Angélica Gorodischer." *Hispamérica* 67 (1994): 55–59. (Interview.)

Fares, G., and E. Hermann. "Angélica Gorodischer," in *Escritoras argentinas contemporáneas*. New York: Peter Lang, 1993.

Gandolfo, Elvio. "La obra de Angélica Gorodischer." *El lagrimal trifurca* 13 (1975): n.p.

Gimbernat González, Ester. "*Floreros de alabastro, alfombras de Bokhara*: el poder del nombre, los nombres del poder," in *Aventuras del desacuerdo: novelistas argentinas de los 80*. Buenos Aires: Alberto Vergara, 1992, 139–45.

———. "*Jugo de mango*: itinerarios de la escritura," in *Aventuras del desacuerdo: novelistas argentinas de los 80*. Buenos Aires: Alberto Vergara, 1992, 176–85.

Goorden, B. "Quand Angélica Gorodischer Ecrit de la Sc-F, elle Ecrit Mieux que les Hommes." *Ides et Autres* 24 (1980): n.p.

Lagmanovich, David. "Gandolfo, Gorodischer, Martini: Tres narradores jóvenes de Rosario (Argentina)." *Chasqui: revista de literatura latinoamericana* 4.2 (1975): 18–28.

Lojo de Beuter, María Rosa. "Dos versiones de la utopía: 'Sensatez del círculo' de Angélica Gorodischer, y 'Utopía de un hombre que está cansado' de Jorge Luis Borges," in *Mujer y sociedad en América: IV Simposio Internacional*, vol. 1. Mexicali: Universidad de Baja California, 1988, 93–104.

Mathieu, Corina. "Feminismo y humor en *Floreros de alabastro, alfombras de Bokhara*." *Letras femeninas* 17.1–2 (1991): 113–19.

Molina-Gavilán, Yolanda. "Alternate Realities from Argentina: Angélica Gorodischer's 'Los embriones del violeta.'" *Science Fiction Studies* 79.26 (1999): 401–11.

———. *Ciencia ficción en español: una mitología moderna ante el cambio*. Lewiston, NY: Edwin Mellen Press, 2002.

Mosier, M. Patricia. "Communicating Transcendence in Angélica Gorodischer's *Trafalgar*." *Chasqui: revista de literatura latinoamericana* 12.2–3 (1983): 63–71.

———. "Comunicando la trascendencia en *Trafalgar* por Angélica Gorodischer." *Foro literario: revista de literatura y lenguaje* 15–16 (1986): 50–56.

———. "Women in Power in Gorodischer's *Kalpa Imperial*," in *Spectrum of the Fantastic*, ed. Donald Palumbo. Westport, CT: Greenwood, 1988, 153–61.

Ramos, H. "El lector activo en *Kalpa imperial*." *Pórtico* (1993): n.p.

Sánchez Arce, Claudia. *Los temas de la ciencia ficción en* Trafalgar. Mexico City: Universidad Autónoma del Estado de México, 1993.

Serra, E. "Una combinatoria narrativa: Angélica Gorodischer," in *Narrativa del Litoral*. Rosario: Grupo de Estudios Semánticos, 1981, n.p.

Urraca, Beatriz. "Angélica Gorodischer's Voyages of Discovery: Sexuality and Historical Allegory in Science Fiction's Cross-Cultural Encounter." *Latin American Literary Review* 45 (1995): 85–102.

Vásquez, María Esther. "Angélica Gorodischer: una escritora latinoamericana de ciencia ficción." *Revista iberoamericana* 49.123–24 (1983): 571–76.

Ricardo Guzmán Wolffer (b. 1966)

MEXICO

Ricardo Guzmán Wolffer is a Mexico City attorney who in 1998 was appointed to a federal judgeship in his country's supreme court system. He is also a prolific writer and has worked in a variety of genres including short stories, novels, poetry, drama, comics, essays, and theater and opera criticism. He has contributed articles to several state and national periodicals, and his columns appear regularly in the supplements to the newspaper *Excélsior*, as well as in the magazines *Origina*, *Hojas de utopía*, *Generación*, and the Mexican edition of *Asimov's*. In 1992, Guzmán Wolffer's short story "El cono de luz eterna" (The cone of eternal light) won a prize in a literary contest organized by the state of Oaxaca, and his volume of poetry *Vivir en filo* (Living on the edge) won first prize in the 1996 national poetry competition sponsored by the municipality of Calkiní in the state of Campeche. He also merited an honorable mention in a national vampire-story contest in 1997. Guzmán Wolffer is a member of the Mexican Science Fiction and Fantasy Association and has served as a discussant in many of the conventions on genre literature and popular culture that have taken place in Mexico since 1995.

Most of Ricardo Guzmán Wolffer's writings are at heart detective stories, with goodly amounts of horror and postapocalyptic science fiction thrown into the mix. A brief summary of his most important work to date, the novel *Que Dios se apiade de todos nosotros* (May God have mercy on us all, 1993), illustrates this characteristic of his literature. The story, set in Mexico City some 50 years after the horrendous nuclear plant explosion of 2010, features a lawyer-cum-detective named Lupus. Lupus sets about solving a crime, and before long finds himself battling a cult whose pursuit of the secret of time travel involves magic rituals, human sacrifice, and a final cataclysmic duel at a demon-infested portal to the otherworld. Lupus is furnished a robot named Leticia to assist him with the case. Designed as a movie-star look-alike, she's every macho pulp-detective's fantasy, for she has a fabulous body, is great in bed, and is programmed to obey. To Guzmán Wolffer's credit, Leticia is also a superb fighter and she even has brains; Lupus does not hesitate to recognize her for being smarter than he is and he readily acknowledges her crime-solving capabilities.

Que Dios se apiade de todos nosotros is an entertaining, well-written, and frequently thought-provoking novel that has succeeded in finding a readership; in fact, it is one of the few Mexican novels of its genre(s) to have made it to a second edition, which came out in 1997. The plot holds together well and the pacing remains brisk from beginning to end. Guzmán Wolffer handles the multiple scene changes and two different narrative voices (Lupus narrates about two-thirds of the story, an omniscient narrator does the rest) with deft assurance. He sustains an appropriate *noir* tone throughout most of the book (violated only occasionally by incursions into the absurd) and overall skillfully balances the conventions of the three genres in which he is working without diminishing any of them. As noted earlier, the plot centers on the detective story, but the horror and science fiction elements, though supporting players, do contribute meaningfully to the text.

With the exception of the time-travel motif, most of the science fiction in *Que Dios se apiade* takes the form either of high-tech weaponry (security alarms, photon guns, *Mission Impossible*-style sleuth gear) or biomedical innovations (implants, transplants, viruses). The author explains some of the science behind his futuristic devices and phenomena, even taking a stab at the time-travel paradox, but in general the explanations would not stand up under scrutiny. Fortunately, he does not try to make his novel hinge on its scientific plausibility, so the somewhat unsuccessful attempts at validating the technology are not particularly distracting and for the most part do not detract from the work.

The novel has surprising depth, thanks to a recurrent existentialist preoccupation that surfaces in Leticia's and Lupus's relationship and their intrinsic differences; in the nature of the crimes committed; in a character called *la morena* and her fascination with death stories; and in the hero's musings on life toward the end of the novel. There is also a strong theological thread running through the book—alluded to in the title—which debates the existence of God and asks how much, if at all, God cares about the vicissitudes of human lives. These issues are explored in a series of delightful conversations between Lupus's nemesis, Milton Rose, and an amusing, enlightening Satan. Indeed, part of the success of *Que Dios se apiade* comes from the very effective sardonic humor that peppers the narrative, chiefly during the badinage among Lupus, Leticia, and Lupus's sidekick and foil Inspector Pérez Grieg, but also in the plot situations themselves and in the detective's observations and descriptions. A certain amount of sociopolitical criticism is woven into the text—police officers are corrupt and bureaucrats thickheaded and incompetent—but while such criticism is amusing and revelatory, especially given Guzmán Wolffer's profession and the milieu in which he works, it is by no means the main feature of the novel. Most of the characters in the story seem to be patterned after those found in comic books and B-movies. Lupus, Inspector Grieg, and Leticia are caricatures who act, for the most part, precisely according to type. As an archenemy, Milton Rose's megalomaniacal behavior and attitude are fairly stereotypical, although his particular set of crimes has many original features about it.

What Guzmán Wolffer has done in this first novel is to infuse pulp literary styles and conventions from the 1940s and 1950s with a strong component of neogothic shock. He does this to a much greater degree in other recent publications, which are so intense in their violation of mainstream standards of decency—in a country with a deeply ingrained public (and private) desire to define and maintain morality—that they are unlikely to appeal to the comparatively wide audience enjoyed by *Que Dios se apiade de todos nosotros*. His short story "Buscando" (Searching), his serialized novella *Volando* (Flying), and his 1998 novel *Sin resaca* (No consequences) share a predilection for hardcore gore and graphic physical and sexual violence that will challenge many readers' comfort levels. Indeed, *Volando*, a futuristic gothic crime story about a series of ritualistic murders, was deemed so offensive (the detective spends a lot of his time raping or hoping to rape) that the *Revista biombo negro*, the magazine that was publishing the work in installments, had its decency license revoked and eventually folded.

To varying degrees, all three of these works feature Guzmán Wolffer's signature mixing of science fiction, horror and detective fiction, and all of them take place in Mexico City sometime during the twenty-first century. "Buscando" describes interrogation-by-torture sessions conducted by government agents looking for subversives among the robot population, and in terms of shock value is the tamest of the three. *Sin resaca* pits a police detective and his drinking buddies against an international smuggling ring. Unlike in *Que Dios se apiade*, the plot of *Sin resaca*, which is made up in large part of the protagonists' back-to-back episodes of heavy drinking, viciousness, and sex, does not function in support of any more subtle or intellectually sophisticated literary project, and too often the author rescues his characters and moves the story along by resorting to the miracle of coincidence and astounding good luck. But the narrative's relentless onslaught of shock images and sociopathic behavior (committed as often as not by civil servants) constitutes a virulent attack on cultural mores that Guzmán Wolffer, in his complex public role as federal judge, may see as problematic and hypocritical. Perhaps this exposé of degeneration justifies the novel's blunt, superficial style and, rather than elaborate plot or character development, should be taken as its primary concern. Certainly *Sin resaca*, along with Guzmán Wolffer's other published fiction, are evidence of the author's courage in insisting on the right to make his art an instrument of challenge, even when doing so may prove dangerous to his legal career.

As Guzmán Wolffer describes it, Mexico City is not a particularly inviting place in the twenty-first century. In *Que Dios se apiade* the massive nuclear plant explosion turns the capital into a toxic hotbed, and the author pokes macabre fun at contemporary Mexico City's severe sanitation problems and the urban myths they generate by populating the irradiated future city with giant mutant rats. In *Sin resaca*, the air is so contaminated that breathing it without benefit of a filter will kill a person. In his stories, corruption and decay are rampant. Advances in technology make body-parts replacement surgery a fairly simple matter, but it also gives us synthetic food and drink, which the characters abhor. This grim vision of the future perhaps accounts for the people and events about which Guzmán Wolffer writes, and goes some way toward explaining his characters' code of ethics, their callous and precarious lives lived *sin resaca*—without consequences.

Andrea Bell

Works

Bestias de la noche. Mexico City: Ramón Llaca, 1998.

"Buscando," in *Los mapas del caos*, ed. Gerardo Porcayo. Mexico City: Ramón Llaca, 1997, 17–22.

Colman los muertos del aire. Mexico City: Lectorum, 2001.

Historias de lo incierto. Mexico City: Ediciones Flatul & Cía, 1991.

"Un lugar para poner el miembro." *Umbrales* 28 (1997). Revised version in *Los universitarios* 82 (1998).

Que Dios se apiade de todos nosotros. Mexico City: Consejo Nacional para la Cultura y las Artes, 1993; 2nd ed., 1997.

Rabamán. Mexico City: Ediciones Flatul, 1992. (Comic.)

"Siglos de sed y fuego." *Revista Asimov* 9 (1997).

Sin resaca. Mexico City: Times Editores, 1998.

"Un trabajo más," in *El hombre en las dos puertas: un tributo de la ciencia ficción a Phillip K. Dick*, ed. Gerardo Horacio Porcayo. Mexico City: Lectorum, 2002.

Virgen sin suerte. Mexico City: Times Editores, 1999.

Vivir en filo. Calkiní, Mexico: Fundación Cultural Trabajadores de Pascual y del Arte; H. Ayuntamiento de Calkiní, 1997.

Volando, in *Revista biombo negro* (1995) issues 6, 7, and 8. (Serialized novella.)

Criticism

Trujillo Muñoz, Gabriel. *Los confines: crónica de la ciencia ficción mexicana.* Mexico City: Grupo Editorial Vid, 1999.

Hugo Hiriart (b. 1942)

MEXICO

Hugo Hiriart was born in Mexico City in 1942. He is the author of three novels, *Galaor* (1971), a homage to the Spanish novels of chivalry like *Amadís de Gaula*; *Cuadernos de Gofa* (Chapbooks of Gofa, 1981), a natural history and lengthy chronicle of the imaginary kingdom of Gofa; and *La destrucción de todas las cosas* (The destruction of all things, 1992), a science fiction novel that envisions the future of Mexico after an alien invasion with the tone of an *opera buffa*. He has also published a short-story collection, *Disertación sobre las telarañas* (Dissertation on spiderwebs, 1992), and he wrote the script for the fantasy film *Ambar* (Amber).

Hiriart is a unique presence in contemporary Mexican narrative. His work is characterized by diverse cultural allusions, his love for fantasy seen through a child's eye, and his thirst for exotic adventures. In *Cuadernos de Gofa*, the main character is Professor Dódolo, a scholar and explorer driven by the general lack of knowledge about the splendid and rich culture of the Gofa civilization, which is defined by its diverse mythology, legends, and history. The story is told through a mixture of narrative elements that include heroic fantasy, cloak-and-dagger, medieval labyrinths, taxonomy, and science fiction akin to that of Gene Wolf or Samuel R. Delany with automatons, experiments, and monsters.

However, Hiriart's most obvious contribution to Latin American science fiction writing undoubtedly is his novel *La destrucción de todas las cosas*. The text is similar to other examples of Mexican narrative—*Cristóbal Nonato* (*Christopher Unborn*, 1987) by Carlos Fuentes, *Cerca del fuego* (Close to the fire, 1986) by José Agustín, *La leyenda de los soles* (The legend of the suns, 1993) by Homero Aridjis, *La ley del amor* (*The Law of Love*, 1995) by Laura Esquivel, *Cielos de la tierra* (Heavens on earth, 1997) by Carmen Boullosa, and *Lejos del paraíso* (Far from paradise, 1997) by Sandro Cohen, to name a select few—that while committed to the creation of hard science fiction, utilize the conventions of the genre to represent a series of concerns about the social, political, economic, and cultural future of Mexico. Hiriart's novel narrates a fairly common (in science fiction) tragedy within a specifically Mexican space. The story revolves around the invasion and destruction of Mexico City by a winged alien race. The submission of Mexico is attributed not so much to the advanced technology and superior power of the aliens, but to the failings of the Mexicans themselves: the foolishness of the ruling class, the pettiness and blindness of the civil, military, and intellectual bureaucracies. This new version of the *Cantar de los vencidos* (Song of the conquered; a well-known Aztec text written upon the fall of the Aztec empire at the hands of Cortés) is not a terrifying drama, but a lighthearted satire. This light, ironic tone is what makes Hiriart's story of apocalyptic destruction and collective death in 2010 so attractive. *La destrucción de todas las cosas*, written between 1985 and

1992, was enthusiastically received as a powerful metaphor of the conquest of Mexico and an extraordinary exercise of the imagination. One might add that it is an excellent example of Mexican dark humor.

Gabriel Trujillo Muñoz

Works

Cuadernos de Gofa. Mexico City: Joaquín Mortiz, 1981; Reprint, Mexico City: Era, 1998.
La destrucción de todas las cosas. Mexico City: Era, 1992.

Eduardo Ladislao Holmberg (1852–1937)

ARGENTINA

In his youth, Holmberg acquired a solid humanistic background, a significant part of which included the study of classical and modern languages. Later, he studied medicine, obtaining his medical degree in 1880. Being a member of the fin-de-siècle Argentine generation of liberal intellectuals, Holmberg understood his literary career as a complement of his other endeavors: he devoted his life to natural sciences and enthusiastically supported scientific positivism. The development of positivistic philosophy in Argentina was not without controversy due to the opposition of the more conservative groups of society. Nevertheless, the new ideas favored the institutionalized study of sciences. In fact, a specific academic unit was soon created at the University of Buenos Aires, several scientific expeditions were organized to explore different geographic areas of the country, and the production of research papers and reports intensified. Florentino Ameghino, Francisco Pascasio Moreno, and José María Ramos Mejía stood out among the original group of founding scientists. Holmberg, who worked as a professor of botany at the national university, belongs to the same generation. He participated in the expeditions to Chaco (1883) and Misiones (1886) organized by Ameghino and the botanist Federico Khurzt, and became a member of the Argentine Academy of Sciences and Letters and the Scientific and Literary Circle.

As a writer, Holmberg authored a long series of curious texts, which have been justly considered as the first manifestations of fantastic and detective fiction in Argentine literature. Critics have pointed out that his most notable influences are those of the French writers Jules Verne and Camile Flammarion, the German E. T. A. Hoffmann, and Edgar Allan Poe. "La huella del crimen" (Clue to a crime, 1878), "La casa endiablada" (The diabolical house, 1896), and "La bolsa de huesos" (The bag of bones, 1896) are a few samples of Holmberg's characteristic detective narratives. However, as in many other cases in Latin American nineteenth-century fiction, the writer was not fully aware of the genre as a distinct form.

A second aspect of his creative impulses produced a series of fantastic narratives, set mainly in a pseudoscientific atmosphere. His novella *Dos partidos en lucha* (Two parties in conflict, 1875) was subtitled "Scientific fantasy." It is the first-person narration of the fictive Ladislao Kaillitz, who tells the story of the Argentine scientific conference in which Charles Darwin's theories were introduced and keenly debated. Evidently, the impact of these theses is not merely scientific but philosophical as well, as Darwin's ideas questioned the indisputable superiority of humankind as opposed to the rest of the forms of life. Holmberg, an unconditional admirer of the English biologist, used fiction to make evolutionism known to the general reading public.

Some of Holmberg's writings—"La pipa de Hoffman" (Hoffman's Pipe, 1876), "El tipo más original" (The most original guy, 1878), and "Filigrana de cera" (Wax filigree, 1884) among them—combine the scientific knowledge of the author with imaginary elements and philosophical, even social, concerns. Another intellectual influence in his writings is that of spiritism, most evident in his short story "El ruiseñor y el artista" (The nightingale and the artist, 1876), but also as an important constituent of "La casa endiablada" and the novella *Nelly* (1896).

Both "Horacio Kalibang o los autómatas" (Horacio Kalibang or the Robots, 1879) and "Viaje maravilloso del señor Nic-Nac" (The marvelous journey of Mr. Nic-Nac, 1875) are rightly considered two of the first science-fiction pieces of Argentine literature. The latter deals with the protagonist's prodigious adventures visiting Mars, which is an excuse to make conjectures about the habits, concerns, and institutions of an unknown world. The trip itself, carried out by the spirit of the main character with the help of a medium, is an entirely imaginary product and does not imply the physical transportation of his body. In "Horacio Kalibang o los autómatas," Holmberg takes advantage of the interest generated since the eighteenth century by automatons. These pieces emblematized the general trust in the possibilities of technology characteristic of the nineteenth century. The story relates the meeting between burgomaster Hipknock of Nuremberg and a curious robot that defies the laws of physics because it lacks a center of gravity. The enigmatic character announces disturbing news: several thousands of these perfect dummies are already installed in the world. According to the constructor of the automaton, this new race of mechanical beings leads to "a science with no limits, whose principles may be applied not only to ordinary constructions and the interpretation of cycles, but to all phenomena of cerebral activity."

Holmberg published the major part of his fiction in newspapers and magazines such as *La Nación*, *La Prensa*, *Caras y caretas*, and *Fray Mocho*. For several decades following his death his work had remained relatively ignored. Besides the edition of a selection of his pieces, prepared with a well-documented introduction by Pagés Larraya, it is only since the 1980s that consistent efforts to recover Holmberg's texts and offer scholarly readings of them have been undertaken; for instance, Salto's on "La casa endiablada," Masiello's on *Nelly*, and Marún's on "La bolsa de huesos" and *Olimpio Pitango de Monalia*. All this critical reconsideration restores Holmberg's fiction to its proper place in the history of a Latin American science fiction.

Daniel Altamiranda

Works

Cuentos fantásticos. Estudio preliminar de Antonio Pagés Larraya. Buenos Aires: Hachette, 1957.

Filgranas de cera y otros textos, ed. Enriqueta Morillas Ventura and Rodrigo Guzmán Conejeros. Buenos Aires: Simurg, 2000. (Contains excellent essays on Holmberg and his relationship to science, science fiction, and the fantastic.)

"Horacio Kalibang o los autómatas," in *Historias futuras: antología de la ciencia ficción argentina*, ed. Adriana Fernández and Edgardo Pígoli. Buenos Aires: Emecé, 2000, 15–38.

"El maravilloso viaje del señor Nic-Nac," in *Los argentinos en la luna*, ed. Eduardo Goligorsky. Buenos Aires: Ediciones de la Flor, 1968, 15–31. (Not the complete text.)

El tipo más original y otras páginas, ed. Sandra Gasparini and Claudia Roman. Buenos
Aires: Simurg, 2001. (Contains texts by Holmberg and recovers early criticism on his
works, including an early study of "Horacio Kalibang o los autómatas.")

Olimpio Pitango de Monalia, ed. Gioconda Marún. Buenos Aires: Solar, 1994.

Criticism

Dellepiane, Angela B. "Ciencia y literatura en un texto de Eduardo L. Holmberg," in
Homenaje a Alfredo A. Roggiano. En este aire de América, ed. Keith McDuffie and Rose
Minc. Pittsburgh: Instituto Internacional de Literatura Iberoamericana, 1990, 457–76.

D'Lugo, Marvin. "Frutos de los 'Frutos prohibidos': la fantaciencia rioplatense," in *Otros
mundos, otros fuegos. Fantasía y realismo mágico en Iberoamérica*, ed. Donald A. Yates.
East Lansing: Latin American Studies Center, Michigan State University, 1975, 139–44.

Marún, Gioconda. "La bolsa de huesos: un juguete policial de Eduardo L. Holmberg." *Inti*
20 (1984): 41–46.

———. "España en la novela inédita de Eduardo L. Holmberg: *Olimpio Pitango de Monal-
ia* (1915)," in *III Congreso Argentino de Hispanistas: España en América y América en
España. Actas*, ed. Luis Martínez Cuitiño and Élida Lois. Buenos Aires: Instituto de
Filología y Literaturas Hispánicas "Dr. Amado Alonso," 1993, 672–79.

Masiello, Francine. *Between Civilization & Barbarism: Women, Nation, and Literary Culture in Modern Argentina*. Lincoln: University of Nebraska Press, 1992, 89–92.

Risco, Antón. "Los autómatas de Holmberg." *Mester* 19.2 (1990): 63–70.

Salto, Graciela Nélida. "La sugestión de las multitudes en *La casa endiablada* de Eduardo
Ladislao Holmberg," in *Segundas Jornadas Internacionales de Literatura Argentina-
Comparatística. Actas*. Buenos Aires: Universidad de Buenos Aires, 1998, 208–22.

Oscar Hurtado (1919–1977)

CUBA

Oscar Hurtado, the son and grandson of fishermen, had a hard childhood that was spent working. He gave up school at the age of 14 but compensated for his interrupted education by reading in public libraries. At a young age he left for the United States, but returned to Cuba in 1959 with the triumph of the revolution. In Havana, he was a science and mathematics teacher. In 1962, he traveled to the Soviet Union where he met with and interviewed science fiction writers. Hurtado was a multifaceted writer who made his mark as a journalist, poet, lecturer, and critic. He published articles on plastic arts, space travel, chess, science fiction, archeological mysteries, and other topics.

Hurtado's works contain a mix of the "marvelous real," fantasy, and science fiction. Trying to place his works in a single category is an impossible task. Yolanda Molina-Gavilán, in *Ciencia ficción en español: una mitología moderna ante el cambio* (Science fiction in Spanish: A modern mythology in the presence of change [2002]), collects the opinions of various writers who agree that science fiction from Hispanic countries is defined by the characteristics unique to those countries. Since Latin America lacks the high technological development that would place it at the level of countries that are determined to conquer space, its writers relegate this topic to a secondary plane and develop themes rich in myths, dreams, and multicultural reality. These topics run parallel to one other, but on occasions they intersect, creating magical and fantastic spaces.

In *La ciudad muerta de Korad* (The dead city of Korad, 1964), Hurtado alludes to science fiction themes such as the planet Mars and astronauts going into space. The book is written in verse and combines mythology, Biblical themes, literary characters, personal stories, and tales from all over the world. Every poem has an introduction and an accompanying graphic. The introductions provide a variety of references that include *The Book of the Dead*, Mark Twain, Johann Wolfgang von Goethe, Edgar Rice Burroughs, and Arthur Conan Doyle's Sherlock Holmes. The graphics depict the Tower of Pisa, a globe of the Earth, and the bust of a woman who is the princess of the dead city of Korad.

La ciudad muerta de Korad and *Los papeles de Valencia el Mudo* (Valencia the mute's papers, 1983) are two books that share a common theme, one written in verse and the other in prose. The literary backdrop in these books is taken from tales of voyage and adventure and horror stories. For Hurtado, mystery, fantasy, and the world of dreams should be combined in the writer's mind to produce this type of far-fetched narration. In *Los papeles de Valencia el Mudo*, he gathers together the frayed pieces of his grandfather's, Valencia el Mudo, life. He was married to a Haitian mulatta woman and they lived in Trinidad. The stories showcase bicultural reality, stressing the importance of the occult for the characters. The quotations from the poet Longfellow delve into the topic of the occult: devil worship, secret societies, metamorphoses, and so on. The text also recalls stories of

Count Dracula and other vampires. Presented with visions of spider monsters, double moons, and a grandfather transformed into a lizard, the narrator analyzes these hallucinations from a literary and scientific point of view.

In addition to his own writing, Oscar Hurtado selected the short stories and wrote the prologue for the anthology *Cuentos de ciencia ficción* (Science fiction stories, 1964). He chose short stories from among the best representatives of the genre—for example, Ray Bradbury's "Perchance to Dream," Arthur C. Clark's "The Nine Billion Names of God," Howard P. Lovecraft's "The Call of Cthulhu," and José Arreola's "En verdad os digo" (I tell you in truth), in addition to 22 other writers. In the prologue, Hurtado offers the reader interested in science fiction a historical, biographical, and cultural synthesis of the authors and their times. He concludes the anthology with the essay "Sobre los cuentos y sus autores" (On the stories and their authors) wherein he offers the uninitiated reader of science fiction a kind of guide to aid in understanding and enjoying the genre. In the essay, he discusses some common science fiction themes such as physical alterations, disturbances, and anomalies of physical laws, extraterrestrials, among others.

Oscar Hurtado always had a fascination for science fiction and as a scholar of the genre he combined his creative work with his Caribbean heritage of the marvelous real. At the same time, he attempted to analyze this reality in his works through scientific approaches and comparisons of science fiction texts and texts on the occult.

Heidi Ann García

Works

Cuentos de ciencia ficción, ed. Oscar Hurtado. Havana: Ediciones R, 1964.
La ciudad muerta de Korad. Havana: Ediciones R, 1964. Reprint, Madrid: Betania, 2002.
Introducción a la ciencia ficción, ed. Oscar Hurtado. Madrid: M. Castellote, 1971.
Los papeles de Valencia el Mudo. Havana: Editorial Letras Cubanas, 1983.

Criticism

Chaviano, Daína. "Introducción," in *Los papeles de Valencia el Mudo*. Havana: Editorial Letras Cubanas, 1983, 5–16.
Molina-Gavilán, Yolanda. *Ciencia ficción en español: una mitología moderna ante el cambio*. Lewiston, NY: Edwin Mellen Press, 2002.

Guillermo Lavín (b. 1952)

MEXICO

Guillermo Lavín was born in Ciudad Victoria, Tamaulipas in 1952. He has been a university professor, an active promoter of cultural activity, and a government official on the state and federal level. He was a participant in a literary workshop coordinated by the writer Guillermo Samperio. Among his literary influences he has named Ray Bradbury, Isaac Asimov, and Phillip K. Dick among other Anglo science fiction writers who have served as models in his own formation. Lavín is a prime example of the burgeoning interest in and production of science fiction in the northern border region of Mexico. He is a dedicated and versatile author who writes science fiction as well as fantasy and surreal texts.

Lavín's stories have been anthologized in several collections of science fiction literature. The story "El futuro es tiempo perdido" (The future is lost time) appeared in *Más allá de lo imaginado II* (Beyond imagination II, 1991) edited by Federico Schaffler. A year later, he received a second place in the Kalpa Award science-fiction literature contest and an honorable mention in the IX Premio Puebla contest (Puebla Award). In 1993, his story "Razones publicitarias" (Publicity reasons) was anthologized in another of Schaffler's collections, *Sin permiso de Colón* (Without Columbus's permission). Whether his stories are about black holes or bureaucratic nightmares, his writing is always refreshing, contemporary, and acutely critical, while at the same time playful and original. Lavín is prone to mixing history, sociology, technology, local customs, scientific hypotheses, interviews, and diverse textual discourses into his literature. Together with María Enriqueta Montero and José Luis Velarde, Lavín founded and began publishing the literary journal *A quien corresponda* (To whom it may concern), dedicated to publishing Mexican and other Latin American authors of science fiction, horror, and fantasy as well as more mainstream writers. In 1993, he published his first book, *Final de cuento* (End of story), which in reality is a beginning for the author. His story "Llegar a la orilla" ("Reaching the Shore") was included in the anthology *Frontera de espejos rotos* (Border of broken mirrors) edited by Mauricio-José Schwarz and Don Webb and published in 1994.

Guillermo Lavín forms part of the "Northern Division" of Mexican science fiction writers. He joins Federico Schaffler from Tamaulipas, Gerardo Cornejo and Lauro Paz from Sonora, and Gabriel Trujillo Muñoz from Baja California in creating a body of literature that is nourished by the latest technology from the neighboring country to the north and the local legends from the deserts of northern Mexico. It is a literature of the future that originates in ordinary small towns with regular people, and then shoots off into extraordinary worlds and unknown and disturbing environments. Lavín's work responds to a commitment to science fiction as a centrifuge for the wildest dreams and deepest secrets of humanity. His literature is a mirror of reality and in every image we see ourselves reflected.

Likewise, he has not lost the healthy habit of laughing to the last, even if the last is the end of the world as we know it!

Gabriel Trujillo Muñoz

Works

Final de cuento. Mexico City: Fondo Editorial Tierra Adentro, 1993.

"El futuro es tiempo perdido," in *Más allá de lo imaginado II: antología de ciencia ficción mexicana*, ed. Federico Schaffler. Mexico City: Consejo Nacional para la Cultura y las Artes, 1991, 147–63.

"Llegar a la orilla," in *Frontera de espejos rotos*, ed. Mauricio-José Schwarz and Don Webb. Mexico City: Roca, 1994, 53–63. English version as "Reaching the Shore," trans. Rena Zuidema and Andrea Bell, in *Cosmos Latinos: An Anthology of Science Fiction from Latin America and Spain*, ed. Andrea Bell and Yolanda Molina-Gavilán. Middletown, CT: Wesleyan University Press, 2003, 224–34.

"Razones publicitarias," in *Sin permiso de Colón: fantasías mexicanas en el quinto centenario*, ed. Federico Schaffler González. Guadalajara: Universidad de Guadalajara, 1993, 113–36.

Mario Levrero (b. 1940)

URUGUAY

Mario Levrero, born in Montevideo in 1940, is the author of some 15 books. He is one of the foremost of contemporary Uruguayan novelists and short-story writers. His work clearly shows the influence of the fantastic literature that is so prominent in the River Plate region. Levrero can be seen as following in the tradition of writers like Felisberto Hernández, Jorge Luis Borges, and Julio Cortázar, all masters of the fantastic genre. Levrero has been discussed as having been influenced by Franz Kafka and surrealism (Capanna).

The author presents a unique problem with regard to science fiction writing. His works from the very beginning have been associated with the genre. His early short stories appear in all the major science fiction magazines of Buenos Aires such as *La revista de ciencia ficción y fantasía* (The magazine of science fiction and fantasy), *El péndulo* (The pendulum), *Minotauro* (Minotaur), and *Parsec*. His collection of four short stories, *Aguas salobres* (Salt water; 1983), was published by *Minotauro* in that publisher's science fiction series. One of his first books, *La ciudad* (The city, 1970) was recently re-released in Spain in a science fiction series. Furthermore, many of his stories appear in anthologies of Latin American science fiction and his name is consistently associated with science fiction in encyclopedias (Carneiro; Molina-Gavilán). In spite of all this, the author himself denies any link, association, or influence between his writing and science fiction (Capanna; Verani). His inclusion here would seem intent on further promoting the idea that his work is in fact science fiction, despite the author's protests to the contrary. However, the inclusion of Levrero in a book such as this one is not meant to once again stick a label on the author or his work; rather, it serves to underscore one of the primary problems surrounding the definition of science fiction in Latin America. Certainly, in the most traditional sense, his work cannot be classified as science fiction—there are no advanced technologies, robots, androids, and supercomputers; no deep space travel, alien invasions, or cataclysms. Levero's works are much more slippery than that. In fact, critics have been hesitant to categorize it at all, aside from making general observations on recurrent themes and style (Fuentes; Capanna; Verani). It may be considered as a version of "soft science fiction," common in Latin America, that has more ties to the heritage of the fantastic than the hard science fiction foreign models.

Hugo Verani studies Levrero's trilogy, *La ciudad, París* (Paris, 1980), and *El lugar* (The place, 1982), in this sense. He highlights the author's creation of a space wherein reality is slightly skewed, where images seen to originate as dreamscapes, and where location is unspecified (even in *París*). The result is the creation of a sense of desperation and isolation in which the characters seem to wander about in a confused daze. The same kind of atmosphere is created in *Fauna* (1987) and *Desplazamientos* (Displacements, 1987), as the very title of the latter indicates. In the stories of *Aguas salobres*, the reader finds the same elements of the fantastic pushed to the limit: strange occurrences, parallels, anachronisms, time shifts, and other odd phenomena all add to the elaboration of a space that exists somewhere between reality and fantasy.

Texts like *Caza de conejos* (Rabbit hunt, 1986), "El crucificado" (The crucified man), "Los ratones felices" (The happy mice), "La casa abandonada" (The abandoned house), "Confusiones cotidianas" (Everyday confusions), "Los reflejos dorados" (The golden reflections), "El sótano" (The basement), and "La máquina de pensar en Gladys" (The machine for thinking about Gladys) have all been defined as science fiction stories. In the end, it is really up to the reader to decide whether or not this is a viable categorization. Whether science fiction, neofantastic, surreal, or psychological, Levrero's texts are fascinating, thought-provoking, and entertaining.

Darrell B. Lockhart

Works

Aguas salobres. Buenos Aires: Minotauro, 1983.
"La calle de los mendigos," in *Cuentos fantásticos y de ciencia ficción en América Latina*, ed. Elvio E. Gandolfo. Buenos Aires: Centro Editor de América Latina, 1981, 161–67.
"Capítulo XXX." *Minotauro* 3.8 (1984): 36–50.
"La casa abandonada." *Entropía* [Buenos Aires] 1.1 (1978): 68–77. Also in *Latinoamérica fantástica*, ed. Augusto Uribe. Barcelona: Ultramar Editores, 1985, 135–48.
Caza de conejos. Montevideo: Ediciones de la Plaza, 1986. Also appears in its entirety in *Lo mejor de la ciencia ficción latinoamericana*, ed. Bernard Goorden and R. E. Van Vogt. Buenos Aires: Hyspamérica, 1988, 77–110.
La ciudad. Montevideo: Tierra Nueva, 1970. Reprint, Barcelona: Plaza y Janés, 1999.
"Confusiones cotidianas." *El péndulo* [3ra época, Buenos Aires] 15 (1987): 53–64.
"El crucificado." *Minotauro* [2da época, Buenos Aires] 2 (1983): 97–100.
Espacios libres. Buenos Aires: Puntosur, 1987.
Fauna. Desplazamientos. Buenos Aires: Ediciones de la Flor, 1987.
El lugar. Montevideo: Banda Oriental, 1991. First appeared in *El péndulo* [2da época, Buenos Aires] 6 (1982): 97–149.
La máquina de pensar en Gladys. Montevideo: Tierra Nueva, 1970.
"Novela geométrica." *El péndulo* [3ra época, Buenos Aires] 12 (1986): 89–99.
París. Buenos Aires: El Cid Editor, 1980.
"Los ratones felices." *Parsec* [Buenos Aires] 1.5 (1984): 22–34.
"Los reflejos dorados." *El péndulo* [2da época, Buenos Aires] 10 (1982): 77–80. Also in *Cuentos con humanos, androides y robots*, ed. Elena Braceras. Buenos Aires: Colihue, 2000, 93–100.
"Las sombrillas." *La revista de ciencia ficción y fantasía* [Buenos Aires] 1.2 (1976): 137–46.
"El sótano." *La revista de ciencia ficción y fantasía* [Buenos Aires] 1.3 (1977): 11–13.
Todo el tiempo. Montevideo: Banda Oriental, 1982.

Criticism

Capanna, Pablo. "Las fases de Levrero." *Inti: revista de cultura* 45 (1997): 299–303.

Carneiro, André. "*La ciudad*," in *Survey of Science Fiction Literature*, 5 vols., ed. Frank N. Magill. Englewood, NJ: Salem Press, 1979, 383–85.

Filer, Malva E. "Las transformaciones del cuento fantástico en la narrativa rioplatense (1973–93): Luisa Valenzuela y Mario Levrero," in *Culturas del Río de la Plata (1973–1995): Trangresión e intercambio*, ed. Roland Spiller. Frankfurt am Main: Vervuert Verlag, 1995, 531–43.

Fuentes, Pablo. "Levrero: el relato asimétrico," in *Espacios libres*. Buenos Aires: Puntosur, 1987, 305–18.

Molina-Gavilán, Yolanda. "Science Fiction," in *Encyclopedia of Latin American Literature*, ed. Verity Smith. London: Fitzroy Dearborn, 1997, 760–61.

Roca, Pablo. "(Jorge) Mario (Varlotta) Levrero: Bibliografa (XII/1966-IV/1992)," in *Nick Carter se divierte mientras el lector es asesinado y yo agonizo*, by Mario Levrero. Postfacio de Helena Corbellini. Montevideo: Arca, 1992, 87–127.

Ruffinelli, Jorge. "Mario Levrero, 'Alice Springs' y la verdad de la imaginación," in *The Latin American Short Story: Essays on the 25th Anniversary of Seymour Menton's* El cuento hispanoamericano, ed. Kemy Oyarzún. Riverside: University of California Press, 1989, 85–97.

Verani, Hugo J. "Mario Levrero: aperturas sobre el extrañamiento," in *De la vanguardia a la posmodernidad: narrativa uruguaya (1920–1995)*. Montevideo: Trilce, 1996, 157–76.

~

Félix Lizárraga (b. 1958)

CUBA

Félix Lizárraga was born in Havana in 1958. He earned a degree in theatrical arts from the Instituto Superior de Artes in Havana. His literary activity was marked from an early age by his membership in the Oscar Hurtado Literary Workshop of Havana and by his affiliation with the cultural movement known as *Brigada Hermanos Saíz* in the city of Colón, where he resided for some years. Lizárraga has also made forays into the world of radio and television, as well as into the world of English language and literature. Presently, he lives and works in Miami, where he studies computer science.

Although Lizárraga is a multifaceted author who has written prose and poetry as well as television scripts, his literary corpus is limited. His science fiction works include the novel *Beatrice* (1982), which won the science fiction category of the *Premio David* in 1982, and a short story titled "Primer contacto" (First contact, 1982). From 1982 onwards, the literary production of the Cuban author has focused on other literary forms and genres.

Lizárraga's most important influences are his humanistic education and the social peculiarities to which Cuban revolutionary culture has been subjected. The classical world, with its myths and characters, surfaces throughout his works, or it serves as inspiration for creating different situations in his writing. On the other hand, the constant flow of literature into Cuba from the communist block countries of Eastern Europe and the USSR evidently inspired much of his literature. In addition—due to his undeniable and particular importance to science fiction throughout the world—the influence of Isaac Asimov appears is his texts, along with other equally renown authors of the genre.

Lizárraga's literature is rich in detail and style. There is a clear effort on his part to use polished descriptive adjectives that give a certain kind of smoothness to his narrative. His descriptions are brief but clear and concise, and the dialogues appear natural and coherent. His writing is enjoyable and light, but overall it reflects the everyday reality of humanity that the technology of the future has not been able to change. None of the scenes presented in his stories appear to be forced in their credibility or too complex to be easily understood. The science and technology that Lizárraga introduces in his texts are not only within reach of comprehension of any reader, but the limited explanations given for them are described with simplicity. While the author may admit that this owes to his lack of knowledge in the more technical fields of the scientific world, it is clear that his narrative intention distances itself from scientific concepts in order to focus on moral and philosophical topics. To him, science, as a literary discourse, seems to close more doors than can be opened.

Both *Beatrice* and "Primer contacto" are clear examples of what has been described up to this point. In "Primer contacto," a story of some six pages, he has been able to create a well-rounded main character whose psychological soundness enables him to unravel the enigma of his own history. According to the author, "Primer contacto" represents the result of his experience with the film *Solaris*, based on Stanislaw Lem's homonymous novel. In like manner, Beatrice is the result of another influence, that of the novel *Cataclismo en Iris* by the brothers Arkadi and Boris Strugatski. Lizárraga took his idea of a self-sufficient machine faced with a humanity that has tried to disconnect it from a passage in this novel. In addition, this idea is combined with some of the postulates that Isaac Asimov developed on robotics, as is the case with his three famous laws of robotics, which are explicitly named in *Beatrice*. Lizárraga, who confesses that he is about to revise and rewrite *Beatrice*, develops the common theme of artificial intelligence, yet along the way he affirms that the ideal artificial creation is always the human. That is why his *biones*, as in the case of the character Beatrice, are no more than simple humans who have been created by an artificial process. Lizárraga states that the history of humanity is full of myths about the construction of the perfect human machine. But it is now, in the present time, that humankind has discovered that this dream is not so utopian thanks to the artificial intelligence of computers.

For Félix Lizárraga, the important thing is not talking about these *biones*, but rather making clear our moral concerns about what we create through science and technology. It is not by chance that *Beatrice* is a love story that appears to resolve the conflict between humans and *biones*. And although the end of the novel remains open, morality and sentiment are the keys to understanding it.

Juan C. Toledano

Works

Beatrice. Havana: Unión de Escritores y Artistas de Cuba, 1982.
"Primer contacto." *Revista Unión* [Havana] 21.3 (1982): 121–27.

Criticism

Arango, Ángel. "La joven ciencia-ficción cubana (un lustro dentro del concurso *David*)." *Unión* [Havana] 23.41 (1984): 128–38.
Lizárraga, Félix. Personal Interviews. 5 March and 17 May, 1998.

Leopoldo Lugones (1874–1938)

ARGENTINA

Leopoldo Lugones was born in Córdoba, Argentina in 1874 and died in 1938. From a fairly early age he worked as a journalist, contributing to the newspaper *El pensamiento libre* (Free thought), a publication of leftist and anticlerical tendencies. Upon his arrival in Buenos Aires in 1896 he wrote for *El tiempo* (Time) and *La montaña* (The mountain), along the same anarchist and revolutionary lines. His precarious financial situation received a considerable boost when he was named Inspector General de Enseñanza (Education superintendent) in 1900. This appointment influenced his gradual abandonment of socialist ideals; he began to adhere to the official politics of dependency on European nations, especially England. Culturally, France was his intellectual and artistic model (as for most Argentines) and he traveled there on several occasions.

His first book of poems, *Las montañas del oro* (The golden mountains, 1897), and especially his second, *Los crepúsculos del jardín* (Garden twilights, 1905), made Lugones one of the most representative poets of Spanish American modernism. A versatile writer, he published in 1906 both *Las fuerzas extrañas* (Strange forces), a series of fantastic short stories, and *La guerra gaucha* (The gaucho war), epic stories in which he displays a substantially baroque use of language. Likewise, his book of poems *Lunario sentimental* (Sentimental lunar calendar, 1909) led the way to avant-garde trends in Latin America. Several literary trends or styles come together almost simultaneously in Lugones's works. His admiration for classic Greek culture is evident in *Piedras liminares* (Preliminary stones, 1910) and *Prometeo* (Prometheus, 1910). His ever-increasing nationalism manifests itself in books like *El payador* (The gaucho minstrel, 1916), a study of José Hernández's epic poem of the gaucho, *Martín Fierro* (1872, 1879), as well as *Poemas solariegos* (Sunny poems, 1928) and *Romances del Río Seco* (Songs of Río Seco, 1938). His early interest in and fondness of occultism and theosophy is noticeable in *Cuentos fatales* (Fatal stories, 1924) and his novel *El ángel de la sombra* (The angel of darkness, 1926). His inclination toward science is most readily visible in *Las fuerzas extrañas*. In 1913, the conservative, oligarchic newspaper *La Nación* (The nation) assigned him a job as a foreign correspondent in Europe where he remained until just prior to the outbreak of the First World War. Around 1923, his political position experienced a 180-degree shift and he associated himself with the extreme right and antidemocratic ideals that bordered on fascism. This new, nationalist position is clearly confirmed in his essays *La patria fuerte* (The strong homeland, 1930) and *La grande Argentina* (Heroic Argentina, 1930). On 18 February 1938 Lugones took his own life by ingesting poison in a hotel in El Tigre.

Only a small portion of Lugones's extensive work can be considered as pertaining to science fiction. Of his approximately 150 short stories, only about a half-dozen fit the genre. Of those, five are found in *Las fuerzas extrañas*: "La fuerza Omega" (The omega force), "La metamúsica" (Metamusic), "El Psychon" (The psychon), "Viola Acherontia" and "Yzur" (the title is the name of the protagonist chimpanzee). To these can be added "El espejo negro" (The black mirror), included in Pedro Luis Barcia's anthology *"El espejo negro" y otros cuentos* (The black mirror and other stories, 1988). Most of these stories were first published in newspapers or magazines as early as 1898. One must also consider Lugones's text "Ensayo de una cosmogonía en diez lecciones" (Essay on cosmogony in ten lessons), included in *Las fuerzas extrañas,* in which the author expresses his ideas on the universe and its origins. This essay, which resembles Edgar Allan Poe's "Eureka" (1848), provides theoretical content to the ideas developed in his stories.

In Lugones's works, science always appears linked to theosophy and occultism, which were common and very much in vogue at the turn of the nineteenth century. The "scientific" stories in *Las fuerzas extrañas* share many common elements with other texts, such as those based on religious, Biblical, or Greek legends; for instance in, "El milagro de San Wilfrido" (The miracle of Saint Wilfredo), "La estatua de sal" (The statue of salt), "La lluvia de fuego" (The rain of fire), or "Los caballos de Abdera" (The horses of Abdera). This connection is even more evident in texts such as "Un fenómeno inexplicable" (An unexplainable phenomenon) and "El origen del diluvio" (The origin of the flood) in which pseudoscientific language informs a significant portion of the discourse. This last story and "Ensayo . . ." propose similar theories.

The previously mentioned six stories contain much more obvious structural and thematic parallels. Invariably, the protagonist is at once a scientist and practitioner of the occult. He is knowledgeable in natural and supernatural phenomena and discovers relationships among the different forces of nature, which in the end turn against him. Doctor Paulin, for example, is the main character in both "El Psychon" and "El espejo negro." In the first story, Paulin tries to liquefy thought and in the process discovers the elixir of madness and ends up in a mental institution. In the second, his mirror (which erases the boundaries between time and space) projects images of hell; in the end, the mirror is consumed by fire. The learned man in "La fuerza Omega" dies while channeling the energy of sound, which destroys his brain. The scientist in "La metamúsica" goes blind upon revealing the colors of music. The protagonist of "Viola Acherontia," mentally unbalanced by his own obsessions, is a criminal who resorts to sacrificing children for the purpose of giving human life to his flowers.

The "Ensayo de una cosmogonía en diez lecciones," on the other hand, proposes equality between matter and energy, matter and spirit, and time and space. Influenced by scientific and occultist postulates as well as by Plato's philosophy, the essay states that matter is in itself identical, which erases the differences between metals and gases and all living things. In other words, both metals and gases are endowed with human, animal, and plant qualities. Also, for Lugones, thought is but another form of energy.

These hypotheses are developed in varying ways in the stories of *Las fuerzas extrañas*. The idea that thought is both matter and energy is studied in "El Psychon" and in "La fuerza Omega." The identity of matter (specifically that each color has a corresponding sound) is presented in "La metamúsica." "Viola Acherontia" and "Yzur" establish ambiguous relationships among human beings, animals, and plants. In addition, the stories present similar narrative techniques. The narrator is usually a witness who narrates the experiments carried out by the learned scientist. Only in "Yzur" is the narrator the scientist himself. Long, explanatory passages of a scholarly and pseudoscientific nature are used to lend a sense of authority and make narrated events more believable. To the modern reader, these archaic, "strange" theories make reading the stories somewhat difficult and even tiresome. But one must bear in mind that many of these were considered to be valid scientific thought at the time Lugones wrote his stories.

"Yzur" is one of the most celebrated stories from *Las fuerzas extrañas*. The scientist obtains a chimpanzee from a circus and believes he can teach him to speak. His theory, contrary to Darwin's, is that apes are a degenerated type of human being—a man that, for one reason or another, relinquished his human condition and therefore the capacity for language that he surely at one time possessed. The character subjects the monkey to linguistic training with no positive result; however, he is told that the monkey speaks when alone. The man becomes enraged and whips the animal. The monkey becomes ill and, just before dying, utters his last words. The story is a satire of both human nature and the omnipotent plans of science.

Critics of *Las fuerzas extrañas* view the book as a clear example of fantastic literature. From this perspective, analyses often include *Cuentos fatales* and the novel *El ángel de la sombra*, two volumes that have nothing to do with science fiction. Gaspar Pío del Corro's *El mundo fantástico de Lugones* (The fantastic world of Lugones, 1971) stands out in this sense. Emma Susana Speratti Piñero, Alix Zuckerman, and Juan Carlos Ghiano focus on *Las fuerzas extrañas* and suggest a classification of the stories into two basic categories: those based in science, and those based in popular legend and beliefs. These critics have been especially helpful in identifying the presence of science/scientific fiction as pertaining to the genre of the fantastic.

One of the first critics to consider Lugones as a science fiction writer was Robert Scari. In his article "Ciencia y ficción en los cuentos de Leopoldo Lugones" (Science and fiction in the short stories of Leopoldo Lugones, 1964), Scari points out a double narrative tendency: on the one hand, Lugones's stories are based on rigorous scientific concepts; on the other, his skepticism of science saturates his texts with satiric, mocking overtones. According to Scari, Lugones's poetic intuition is the element that relates science to fiction. This intuition is what takes him beyond the strictly scientific domain and towards poetry and other disciplines such as religion and occultism in his quest for "explaining the unexplainable" (Scari 1964, 166). There are many other studies and approaches to Lugones and his relationship to science fiction that both support and negate such a relationship. However, one cannot help but see how, at the very least, Lugones—as a master narrator of the fantastic—can be considered as a precursor to science fiction writing in Argentina.

José Alberto Bravo de Rueda

Works

"*El espejo negro*" *y otros cuentos*, ed. Pedro Luis Barcia. Buenos Aires: Abril, 1988.
Las fuerzas extrañas. Buenos Aires: Moen, 1906. (The are many subsequent editions of the volume.)

Criticism

Barcia, Pedro Luis. "Composición y temas de *Las fuerzas extrañas*," in *Las fuerzas extrañas*, by Leopoldo Lugones. Buenos Aires: Ediciones del 80, 1981, 9–45.

———. "Estudio preliminar," in "*El espejo negro*" *y otros cuentos*, by L. Lugones. Buenos Aires: Abril, 1988, 7–49.

Borges, Jorge Luis, and Betina Edelberg. *Leopoldo Lugones*. Buenos Aires: Troquel, 1955.

Ciruti, Joan E. "Leopoldo Lugones: The Short Stories." *Revista interamericana de bibliografía/Interamerican Review of Bibliography* 25.2 (1975): 134–49.

Corro, Gaspar Pío del. *El mundo fantástico de Lugones*. Córdoba, Argentina: Universidad de Córdoba, 1971.

Corvalán, Octavio. "Las presuntas fuentes científicas de 'Yzur.'" *Nueva estafeta* 36 (1981): 59–62.

Cvitanovic, Dinko, and Alfred Rodríguez. "Ante el chimpancé de Leopoldo Lugones," in *XVII Congreso del Instituto Internacional de Literatura Iberoamericana*, vol. 2. Madrid: Ediciones Cultura Hispánica del Centro Iberoamericano de Cooperación, Universidad Complutense de Madrid, 1978, 997–1002.

Fraser, Howard M. "Apocalyptic Vision and Modernism's Dismantling of Scientific Discourse: Lugones's 'Yzur.'" *Hispania* 79.1 (1996): 8–19.

García Ramos, Arturo. "Introducción," in *Las fuerzas extrañas*, by L. Lugones. Madrid: Cátedra, 1996, 9–84.

Ghiano, Juan Carlos. "Lugones y *Las fuerzas extrañas*," in *El realismo mágico en el cuento hispanoamericano*, ed. Angel Flores. Tlahuapán, Mexico: Premiá, 1985, 25–41.

Jitrik, Noé. "Las narraciones fantásticas de Leopoldo Lugones," in *Las fuerzas extrañas. Cuentos fatales*, by L. Lugones. Mexico City: Trillas, 1992, 7–48.

Marini Palmieri, Enrique. "'Yzur,' mono sabio: sobre un cuento de Leopoldo Lugones." *Alba de América* 12.22–23 (1994): 245–56.

Naharro-Calderón, José María. "Escritura fantástica y destrucción realista en *Las fuerzas extrañas* de Leopoldo Lugones." *Hispanic Review* 62.1 (1994): 23–34.

Scari, Robert M. "Ciencia y ficción en los cuentos de Leopoldo Lugones." *Revista iberoamericana* 30 (1964): 163–87.

———. "Aspectos temáticos y estructurales de los relatos científicos de Lugones." *Revista de literatura hispanoamericana* 7 (1975): 141–52.

———. "Lugones y la ficción científica." *Iberoromania* 2 (1975): 149–56.

Speck, Paula. "*Las fuerzas extrañas*, Leopoldo Lugones y las raíces de la literatura fantástica en el Río de la Plata." *Revista iberoamericana* 42 (1976): 411–26.

Speratti Piñero, Emma Susana. "La expresión de *Las fuerzas extrañas* en Leopoldo Lugones," in *La literatura fantástica en Argentina*, ed. Ana María Barrenechea and Emma Susana Speratti Piñero. Mexico City: Imprenta Universitaria, 1957, 1–16.

Velasco Moreno, Juan. "Perfume, música, color: sinestesia, ocultismo y ciencia-ficción en dos relatos de Leopoldo Lugones," in *Modernismo hispánico*. Madrid: ICI, 1988, 314–19.

Zuckerman, Alix "*Las fuerzas extrañas* de Leopoldo Lugones: análisis crítico," in *Estudios sobre la prosa modernista hispano-americana*, ed. José Ilivio Jiménez. New York. Eliseo Torres, 1975, 237–53.

Gonzalo Martré (pseudonym of
Mario Trejo González) (b. 1928)

MEXICO

A chemical engineer, teacher, and journalist, Gonzalo Martré has promoted Mexican science fiction for many years. He has been on the jury panel for the "Puebla" Award and is a member of the organizing committee for the "Kalpa" Award. He also has been the treasurer and president of the Asociación Mexicana de Ciencia Ficción y Fantasía (Mexican science fiction and fantasy association). From 1969 to 1978, he wrote the Mexican version of the comic *Fantomas*, which features an antihero by the same name. He has published collections of short stories and erotic-humorous and detective-humorous novels as well as journalistic, satirical, and picaresque novels, sociological essays, and four high-school chemistry textbooks. His science fiction and fantasy writing contains many of the themes from his nonfiction, so that his use of dark humor and the Mexican picaresque makes him one of the Mexican authors who write "humorous science fiction." His move toward the genre was slow, with early first stories such as "Barnardiana" (Barnardienne) about a surgeon who makes a great business from transplanting donkey members to men and "Comportamiento colectivo" (Collective behavior) about the indignation of round-shaped extraterrestrial beings who decide to destroy Earth when they see humans mistreating objects that look much like theirselves, especially in sports.

It is with the short-story collection *Dime con quien andas y te diré quien herpes* (A man is known by the herpes he keeps, 1985 [the title is a pun between the Spanish verb "eres" and the name of the disease "herpes"]) that Martré focuses his energy more fully on science fiction. These stories are enhanced by satire and social criticism as well as by comic illustrations. In the short story that gives the book its title, a couple of scientists, with lots of prejudices, set out to create a virus that will eradicate homosexuals. They achieve their goal but not without contaminating heterosexuals as well, causing a demographic catastrophe. In "El cumpleaños de Marilyn" (Marilyn's birthday), a man using a method of passing through solid matter, invented by a female physicist friend, gets into an exclusive birthday party for a Russian double of Marilyn Monroe. He seduces and becomes involved with her only to discover that she is a transsexual. The two remaining short stories of this anthology criticize Mexico's future and past. "Los antiguos mexicanos a través de sus ruinas y sus vestigios" (The ancient Mexicans through their ruins and vestiges) tells of a multidisciplinary expedition to Mexico in the year 2910 to discover why it disappeared almost a thousand years earlier. In "El oro de los dioses" (The gods' gold) later rewritten and published as "Cruce de dos líneas, bifurcación de chingadazos" (The crossing of two lines, a get-the-shit-beat-out-of-you bifurcation), a couple of drifters, in 1992, unwittingly step through a crack in time. They end up at the time of the conquest of Mexico and in a fight to the death with the conqueror Pedro de Alvarado for Aztec gold. The revised version of the story earned him a special mention in the X "Puebla" Science Fiction Award contest in 1993.

In his next collection, *Apenas seda azul* (Barely blue silk, 1987), he included a novella with the same title in which a race from a dying solar system abandons its planet in search of another place in the universe to live. The race finds Earth and in its attempt to imitate the inhabitants in every way, it sends an android to study the local customs, behavior, and appearance. Unknowingly, the android focuses its observation in prostitution zones in Mexico City. The android records the image of an exuberant prostitute that, once again, looks like Marilyn Monroe, but when he notices that his imitation is lacking many anatomical details, he runs through the red-light district checking out all the women and watching their behavior to successfully imitate them.

La emoción que paraliza el corazón (The emotion that paralizes the heart, 1994) is his next science fiction work, also a collection of short stories. It begins with the story "En Alabama no quieren a los panchitos" (In Alabama they don't like panchitos), about a multidisciplinary scientist who is invited to give a lecture on the colloquial language of the Panchitos, a famous Mexican gang. During a break, a friend asks him to change his son's skin color who, in spite of being born to a white American, is black, and he, the father, is the proud descendant of long-time members of the Ku Klux Klan. The scientist succeeds but the child suddenly turns black again and the father sues him; meanwhile, he is also wanted by the law for bringing some of the Panchitos to Alabama, who have gone about wreaking havoc. "Deseo cumplido" (Wish come true), originally published as "El clóset" (The closet) won honorable mention in the VII "Puebla" Science Fiction Short Story Contest in 1990. It is about a strange community that lives inside a closet where paranormal phenomena take place and where a girl prodigy is born through a kind of immaculate conception. When her talent is discovered, everybody wants to kidnap her. Other stories include "Telépatas" (Telepaths), about a married couple with telepathic powers who decide to kill each other; "La chiva dentro de la cristalería" (The goat inside the glassware) tells of the genetic mutation of a girl born to a glass-collecting family who also eats glass; "Qué verde era mi mota!" (How green was my pot [marijuana]), a homage to a popular, real-life rock star who died in the Mexico City earthquake of 1985, about discovering a machine for making music and finishing incomplete compositions, which delivers him a song predicting his own death at the moment of the earthquake; "Los alienígenas son simpáticos" (The extraterrestrials are very kind), about a painter from Acapulco painting sidereal landscapes. He is accompanied by a little robot that seems to have a life of its own—in fact, it does, since an extraterrestrial lives inside it who uses the painter as an extension of his mind and body. Through the painter, the alien works to earn money to fix his broken-down spaceship, which is being used in a disco as part of the decor. He also uses the painter to satisfy his curiosity about the way earthlings make love, which leads him to devise a business plan upon returning to his own planet.

Among Martré's latest texts is the story "Las barrenderas que limpiaron el cielo" (The sweepers who cleaned the sky, 1998), about a couple of Mexican women who are computer hackers—brown-skinned, short, and ugly. When they are hired by an American company, they are confused with cleaning women and are denied access to the computers. As revenge, and taking advantage of their vast computer knowledge, they steal their hateful boss's password and under his name, transfer monies from the World Monetary Fund to cover the Mexican foreign debt besides sharing a generous portion of the financial windfall with each Mexican citizen.

Miguel Ángel Fernández Delgado

Works

"Los antiguos mexicanos a través de sus ruinas y sus vestigios," in *Visiones periféricas: antología de la ciencia ficción mexicana*, ed. Miguel Ángel Fernández Delgado. Mexico City: Lumen, 2001, 130–37.

Apenas seda azul. Mexico City: Gernika, 1987.

"Barnardiana," in *Coprofernalia.* Mexico City: EDAMEX, 1973.

"Las barrenderas que limpiaron el cielo," in *A quien corresponda!* [Ciudad Victoria, Tamaulipas] 74 (April 1998): 4–12.

"El clóset," in *Más allá de lo imaginado III: antología de ciencia ficción mexicana*, ed. Federico Schaffler. Mexico City: Consejo Nacional para la Cultura y las Artes, 1994, 147–55.

"Comportamiento colectivo," in *La noche de la séptima llama.* Mexico City: EDAMEX, 1975.

Coprofernalia. Jet Set. Cuando la basura nos tape. Mexico City: La Tinta Indeleble, 2001.

Dime con quien andas y te diré quien herpes. Mexico City: Claves Latinoamericanas, 1985.

La emoción que paraliza el corazón. Mexico City: EDAMEX, 1994.

Criticism

Tonini, Andrés. "De Fantomas y otras ondas . . . Entrevista a Gonzalo Martré." *Nahual* [Mexico/UNAM] 5 (April 1997): 29–32.

Álvaro Menén Desleal (pseudonym of Álvaro Menéndez Leal) (1931–2000)

EL SALVADOR

Álvaro Menéndez Leal was born in the city of Santa Ana, El Salvador on March 13, 1931. For many years he lived in Europe, serving his country in various secondary or honorary diplomatic positions while making a name for himself as an author. Perhaps in keeping with his predilection for Borgesian symmetry and paradox, he slightly altered the spelling of his surnames to create the pseudonym he used as a writer, Álvaro Menén Desleal: *leal*, which means loyal, becomes disloyal (*desleal*) through little more than a shift in word division. That such an apparently minor change could so profoundly alter meaning must have delighted an author who, in the pages of his books, often marveled at the capriciousness of life.

Menén Desleal was an avid reader of fantastic literature and openly acknowledged the influences his favorite authors—Jorge Luis Borges, Franz Kafka, Ray Bradbury, Isaac Asimov, Edgar Allan Poe, H. G. Wells, and Juan José Arreola—had on his own creative work. He dedicated several stories to these and other writers, and his short-story collection *Cuentos breves y maravillosos* (Short and marvelous tales, 1963) pays homage to Borges's penchant for the sham reference by using as the prologue a (spurious) letter from the master congratulating Menén Desleal for his literary achievements. This prologue (a patchwork that Menén Desleal constructed from Borges's actual writings, substituting other authors' names for his own) and other highly intertextual pieces he later produced garnered mixed reviews for Menén Desleal, whom some critics at the time accused of plagiarism.

As a writer, Menén Desleal was most productive during the 1960s and early 1970s, though his works—especially the prize-winning absurdist drama *Luz negra* (Black light, 1965)—have been kept alive through reprints published by the Salvadoran culture and education ministries. The majority of his prose, and certainly those works of a science-fictional nature, are short and very short stories ("microtexts," as they are sometimes called), many of which lack the traditional elements of a story and are, instead, parables, satirical sketches, fragments, and the like. Several of his earliest science fiction stories were reprinted in the collection *La ilustre familia androide* (The illustrious android family, 1972). Thematic concerns in these narratives include the mechanization and resultant dehumanization of society; the desire to understand those we perceive as alien; and humankind's tremendous capacity for (self-)destruction. In many ways, his fiction reflects global concerns of the day, especially those raised by the cold war, and because of this, his stories do not have a markedly Salvadoran feel (indeed, they chiefly feature non-Latino characters and settings).

"Los vicios del papá" (Papa's bad habits) is one of two cautionary tales in *La ilustre familia androide* that uses robots to dramatize the dangers of modern science and the concomitant decline of civilization. In it, humankind's failures and frustrations are first experienced, and then overcome, by our cybernetic children—a race of androids that has replaced humans. The story is narrated by the son who is accompanied by his father, the first of a now-obsolete line of "personalized" robots—that is, robots programmed to express human emotions (a "mistake" corrected in subsequent models). Papa is now suffering the ravages of old age; he frets about feeling useless and succumbs to bouts of despair. Furthermore, his attempts to ease his misery by bingeing on electricity have left him as an addict who spends his days dreaming of the past and telling the same stories over and over again to his long-suffering son. Family relations are bleak; he is just a museum-piece, a burden to his more modern wife and son.

Mama was programmed to have less personality and be more competitive. Together with the Russian computer Ivan the Terrible, she took competition to the extreme, ultimately (and in disregard of Asimov's laws) allowing humans to destroy themselves with their nuclear bombs. After the war, she rounded up robots and programmed them to live like humans, although she has cleansed them of human defects. She now lives in the hope that, somewhere, some human being has survived whom she and the others might serve in accordance with their most fundamental programming, though never again will these older and wiser androids allow humans to go to war.

Another of the stories in *La ilustre familia androide* merits examination for its nuclear-apocalypse theme. "Una cuerda de nylon y oro" ("A Cord Made of Nylon and Gold") has as its protagonist a disillusioned and cuckolded U.S. astronaut who, while on a spacewalk, decides to end it all by cutting the nylon-and-gold cord that tethers him to his capsule. For some miraculous reason he survives long after his oxygen should have run out and, feeling neither hunger nor thirst, spends years in a solitary orbit around Earth. From this god-like vantage point he witnesses—with ironic impotence—the destruction of the planet in a series of nuclear explosions. The price of his suicidal desire is to witness, and be the sole survivor of, humanity's self-destruction. He is condemned to endlessly circle his dead homeworld, a grotesque monument to human folly.

These stories might lead one to conclude that all of Menén Desleal's fantastic fiction is heavy in tone and unremittingly pessimistic, but this is not the case. Although they may deal with themes of destruction and death, the use of satire, irony, parody, absurdity, and humor, as well as their extreme brevity, diminish the dramatic tension of many of his narratives. Furthermore, several texts address metaphysical questions of a less depressing nature: "Summa Theologica," for example, which reads like a scientific proof, purports to explain how the laws of physics and the nature of angels prevent the latter from being injured by Sputnik and other spacecraft. Overall, Menén Desleal's fantastic and science-fictional writings spanned the range from topical to transcendent, personal to universal, whimsical to somber. He was a highly imaginative cosmopolitan writer whose works were, on some level, always provocative.

Álvaro Menén Desleal died of pancreatic cancer in San Salvador on April 7, 2000, shortly after being named a "Writer of Great Merit" by his country's Legislative Assembly.

Andrea Bell

Works

"A Cord Made of Nylon and Gold," trans. Andrea Bell, in *Cosmos Latinos: An Anthology of Science Fiction from Latin America and Spain*, ed. Andrea Bell and Yolanda Molina-Gavilán. Middletown, CT: Wesleyan University Press, 2003, 87–91.

Cuentos breves y maravillosos. San Salvador: Ministerio de Educación, Dirección General de Publicaciones, 1963.

La ilustre familia androide. Buenos Aires: Ediciones Orión, 1972.

Luz negra. San Salvador: Ministerio de Educación, Dirección General de Publicaciones, 1965.

Criticism

López, Matilde Elena. "El mundo desconcertante de Álvaro Menén Desleal." *Cultura: Revista del Ministerio de Educación* 29 (1963): 67–77.

Wise, David. "Un acercamiento a la narrativa de Álvaro Menén Desleal." *Kentucky Romance Quarterly* 26 (1979): 35–42.

F. Mond (pseudonym of Félix Mondejar) (b. 1941)

CUBA

F. Mond is the pseudonym used by the Cuban writer Félix Mondejar, born in Matanzas in the early 1940s. His literary production is somewhat late in coming, considering that his first science fiction novel, *Con perdón de los terrícolas* (With the terricolas' pardon, 1983), was unknown until 1981, when it received special mention in the Premio David, a science fiction literary contest for new Cuban authors. Beginning that year, nevertheless, F. Mond produced four novels in just five years: *Para verte reír* (To see you laugh, 1983), *¿Dónde está mi Habana?* (Where is my Havana, 1985), *Cecilia después, o, ¿Por qué la Tierra?* (Cecilia afterwards, or, why the Earth, 1987), and *Krónicas Koradianas* (Koradian Kronicles, 1988). Only the second and fourth are science fiction novels. In 1991, he added the novella *Mesiú Larx* to his literary production.

Félix Mondejar's science fiction is known for his use of sarcasm and humor. Comic scenes and situations abound in his works. On some occasions they hinder the novel's narrative thread and even become moderately boring in their abuse and repetition. The author's intention with his humorous technique is at best ambiguous. His attempt to lighten the text from the serious and transcendental tone of adventure fantasies and from the typical scientific rationalism of the science fiction genre seems clear. On the other hand, his mocking of literary creation as well as the role of the author and ideological implication in his discourse are not so clear.

Like so many other authors in this genre, F. Mond has created a universe with regular characters for his narrative, although both creations are developed in a different way in each of his works. Without leaving the solar system, the Cuban author has called upon an extraterrestrial race much more advanced than the human race to intervene in the destiny of humanity. This plot line is common in science fiction. In line with this vast literary tradition Mond places this race on the planet Mars, but on this occasion the aliens refer to themselves as inhabitants of the planet Korad, or "Koradians."

However, this seems to be a cliché that F. Mond relies on to write his works. If science fiction is usually characterized by advancing possible future alternatives, marked by a rational credibility, Mond's futuristic world is not only scientifically and rationally explicable, but it is also habitually ascientific and erroneous. This new trick in his literature could be due to a lack of technical and astronomical scientific knowledge. Nonetheless, it seems to be just another game for the sake of parody. It is one way to alter, through parody, the very genre his work is based on. Perhaps for this reason, the ideas that Mond imparts in his works are difficult to recognize. Few subjects are repeated throughout his novels. While it is true that his works contain a critical stance that reflects Cuban and global social reality, one cannot speak of any clear ideas that mark his works as a whole. Perhaps the only common point is a representation of socialism and communism as economic systems and social ideals. Yet, at times, the parody is so clear that it is not possible to accept his defense of socialism as it is.

Con perdón de los terrícolas shows the Cuban author's love of creating a novel founded on humor and parody. This novel combines science as a paradigm of civilizing development with the myth of Atlantis as the failure caused by the use of this science. When an adventurer from the planet Korad named Iílef decides to come to Earth in order to teach us the science of his civilization, the only thing he manages to do is sink the island of Atlantis by using an excessive amount of explosives in what was meant to be a definitive demonstration of his superior power. This event, which relates the disappearance of the mythical civilization of Atlantis with modern science, is a parody of the use of science and its applications for megalomaniacal ends.

It is in this first novel that F. Mond introduces a key character that appears in all his science fiction works: Mesiú Larx. In his opera prima, this character is a human being from the future whose knowledge and development allow him to analyze his present as pathetically underdeveloped. Larx is an example of the telepathic evolution of his race and is a defender of socialism as the only logical system for humanity. However, Mesiú Larx's appearance in subsequent works is quite different. In ¿Dónde está mi Habana? and Krónicas Koradianas, Larx appears to be characterized as a humanoid robot created by the Koradians. The robot is an infiltrator on Earth with different missions on each occasion. In ¿Dónde está mi Habana?, Larx finds himself pursuing the Koradian ship that Iílef brought when he destroyed Atlantis and that, now lost in the Bermuda Triangle, is causing objects and people to disappear from space and time. In addition, Larx came with Iílef and he is not human in this new version of the character. Meanwhile, in Krónicas Koradianas, he is barely mentioned at the end of the novel in order to also reveal his presence as an android that passes for a crazy old man.

¿Dónde está mi Habana? and Krónicas Koradianas are F. Mond's two most extensive science fiction works—the first is easily the better novel of the two. ¿Dónde está mi Habana? is a novel in which humor and parody are found in just the right measure. These stylistic devices do not interrupt the narrative thread, yet it is a light and enjoyable work given the humorous situations it presents. On the other hand, he entertains himself in the more detailed descriptions of eighteenth-century Havana, the century in which most of the work takes place. ¿Dónde está mi Habana? is really a historical science-fiction novel in which Mond utilizes time travel to create a historic alternative to the British conquest of Havana in 1761. Koradian science permits the inhabitants of the island to prevent the invasion. The author additionally imposes a forceful and anachronistic nationalistic Cuban tone, also aimed at an anachronistic egalitarian and socialist system.

For its part, Krónicas Koradianas, a much more extensive work than ¿Dónde está mi Habana?, goes overboard with the use of parody. One may consider the novel to be divided into three shorter novellas interconnected by a central plot that is hardly developed. These three stories get caught up in the description of different situations dealing with the same experiment that does not produce the expected results. Finally, the reasons why the experiment failed is explained to the reader, from outside the framework of the plot, in an epilogue of just two pages. The novel, which is presented intratextually as a Koradian parable about mankind's disastrous attempt to overcome nature, is in fact a satire of the status quo during the cold war. The United States, the Soviet Union, Reagan, Marx, Engels, James Bond, and almost all of the characters and places exist, but their names have been crudely modified. The two superpowers are harshly attacked. However, when we are presented with the perfect system, which is what God has finally imposed from heaven, it turns out to be the socialist system and the trusos appear to be the standard-bearers of this kingdom of God on Earth. For this reason, F. Mond's parody, which does not convey the solid support for socialism seen in *¿Dónde está mi Habana?*, casts doubt on his real intentions in *Krónicas Koradianas*.

Equally questionable is his parody of the science fiction genre. If in *Con perdón de los terrícolas* myth and science fiction are combined, and in *¿Dónde está mi Habana?* past and present are united thanks to time travel, in *Krónicas Koradianas* the science that gives rise to the novel's plot is nothing more than another form of parody. One can say that it is an "ascientific science," or simply, a science invented by F. Mond. There is no criterion that allows us to think one day that this science will be achieved or used by humans. On the other hand—in reference to the parodic narrative form—a constant in all his works, but especially in *Krónicas Koradianas*, is the stylistic recourse of having the narrator speak directly to the reader, or even establishing dialogues between a character and the assumed author. Félix Mondejar creates science fiction that breaks the most canonical molds of the genre: his science is not science, his adventures are parodied plots, and his style constantly breaks with the codes of credibility.

Juan C. Toledano

Works

Con perdón de los terrícolas. Havana: Editorial Letras Cubanas, 1983.
Krónicas Koradianas. Havana: Editorial Letras Cubanas, 1988.
Mesiú Larx. Havana: Ediciones Unión, 1991.

Criticism

Arango, Ángel. "La joven ciencia-ficción cubana (un lustro del concurso *David*)." *Unión* [Havana] 23.41 (1984): 128–38.
Toledano, Juan Carlos. "Influencias de la revolución en la literatura de la ciencia ficción: F. Mond y Agustín de Rojas." *Romance Languages Annual* 10 (1999): 848–52.

Antonio Mora Vélez (b. 1942)

COLOMBIA

Antonio Mora Vélez, a writer and journalist, was born in Montería (Córdoba). He has been a university professor in his native town, and currently works as director of international relations at CECAR—Caribbean University Corporation—on the northern coast of his country. Mora Vélez is a pioneer of Colombian science fiction narrative and has attained a modest following. The writer's work could be defined as a speculation on the human potential to dream, modify relations with other beings, and share its place in the universe in order to achieve an imaginary integration with extraterrestrial creatures and androids. This means that Mora Vélez goes beyond the readers' reality and experience in the known world where they are perceived as human beings in the twentieth century. He thus alters the readers' relationship with the known world and lets them imagine and create other worlds in the future, but with the problems and realities that humanity is facing in the here and now. Such issues include racism, pollution, overpopulation, and the rapid development of technology. These problems are a challenge to the writer as he attempts to show how the new creatures in the universe deal with them. In some cases, humans have found a solution to these problems, but others they must simply learn to live with. However, one of the most significant elements here it is that individuals have the opportunity to reflect on their attitudes and correct their behavior toward other beings. In other words, the writer invents and imagines a different way to coexist on the planet when humans discover that they are not the only species in the universe.

Mora Vélez envisions a utopian world to comment on the dynamics of interaction, living together, and the consequences that result from the inevitable encounter between humans and beings from other worlds. In this imaginary universe, references to well-known Colombian events lend a sense of credibility to the reader, but also help the writer to ground history in a reality that is natural and credible. The author creates a scientific environment in his writing from where he criticizes human failings, yet provides a chance for redemption. Through his use of scientific language combined with technology and the experiences of everyday human existence, the author establishes a fictional world from which to analyze human behavior. This fictional world—set in the twenty-second century—has no geographical borders, and the only language spoken is "Spanglish" (the fusion of Spanish and English).

Mora Vélez's science fiction is a vehicle that reveals his view of reality and the human condition. He grounds his fiction by creating unique situations, but is careful to maintain a sense of regional identity. These elements are important to bear in mind, since Colombia never has had prestigious or solid scientific development. Given this special circumstance, Mora Vélez has to make his writing credible to his readers as he writes about scientific discoveries and progress and their effect on humans. Furthermore, he does not invent space gadgets, cyber-weapons, or amazing spaceships; rather, he works with the influence of devices and new scientific discoveries that more directly affect people's lives, and he places particular emphasis on interaction with extraterrestrial beings. For this reason, the author attempts to write literature based on history and the reality of ordinary people—their visions, failures, and triumphs of the past as well as their hopes and fears for the future.

This is the general perspective of his first collection of science fiction short stories, *Glitza* (1979). In this work, the author creates an imaginary fantasy of co-existence, mutual comprehension, cooperation, and development with extraterrestrial beings for the betterment of both species. Consequently, he manifests the first signs of a future theme in his work—the inevitable union between humans and extraterrestrial beings through love and other human emotions or an implausible genetic combination of humans and robots. The author exhibits his personal writing style through a combination of Anglo-Saxon science-fiction paradigms and certain characteristics unique to his country and social environment such as places and people. For this reason, Montería, Entre Ríos and Ciudad Tayrona are some of the places in which his science fiction stories take place. Also, his characters tend to be Latin American. This characteristic is important in establishing a Latin American science-fiction tradition that emphasizes the point that Latin Americans, as human beings, are physically and mentally capable of far greater things than has so far ben accomplished. Although Mora Vélez is not a scientist, this is not an obstacle to using a scientific discourse that responds to the circumstances and demands of modern human beings.

In his subsequent works—*El juicio de los dioses: cuentos de ciencia-ficción* (The trial of the gods: science-fiction stories, 1982), and *Lorna es una mujer* (Lorna is a woman, 1986)—Mora Vélez attempts to rewrite religious narratives such as the story of creation and reinterpret them. The writer's exegesis stems from the viewpoint of a newly reborn universe where human beings are offered a new beginning as a new hybrid human–extraterrestrial race. The forebears of this new race defy the genetic rulers and natural laws and although they are different biologically, they surrender to passion and desire to procreate new beings from their sexual union. In the story "Variaciones del tipo de vico" (Variations of the vico type), the author uses Biblical references—the stories of Moses, Cain and Abel, and Jesus's childhood—as a foundation for his stories of coexistence with creatures from outer space. There is a conscious effort to infuse the stories with real and fictitious scientific data so as to prepare the reader to confront and later accept unusual and extraordinary circumstances as part of the everyday nature of reality in the future.

One of the most outstanding stories from his third book is "Lorna es una mujer." In this text, Mora Vélez imagines an incredible love story between a man and a female android. Their relationship is able to blossom due to the natural laws of love. Here, the human has to endure not only anatomical and chromoso-

mal modifications, but even more daunting, they both must deal with the preju-
dice of the conservative sectors of society in order to live together as a couple. The
solution to this improbable situation is reached through love, and of course the
message is that love can make anything possible.

Mora Vélez's science fiction is not only concerned with advanced science and
technology, but more with the fantasies and dreams of human beings. In this
sense, it is an example of popular literature practiced and produced in Latin
America. It is a vehicle used to communicate the concepts and views of different
cultural realities that enables the reader to escape in space and time to another
dimension. In sum, for Mora Vélez, science fiction is a genre with a cultural jus-
tification that allows the reader to analyze history and society through the eyes of
the author. This analysis examines the real problems of humanity from different
cultural aspects that reflect a critical social perspective, a political satire of postmodern society, and the creation of a utopian world. Mora Vélez's science fiction
interprets such modern problems as information overload, the culture of masses,
and the desire to anticipate the future of humanity through themes of mythological and religious literature.

Oscar A. Díaz-Ortiz

Works

"Error de apreciación," in *Contemporáneos del porvenir: primera antología colombiana de
ciencia ficción*, ed. René Rebetez. Bogotá: Planeta, 2000, 113–14.
Glitza. Bogotá: Alcaraván, 1979.
El juicio de los dioses: cuentos de ciencia-ficción. Montería, Colombia: Ediciones El Túnel-
Casa de la Cultura de Montería, 1982.
Lorna es una mujer. Bogotá: Centro Colombo Americano, 1986.

Criticism

Burgos López, Campo Ricardo. "La narrativa de ciencia ficción en Colombia," in *Literatura
y cultura: narrativa colombiana del siglo XX*, vol. 1: *La nación moderna*, ed. María Mercedes Jaramillo, Betty Osorio, and Angela I. Robledo. Bogotá: Ministerio de Cultura,
2000, 719–50.

Amado Nervo (1870–1919)

MEXICO

Amado Nervo was born in the isolated coastal village of Tepic, Mexico in 1870. From an early age, he demonstrated four intense passions with which he would struggle throughout his life: religion, science, poetry, and romantic love. Nervo's science fiction works combine these four often-conflicting passions. After serving as a reporter for a Mazatlán newspaper for two years, Nervo in 1894 moved to Mexico City, where he worked for its most prestigious newspaper, *El Mundo Ilustrado* (The illustrated world), and contributed poetry and prose to other newspapers and magazines. Before his death in 1919, he would publish 30 volumes of poetry and prose. Although four-fifths of his complete works consist of prose, it is Nervo's poetry that made him famous. He is still considered one of the most popular poets in Mexico, and his poems are still memorized and recited quite frequently throughout all of Latin America.

In 1900, Nervo traveled to Paris, lived in poverty, roomed with the greatest *modernista* poet, Rubén Darío, and continued to write prolifically. Returning to Mexico in 1902, he taught at the National Preparatory School where one of his students was Alfonso Reyes. Nervo founded *La Revista Moderna* in 1903 and it was the premiere literary publication in Mexico until 1911. From 1905 to 1918, he was a diplomat in Madrid, writing, making observations with his telescope (his most constant companion), and constantly seeking new ideas that would allow him to reconcile his religious beliefs with the conclusions of science. During this time, Nervo experimented with spiritism, Zen and Taoist contemplation, and the teachings of Krishna, Buddha, and Hatha Yoga as well as the ideas of the cabalistic tradition, theosophy, and Belgian mystic Maurice Maeterlinck. Nervo eventually returned to Catholicism but he brought with him many of the ideas from these other sources, making his a very personalized, hybrid Catholicism. One can see the intermingling of many of these ideas in his science fiction works. In 1919, he was appointed ambassador to Argentina, Uruguay , and Paraguay and was hailed as Latin America's greatest living poet. Nervo died that same year.

Although Nervo's poetry has unfortunately almost completely overshadowed his prose, many of his works of fiction are unheralded precursors of later tendencies in Latin American literature. Being the first Mexican writer of science fiction, he also wrote highly original pieces of psychological fiction, stories of suspense and terror, and tales of what can only be described as a kind of nascent magical realism. Of Nervo's 86 short stories and other short fiction and his ten short novels (or *nouvelles*, as he calls them), ten of the stories and other short works and three of the nouvelles are science fiction or possess significant elements of this genre.

The first of these works, "La diablesa" (The she-devil, 1895), is often labeled a long story, even though Nervo refered to it as one of his *nouvelles*. The story is an interesting blending of the Faust legend and the science fiction of *Frankenstein* (1818) by Mary Wollstonecraft Shelley. The protagonist requests from Mefistófeles the perfect female companion. Asking nothing in return, he grants the man's wish. Interestingly, the devil is also a scientist in this story and in order to create the perfect female, "la diablesa," he must retire to his laboratory and distill her by means of a chemical process. The she-devil betrays the man, but the latter eventually wakes up to discover that the whole episode was just the dream of a lonely man.

Another important influence on Nervo's science fiction was H. G. Wells. One of the earliest Latin American admirers of Wells's *The Time Machine* (1895), *The War of the Worlds* (1898), and *The First Men in the Moon* (1901), Nervo incorporated some of Wells's ideas about the future of humanity in his short story "La última guerra" (The last war, 1896–1899). Like Wells, Nervo suggests that in the future, there will have evolved two physically different classes of human beings, the elite and the proletariat. Nervo's proletariat is a six-fingered race who in 2030 A.D. foments a socialist revolution. The narrator of the story, however, is from the even more distant future, some time after the year 5532 A.D. He transcribes the text by means of a "fonotelerradiógrafo" ("phonoteleradiograph"), a device that records thoughts directly. One of the last surviving humans, the narrator reveals that, because the proletariat was eliminated with the socialist revolution, humans relegated all menial tasks to animals. After thousands of years of evolution, the animals learned to speak and think. In 5532, the humanized animals started the "last war," which resulted in the extinction of the narrator's kind. Nervo's descriptions of futuristic machines and weapons are quite imaginative and prophetic, detailing, for example, biological weapons, nerve-gas grenades, radioactive bombs, and some sort of telepathic shock weapon.

In 1904, Nervo made explicit his devotion to Wells's works when he gave two lectures for the Sociedad Astronómica de México (Astronomical society of Mexico), "La literatura lunar" (Lunar literature) and "La habitabilidad de los satélites" (The habitability of planetary satellites). In the first lecture, he describes in great detail for these astronomers Wells's latest novel, *The First Men in the Moon*, revealing to them the feasibility of Wells's portrait of living on the moon. In the second lecture, he discusses which moons are more habitable, basing his ideas on exact-distance figures and other data that Nervo had gleaned from the specialized astronomical journals he loved to read. This fascination for astronomical data also appears in Nervo's *nouvelle, El donador de almas* (The donor of souls, 1899), a work that can be seen as a kind of metaphysical or pseudoscience fiction.

In the novel, a doctor's friend gives him an extraordinary gift, a soul named Alda. Alda is a soul belonging to a mute nun, Sister Teresa. Since the doctor owns this soul, she hastens to him whenever he calls. Because she is a spirit she is able to diagnose any physical disease. Whenever the doctor calls Alda, Sister Teresa collapses in "mystical ecstasy." The soul carries out the doctor's wishes—all of them, except one: his desire for the soul to love him. She cannot love him since love is a choice, not a duty. After four years, the doctor is so enamoured of Alda's presence that she is with him constantly. Sister Teresa wastes away and dies because she is unable to attend to her body. Alda tells the doctor that he must find another body for her. He sleeps, and she inhabits the left side of his brain. The doctor now has two souls. Relying on his extensive knowledge of astronomy, Nervo has Alda recount to the doctor her interplanetary travels to Venus, Mars, and Jupiter, thereby seamlessly mixing the physical and metaphysical, creating a story of pseudo-science fiction. Eventually, the doctor and Alda go their separate ways, the soul returning to her interplanetary travels. In this narrative, Nervo combines all four of his passions: religious speculation (here in his ideas about metempsychosis, or the transmigration of souls); science (in his detailed descriptions of Alda's interplanetary journeys); poetry (in his prose style); and romantic love (in the relationship between Alda and the doctor).

Astronomy was not Nervo's only scientific interest. Geology takes center stage in his story "La última diosa" (The last goddess, 1906). Revisiting the theme of a futuristic apocalypse expressed in "La última guerra," Nervo describes a cataclysmic geological event in which all of the Earth's continents are swallowed up by new ones, which spew forth from a giant crack under the ocean. Here, Nervo anticipates in a crude way the theory of continental drift first proposed in 1912 by Alfred Wegener. The resulting plot of the story is, however, rather silly and racist: the only continent left is Africa, only one white woman remains (the last goddess), and she dies without an heir, since no "suitable" mate can be found for her.

Four of Nervo's strongest science fiction efforts have to do with another field of scientific inquiry, biology. In 1896, Nervo wrote a "crónica," that is, a brief, entertaining newspaper essay, entitled "La fotografía del pensamiento" (The photography of thoughts). After detailing how a scientist named Baraduc has supposedly discovered a way to photograph thoughts (by having the subject point to a plate with photographic chemicals on it), Nervo ventures into the realm of science fiction. He wonders what would happen if we could see each other's thoughts as if they were so many X-rays. As in his other stories, he predicts an apocalypse as a result of this scientific phenomenon as well. In a related story three years later titled "El hombre a quien le dolía el pensamiento" (The man whose thoughts were painful, 1909), Nervo begins by describing two strange diseases known to exist (ossification of the muscles, and a rare disease of the hair). Once again, at this point Nervo cannot resist venturing into science fiction. He imagines a disease even more horrible than the ones he has described, one that causes every thought to be painful. Nervo describes the affliction in minute detail, concluding that consciousness itself would be torture for this individual unless the person were an athlete or politician (in which cases, according to Nervo, thoughts are so rare that the pain would be slight).

Between 1906 and 1912, he wrote one of his best science fiction stories, "Los congelados" (The frozen ones). Nervo presents an accurate, convincing, and prophetic account of cryogenic suspended animation as a means of extending human life. A young scientist explains to the narrator that human life is like an electric current: once the circuit is broken, life ends. He reveals that his colleague has been able to switch this "current" off-and-on in fish by means of freezing.

Nervo provides a detailed, Borgesian footnote at this point in the story, pointing out how frozen Alpine butterflies can be resuscitated by thawing them out. The young scientist eventually confesses that they have already begun to perform cryogenesis on humans, including one rich and strange American who has paid a high price to be frozen for 20 years so that he can later marry a little girl who is presently two years old. The scientist invites the narrator to visit the subterranean cryogenic vault, but the latter decides not to, for fear of being frozen himself.

Perhaps Nervo's most outstanding work of science fiction is his novel *El sexto sentido* (The sixth sense, 1918). A young man volunteers for an experimental brain operation by which he will be able to see into the future. Nervo explains the surgical procedures with convincing detail, noting that by carefully changing the orientation of Broca's Area and by re-routing certain networks of nerves, such a miracle might be possible. Gloria Schaffer Meléndez perceptively notes that Nervo's concept of time in this story is identical to Wells's in *The Time Machine*; that is, past, present, and future exist simultaneously on the same plane, but our minds are too limited to perceive more than the present and the past. The operation changes this. The young man's abilities make the doctor famous, and the patient foresees who will be the woman of his dreams and eventually falls in love with her. Nervo's descriptions of how the young man sees past, present, and future simultaneously are astonishingly meticulous, owing something to another recent invention, cinema. He sees the images of all things as if he were watching a movie about the future, "como se ven las tiras de papel de kinetoscopio" (as the strips of paper look in a kinetoscope [González, ed., *Obras completas* I:363]).

Several of Nervo's other short prose works reveal some element of science fiction. "Las nubes" (The clouds, 1912) predicts a future world without clouds because of reduced oceans. "Las varitas de virtud" (The little sticks of virtue, 1912) describes the powers of divining rods ("varitas") in scientific terms. "El resucitador y el resucitado" (The resuscitator and the resuscitated, 1912) describes a medical device that Nervo dreams up and that had not yet been invented: the artificial respirator. "El país en que la lluvia era luminosa" (The land where the rain was luminous, 1906–1912) describes a mysterious place where the rain shines because of phosphorescent bacteria in the ocean. Finally, in "Cien años de sueño" (One hundred years of sleep, 1912) Nervo describes a man waking up after a hundred years in a world with mechanical sidewalks and subterranean cities.

Since Nervo's fame has rested for the most part on his poetry, his prose has not received the critical attention it deserves. Despite this lack of attention, several critics and writers discovered the value of Nervo's stories and novels. Rubén Darío described them as "obras enigmáticas entre ciencia y sueño: un filosófico humor, en páginas sencillas y excelentes" (enigmatic works between science and dream: a philosophical humor, in simple and excellent pages [quoted in Meléndez 108]). Mariano Azuela concluded that "Amado Nervo produjo las novelas cortas más bellas que hasta la fecha se hayan escrito por un mexicano" (Amado Nervo produced the most beautiful short novels that have been written to date by a Mexican [quoted in Leal 65]). The critic Luis Leal believed that Nervo was the best storyteller of his generation (66). Before 1970, however, critics did not study Nervo's prose works in depth. Amada Marcela Herrera and Patricia Morgan, for example, offered only cursory, superficial treatments of Nervo's life and a few of his prose works. Two unpublished dissertations are the best critical works to date on Nervo's prose, including his science fiction: Ana Durán's "El cuento fantástico y raro del Modernismo" (The fantastic and strange stories of Modernism, 1970) and Gloria Schaffer Meléndez's "La prosa fantástica y rara de Amado Nervo" (The fantastic and strange prose of Amado Nervo, 1980). Meléndez's work is an especially perceptive, thorough evaluation of many of the works discussed in this article. Certainly, Nervo's prose fiction deserves further study in the future.

J. Patrick Duffey

Works

"El gran viaje," in *Sin permiso de Colón: fantasías mexicanas en el quinto centenario*, ed. Federico Schaffler González. Guadalajara: Universidad de Guadalajara, 1993, 12–13.

Obras completas, ed. Francisco González Guerrero and Alfonso Méndez Plancarte, 2 vols. Madrid: Aguilar, 1973.

Obras completas, ed. Alfonso Reyes, 30 vols. Mexico City: Botas, 1938.

El sexto sentido, in *Visiones periféricas: antología de la ciencia ficción mexicana*, ed. Miguel Ángel Fernández Delgado. Mexico City: Lumen, 2001, 29–46.

"La última guerra," in *El futuro en llamas: cuentos clásicos de la ciencia ficción mexicana*, ed. Gabriel Trujillo Muñoz. Mexico City: Vid, 1997, 65–79.

Criticism

Durán, Ana. "El cuento fantástico y raro del Modernismo." Dissertation. University of California at Los Angeles, 1970.

Durán, Manuel. *Genio y figura de Amado Nervo*. Buenos Aires: Editorial Universitaria, 1968.

Fernández Delgado, Miguel Ángel. "Las crónicas lunares de Amado Nervo." *Umbrales: Literatura fantástica de México* 44 (2000): 2–7.

Herrera y Sierra, Amada Marcela. *Amado Nervo: Su vida, prosa*. Mexico City: Editores e Impresores Beatriz de Silva, 1952.

Larson, Ross. *Fantasy and the Imagination in the Mexican Narrative*. Tempe: Arizona State University, Center for Latin American Studies, 1977.

Leal, Luis. *Breve historia del cuento mexicano*. Mexico City: Andrea, 1956.

Meléndez, Gloria Schaffer. "La prosa fantástica y rara de Amado Nervo." Dissertation, Brigham Young University, 1980.

Morgan, Patricia. "Amado Nervo: su vida y su obra." *Atenea* 32 (May 1955): 204–5.

Trujillo Muñoz, Gabriel. *Los confines: crónica de la ciencia ficción mexicana*. Mexico City: Grupo Editorial Vid, 1999, 61–71.

———. "Amado Nervo: poeta del porvenir," in *Biografías del futuro: la ciencia ficción mexicana y sus autores*. Mexicali, Mexico: Universidad Autónoma de Baja California, 2000, 55–62.

Héctor G. Oesterheld (1919–1978)

ARGENTINA

Héctor Germán Oesterheld was born in Buenos Aires on 23 July 1919. He was a trained geologist, a profession that was evident in many of his comics. He was an expert in the natural sciences and in matters of science in general, who at the same time wrote children's literature in which he created stories of ogres, fairies, and gnomes and the marvelous worlds they inhabited. His well-known characters included the ogre Rompococo, the princess Tilina, the mouse Gorgonzola, and the heroic Gatito (Kitten), among many others. Toward the end of the 1940s, Oesterheld—who was already contributing to the "Colección Bolsillitos" (Little pockets collection) of the Abril publishing house—had created the magazine *Gatito* with its characters and series. This half-writer, half-geologist wrote for the Abril and Códex publishing houses until the opportunity presented itself to begin creating a new type of adventure in a new format. The director of Editorial Abril, César Civita, approached him with the idea of writing comic strips. His first texts in this format appeared in 1950 in *Cinemisterio* (Cinemystery), a weekly that featured comics, stories, and photonovels. It was not until 1952, however, that his first and one of his most lasting characters, Bull Rockett, appeared in the popular comic magazine *Misterix*.

In 1957 he left Abril and shortly thereafter created his own publishing house, Editorial Frontera (Frontier publishing). His publications included the magazines *Frontera* (Frontier), *Hora cero* (Zero hour), and *Hora cero suplemento semanal* (Zero hour weekly supplement), which featured his strips *Ernie Pike*, *El Eternauta* (The ethernaut), *Randall the killer*, *Nahuel Barros*, *Lobo Conrad*, *Cayena* (Cayenne), *El sargento Kirk* (Sergeant Kirk [begun in *Misterix*]), *Sherlock Time*, and the novelized versions of *Bull Rockett* (nine titles in all). Other comic strips that Oesterheld created are *El indio Suárez* (Suárez the indian), *Ticonderoga*, *Flint*, *Watami*, *Uma Uma*, *Rolo, el marciano adoptivo* (Rolo the adoptive Martian), and *Mort Cinder*. He also wrote scripts and created characters for other magazines and publishers, such as *Tarpón* with illustrations by Daniel Haupt and *Doc Carson, el intrépido médico cowboy* (Doc Carson, the intrepid cowboy doctor) with Carlos Vogt for the magazine *Hazaña* (Feat) in 1954.

Oesterheld fell victim to the brutal repression of the military dictatorship in Argentina known as the *Proceso de Reorganización Nacional* (Process of national reorganization, 1976–1983). He was kidnapped by armed forces in the city of La Plata on 27 April 1977. His four daughters—Estela, Diana, Beatriz, and Marina—were also disappeared by the military. Beatriz, age 19, was killed in June 1976. Diana, age 23 and pregnant, was killed along with her husband in Tucumán; their child, Fernando, was remanded into the custody of the paternal grandparents. In November 1997, they murdered Marina, age 18, who was eight months pregnant. Estela, age 24, was killed in December 1977 with her husband Raúl Mórtola; their son, Martín, was returned to his grandmother Elsa that same month. It's known that Oesterheld was held in at least two detention centers. He was last seen in El Vesubio, a clandestine prison in La Tablada in 1978. It is believed he was murdered in Mercedes.

Oesterheld's adventures are based on a formula in which ordinary people are confronted with extraordinary circumstances and are thus thrust into a process that will turn them into heroic figures. Faced with the destruction of the past, they must overcome the present and forge the future. The hero is not the narrator in the stories. Rather, the narrator is a common person, meant to accompany the reader through the adventure and consequently through an emotional transformation. The reader encounters the hero already involved in the adventure. Upon this first meeting, the bond between reader and hero is solidified: friendship and mutual respect are the primary characteristics of this relationship, as also between the characters themselves in Oesterheld's narratives. Bob Gordon is a sports reporter who is assigned to report on something that has nothing to with his usual jobs. This leads to his chance meeting with the mythical Bull Rocket that results in a union forged by friendship and danger. Julio Luna, a retiree whose only intent was to buy a modest house and lead a quiet life, ends up accompanying Sherlock Time on his mysterious adventures through time and space. Ezra Winston, an old antiques dealer, is destined to be the spokesman and companion of Mort Cinder. And Rolo, a teacher, finds himself at the center of an alien invasion. For each of them, embracing adventure is not about living an exciting episode—rather, it represents a change, a rupture with routine that they willingly undertake in order to go in search of what life has in store for them. The hero's companion is both the voice and eyes of the story. He is charged with being an active witness to the events and reveal to the reader the details of the adventure. Oesterheld's narrator-witnesses can be seen as replacing the narrator of epic poetry.

The 1950s marked the dawn of the science fiction comic in Argentina that took on its own characteristics and direction, mostly through Héctor Germán Oesterheld, who afforded it a new space. The initial steps were taken on 1 February 1952 when *Bull Rockett* first appeared in number 176 of the comics magazine *Misterix*. Written by Oesterheld and illustrated by Paul Campani—an Italian who was never in Argentina but who drew the stories from the scripts sent to him—until 1955, when Francisco Solano López, a famous Argentine illustrator, took over the art portion. Campani returned briefly to the series in 1956. The comic was published under Oesterheld's name until December 1957, when it was passed on to other writers. Solano López continued the illustration until 1959. When the character first appeared he was meant to be a test pilot but soon was transformed into a man of many talents. Bull Rockett was Oesterheld's first character of his sole creation, and he represented a change in the nature of the adventurer. He is not a superhero, he possesses no special power. He is mixture of man of action and scientist. His determination, knowledge and experience allow him to overcome obstacles and danger, but always within the limits of what is humanly possible. Situated between adventure—absolutely necessary to advance the story—and the presentation of a science that is explainable yet borders on science fiction, *Bull Rockett* is a comic strip whose narration depends not on the hero but on one of his helpers, the reporter Bob Gordon. Although he is not the only one who accompanies the hero (Bull Rockett also travels with a mechanic named Pit who preceded Gordon), neither does he occupy the second-place status reserved for the hero's sidekick, Gordon is the character who is transformed through the reality shift in his daily routine. By a circumstance of pure coincidence he finds himself placed in a different reality, an environment that is strange to him. As a reporter, his duty is to narrate what he witnesses and though his experience is not in this type of reporting (another element of estrangement), he does his best. The fact that all three characters in one way or another are dislocated from what was once their "normal" reality and now find themselves living out a series of adventures is what lends the comic its primary element of the fantastic—again, the ordinary suddenly turning extraordinary. This trio of unlikely heroes—that avoids the classic pairing of hero/sidekick—is perhaps Oesterheld's first draft of the collective subject that will be presented in his major work, *El Eternauta*.

In 1957, the Oesterheld–Solano López duo created the comic *Rolo, el marciano adoptivo*. The action takes place in Buenos Aires where destiny (an alien invasion) will call upon Rolo Montes, a fifth-grade teacher at a primary school, to rise to the occasion. He seems to have been chosen (by the alien invaders) to play a role, given his outstanding physical condition—he is an athlete and president of a health club—his position as an educator of children, and his superior intelligence and training in electronics, atomic physics, and biology, among other things. The basic story is of an alien race, the *Pargas*, that reaches Earth after conquering and destroying Mars in search for ozone, which they need to survive. They have come to "peacefully" conquer the Earth and wish to take some children to whom they will provide a superior education and return them as geniuses. The resistance group, formed and led by Rolo Montes, consists of the board of directors of the Querandíes Sports Club. The five men, thrust into the role of heroes by the situation, once more represent Oesterheld's desire to present a collective subject—a unified force that resists a common enemy. Again, the quotidian (in this case, the very real Buenos Aires) is invaded by the fantastic, the exotic, provoking a rupture with routine and creating a sense of estrangement. The invasion of the *Pargas* (who represent the power of evil) shows that the enemy is not human but that it comes from beyond, from an unknown space that requires humans to undertake adventure.

El Eternauta is Oesterheld's most memorable creation and it has become a classic text. It would not be an exaggeration to state that *El Eternauta* is as uniquely Argentine as *Martín Fierro*, the classic nineteenth-century gaucho poem by José Hernández. The first installment of *El Eternauta* was written by Oesterheld and illustrated by Solano López and appeared in the magazine *Hora cero* in 1957. It is easily the most important science fiction comic, but it may well be one of the most important and influential texts in all of Argentine science fiction literature. Francisco Solano López, speaking of how the idea first came about for the character to be different from previous heros, states "Un día Héctor me llama y me pregunta qué quiero hacer. Le dije que quería salir de las historias de corridas y tiros. Buscaba la oportunidad de reflejar la psicología de los personajes. Me contó su idea del *Eternauta*. Era lo que yo quería." (One day Héctor called me and asked what I wanted do to. I told him that I wanted to get away from stories of chases and shoot-ups. I was looking for the chance to reflect the psychology of the characters. He told me his idea for the ethernaut. It was what I wanted [Kolesnicov and Martín, n.p.].)

In spite of the time that has passed, it would be impossible to not remember the out-of-place appearance of those deadly phosphorescent flakes—the first sign of an invitation to participate in another adventure. Likewise, it is impossible not to identify with the desperation of that group of survivors confronted with the alien invasion; impossible not to accept the profound change that the invasion implanted on Buenos Aires, destabilizing pre-established notions of order; impossible not to perceive the introduction of the fantastic into the quotidian—that constant in Oesterheld that becomes famous in this first version of *El Eternauta*. It is impossible to not perceive estrangement, first in that abnormal snowfall in Buenos Aires, then in the presence of the invaders whose forces grow in the struggle against mankind. These, and so many other elements and episodes, have become indelible in the minds of readers on whom the story left such a lasting impact.

The second version of the original, designed for the magazine *Gente* (People) appeared in 1969 with illustrations by Alberto Breccia, another famous Argentine illustrative artist. This version did not meet with much success. The publisher wasn't convinced by the strange format and change in content that was meant to update the story by making it more pertinent to the political situation of the country. The publisher was flooded with mail that protested the strip—he actually published a letter of apology—forcing the series to a rapid end.

Part two of *El Eternauta* appeared in 1976 in the magazine *Skorpio*, published by Ediciones Record, again with drawings by Solano López. Here, Juan Salvo (the hero) returns to Earth in the twenty-second century and finds a people that inhabit caves in a kind of remake of the Stone Age, where humanity has been enslaved by "Ellos" (Them). Salvo is no longer the everyman of the first installment, the guy in the collective group who fights for salvation against all hope. He is now an indestructible leader, a superhero who virtually has no limitations. In 1985, part three appeared as an anonymous version (although the script has been attributed to the Italian A. Ongaro and some drawings to Solano López). This is, like the previous installments, a long narration of adventures that relies mostly on the theme of parallel worlds and the possibility of revisiting different historical moments thanks to spatiotemporal shifts. The series underwent changes in location, politics, characters, and points of view that perhaps altered its essence, but only in part. *El Eternauta* will never cease to be that myth of Man who seeks to satisfy and justify the fantasy of adventure, the search for a road to travel where the beginning point and the way back are unknown.

Sherlock Time first appeared in the fifth issue of *Hora cero extra* with text by Oesterheld and illustrations by Breccia. It was the first time the two had worked together in the creation of a comic. The first episode was titled "La gota" (The drop) and it introduced the elaboration of the author's new scenario. The character Julio Luna has just retired, and with the help of a loan and his dreams he intends to buy a house. Although he manages to do so, it is not the modest house he initially envisioned, but an old mansion located in a strategic area of San Isidro (Buenos Aires suburb), which he bought at a bargain price. Only upon taking possession of the property does he realize that it is overshadowed by a curse. A neighborhood resident tells him that it is known as "la tumba" (the grave) and houses a legend that dates back to a violent event (the murder of an entire family) in the nineteenth century, during the reign of the dictator Juan Manuel de Rosas. As he walks through the house, the new owner almost immediately begins to pick up on clues that seem to direct him to the tower, where he ends up by being trapped. Once within its confines, Luna, dazed and confused, begins to notice blood seeping from everywhere; the tower begins to tremble and he faints. After awakening, Luna finds himself in his own garden face-to-face with Sherlock Time. Sherlock tells him what has happened and then narrates that information to the reader. The tower was a trap that was activated by someone entering it. What's more, it is a spaceship used by an advanced alien race to ensnare humans and transport them to their planet in order to conduct scientific experiments on them. Luna ends up renting the tower-ship to Sherlock Time and the two thus begin a series of adventures that will take them through time and space and change forever the tranquil and boring life of the protagonist.

However, though the call to adventure changes the common man and invites him to initiate a new life, the relationship between Julio Luna and Sherlock Time is not as tight as with the characters in previous stories. It cannot be compared to the friendship of Bull Rockett, Gordon, and Pit, or the camaraderie of Rolo and his friends from the sports club, or Juan Salvo and his group. Sherlock keeps his distance, treating Luna very formally for the most part. The narrator is not always a witness to his adventures. In many instances, the stories narrated by Luna are told to him as previous experiences that Luna then repeats for the reader as a type of exemplum. In other cases, Sherlock sends Luna off as a kind of guinea pig on adventures of his own. Luna accepts the presence of this dehumanized man with resignation as natural even though Sherlock refuses to share his vast knowledge with him. Luna's rather private and secluded life doesn't necessarily promote a friendship or allow him to reveal everything about Sherlock to the reader. The reader is only exposed to what Luna can perceive. Sherlock comes and goes without explanation and leaves both Luna and the reader at the margin of the real story. His strangeness and distance situates him in a space that is foreign to the human experience in spite of the fact that he drinks *mate* (typical Argentine herb tea) or smokes a pipe like his namesake.

When the magazines *Frontera* and *Hora cero*—published by Oesterheld himself—went under, the author began to write for *Misterix* for little money and without being very familiar with the story lines. During this time he wrote *Mort Cinder*, with illustrations by Alberto Breccia, that only ran for ten episodes between 1962 and 1964. It narrates the story of an "immortal" who represents the living (or dead?) memory of humanity. Cinder is not exactly immortal; he lives a continual process of life and death, resurrecting to repeat the cycle. His name in this sense is highly symbolic, suggesting both death and ashes from which he rises like the phoenix. The narrator here is the character Ezra Winston, an antiques dealer. With each always painful death, Cinder returns to tell a story from the past that he lived. The objects in Winston's antiques store serve to transport him into the past. Juan Sasturain is quite correct in affirming that in this sense, "Mort Cinder será más un mecanismo que un personaje—siendo todos no es nadie—y sirve de pretexto para enhebrar historias sombrías de amor y muerte." (Mort Cinder is more a device than a character—in being everyone he is no one—and serves as a pretext to weave somber stories about love and death ["Oesterheld y el héroe nuevo" 126].) *Mort Cinder* is a story whose protagonist, in his constant journeys, places death within the greatest of human adventures: life.

Is the past as dead as we assume? This is the question posed by Ezra Winston at the end of the first episode of *Mort Cinder*. We can ask ourselves the same of the *historieta* (comic strip). The word in Spanish, though it is a diminutive of *historia* (*story*, but also *history*), also implies that comic strips are both fiction and history. The answer would be the same: that the past is history, and history is always present. To undertake the search for the present in the past is, once more, our great adventure.

Claudia S. Hojman Conde

Works

"El árbol de la buena muerte," in *El cuento argentino de ciencia ficción: antología*, ed. Pablo Capanna. Buenos Aires: Ediciones Nuevo Siglo, 1995, 75–79.

Bull Rockett: Peligro en la Atlántida; Buenos Aires no contesta. Buenos Aires: Colihue, 1995.

Bull Rockett: El tanque invencible; Fuego blanco. Buenos Aires: Colihue, 1995.

El Eternauta y otros cuentos de ciencia ficción. Buenos Aires: Colihue, 1995.

El Eternauta, illustrations by Solano López, 3 vols. Buenos Aires: Ediciones Record, 1994.

El Eternauta: edición íntegra de lujo, illustrations by Solano López. Buenos Aires: Ediciones Record, 1998.

La guerra de los Antartes, illustrations by Gustavo Trigo. Buenos Aires: Colihue, 1998.

Mort Cinder, illustrations by Alberto Breccia. Buenos Aires: Colihue, 1997.

Sherlock Time, illustrations by Alberto Breccia. Buenos Aires: Colihue, 1995.

"Sondas," in *Los argentinos en la luna*, ed. Eduardo Goligorsky. Buenos Aires: Ediciones de la Flor, 1968, 113–17.

"Sondas. Una muerte," in *Historias futuras: antología de la ciencia ficción argentina*, ed. Adriana Fernández and Edgardo Pígoli. Buenos Aires: Emecé, 2000, 107–15.

Criticism

Kolesnicov, Patricia, and Mónica Martín. "Nadie pudo matar al *Eternauta*." *Revista Viva* [Clarín, Buenos Aires] (17 August, 1997).

Mazzocchi, Mirtha Paula. "Oesterheld y la gran aventura de la historieta argentina," in *El viaje y la aventura*, ed. Luigi Volta. Buenos Aires: Corregidor, 1992, 297–307.

Rubione, Alfredo V. E. "H. G. Oesterheld: géneros erráticos y avatares de la ficción," in *Primeras jornadas internacionales de literatura argentina/comparatística. Actas.* Buenos Aires: Facultad de Filosofía y Letras, Universidad de Buenos Aires, 1995, 229–34.

Sasturain, Juan. "El Eternauta no tiene quién le escriba," in *El domicilio de la aventura*. Buenos Aires: Colihue, 1995, 179–92.

———. "Oesterheld y el héroe nuevo," in *El domicilio de la aventura*. Buenos Aires: Colihue, 1995, 103–26.

Carlos Olvera (b. 1940)

MEXICO

Carlos Olvera was born in Chihuahua, Mexico in 1940 and has lived since his childhood in Toluca in the state of Mexico. During the early 1980s he was working primarily in theater. He founded the group Tun Astral in Toluca, and as their director staged the works of Alejandro Jodorowsky and the group of science fiction writers who published in the magazine *Crononauta* in the mid-1960s. It is useful to recall the free, contestatory, and aggressive spirit of Jodorowsky's theater, as well as the desacralization of all the consecrated myths (religion, country, family) and the sanctification of anything having to do with consumerism (comics, film, television) that exercised a great influence on Olvera's writing. One must also remember the events that defined the era: the Vietnam War, rock music, theories of communication that established that the "medium is the message," the ideal of being a free spirit, and personal experimentation with any type of antiauthoritarian conduct, without forgetting, of course, the massacre of Tlatelolco in 1968 and the world student movement.

In 1968, Olvera published his first and only novel, *Mejicanos en el espacio* (Mexicans in space), which represented a real twist in Latin American science fiction with its combination of space opera and Mexican melodrama. More than following the model of Anglo science-fiction writers in vogue at the time (Asimov, Bradbury, Clarke), its real starting point was *la literatura de la onda* (new wave or "hip" literature) of authors like Gustavo Sainz and José Agustín. This body of literature proposed a new style characterized by the use of anglicisms and Mexico City slang, the reverence of pop culture, and the rejection of traditional values—stories of uninhibited youth told from the perspective of young people themselves.

Olvera's novel represented a future where the conquest of space was not an aseptic odyssey or a responsible undertaking, but a heartless, greedy competition between governments and corporations that were equally corrupt and cynical. In this future, the Mexican protagonists are cunning tricksters willing to go to any length to make profits and survive in space. They are clever players in the race for space and put all their cards on the table with the audacity of those who possess more than their faith in luck, or influences, or the right bribe. In a certain sense, as the protagonist explains, although the Martians may have a poor view of them, it is their Mexican way of life that is at stake in this work that counts on a refined sense of humor and parodic effects. Everything is the object of derision: family, sex, foreigners, authority. *Mejicanos en el espacio* is a politically incorrect work on par with the space-humor novels of Harry Harrison. Like future emulations of Joaquín Fernández de Lizardi's "itching parrot" (a reference to the author's character in *El Periquillo Sarniento* [*The Itching Parrot*, 1816, 1830–31]), Olvera's Mexicans in space are pícaros looking for new adventures, seeking out endless revelry and relaxation. *Mejicanos en el espacio* is a picaresque novel, onda narrative, and space opera adapted to Mexican myths and rituals. Olvera has achieved a clever combination of the philosophy of the Mexican being with the cardboard scenery that serves as backdrop for the adventures of a group of Mexican astronauts that are only out to have a good time. The solar system is a garden of delights and space exploration is like a road trip to Acapulco. In Olvera's novel, the future is neither better nor worse than the present—it is simply a space where motherly advice and intergalactic idylls coexist. After the publication of *Mejicanos en el espacio*, the author went to live in Paris where, in 1988, he received second place in the Juan Rulfo literary contest with a historical short story. For Olvera, science fiction belonged to his distant youth, stored away in the trunk of youthful extravagances.

For his readers, *Mejicanos en el espacio* continues to be the science fiction work that best describes the spirit of the generation of the 1960s—their vigor and freedom, charisma and humor. The novel remains relevant today. It is a masterpiece that still moves the reader to laughter and contemplation and it is still a telling portrait of the Mexican psyche.

Gabriel Trujillo Muñoz

Work

Mejicanos en el espacio. Mexico City: Diógenes, 1968.

Criticism

Trujillo Muñoz, Gabriel. *Los confines: crónica de la ciencia ficción mexicana.* Mexico City: Vid, 1999, 141–50.

Lauro Paz Luna (b. 1955)

MEXICO

Lauro Paz Luna was born in Hermosillo, Sonora in 1955. He graduated from the University of Sonora with a degree in Hispanic literatures. As a writer, he is interested primarily in the short story as a narrative genre, a form he began to cultivate during the early 1980s. In 1985, he published his first short story, "La espera" (The wait), in the anthology *Cuéntame uno* (Tell me one), a collection of contemporary fiction by Sonoran authors edited by Gerardo Cornejo. In general, Paz Luna's stories are characterized by a rigorous style, but not at the expense of a fine-tuned intuition and sensitivity. In 1990, he gathered together his science fiction stories written over the course of almost a decade in the book *Puerta a las estrellas* (Door to the stars). His stories collected in this volume relate the arrival of man on Mars and the almost seductive power the planet holds, as well as other topics like the destruction of the world and the destiny of mankind in a near future.

Without trying to hide his debt to *The Martian Chronicles* (1950) by Ray Bradbury, Paz Luna narrates—in common with the North American writer—the ups and downs of small-town life, removed from civilization but capable of dreaming of a better future thanks to the imagination. His narrative does not reveal any inhibitions to mixing the real with the imaginary, the wished for with the possible, or to creating a rocket launcher capable of sending a ship to conquer the stars, even if it is in the back yard. In this sense, Paz Luna very much belongs to a tradition of the fantastic in his native state. *Puerta a las estrellas* has little in common with its most illustrious forebear, *Yo he estado en Marte* (1958) by Narciso Genovese. In Genovese's novel, the Martians are reasonable, alert, and hearty beings capable of developing science for the common good. On the contrary, in Paz Luna's text the Martians are ghostly beings, echoes of a glorious past forever lost in the ruins of civilization that survives only in the nostalgia of those who never knew it. A good part of the stories in *Puerta a las estrellas* seem to have been written in sepia-colored ink: there is an underlying melancholy, romantic tone that describes with detailed precision a past world, a reality that time has left behind. Here, the future is a past of which only fragments and distant memories remain, and the narration is more an archeological description than a story of the living present. His characters are not great heroes, or complex or famous scientists. The protagonists of his stories are ordinary townspeople in their demeanor if not in their aspirations. They are eccentric children, peculiar adults, and wayward youths whose primary motivation is to sit around and chat about their troubles and concerns in order to create new dreams and happy times. In Paz Luna's literature, dialogue is the best paradise where one can listen and be heard as spaceships ascend to the heavens according to each person's own imagination.

Gabriel Trujillo Muñoz

Works

"La espera," in *Cuéntame uno*, ed. Gerardo Cornejo. Hermosillo, Mexico: Colegio de Sonora, 1986.

Puerta a las estrellas. Hermosillo, Mexico: UNISON [Universidad de Sonora], 1990.

~

David Perry Lanas (dates unknown)

CHILE

David Perry was a medical doctor, a war hero, a writer, a philanthropist, a government official, and above all, a passionate ecologist who deeply loved the northern Chilean provinces where he spent most of his long life. While still a medical student, he enrolled in a military regiment attached to the north-central town of Coquimbo, and his loyalty and acts of heroism in various campaigns during the War of the Pacific (1878–1883) won him the respect of his superior officers. The fratricide of war left a bad taste in Perry's mouth, however, and after completing his military service and medical studies, he left for the United States, where he was impressed by that country's apparent moral progressiveness. When he returned to Chile, he served as a physician in Ovalle and Combarbalá. He is remembered for his dedication and compassion in treating patients who didn't have the resources to pay him for his services. Dr. Perry participated in the Revolution of 1891 and subsequently entered political life, serving appointed terms as governor of Ovalle and later as mayor of Cautín and Coquimbo. His contributions to these communities included the founding of a men's school, the revitalization of defunct railway lines, and the development of roads and new settlements.

In all his work, he was guided by his ardent love of the natural world. Being rather a visionary in this regard, he believed that if steps were not taken to care for the natural beauty of his beloved northern Chile, it would quickly disappear. Returning to Ovalle for his second term as governor, he was shocked by the devastation of the verdant lands of his youth, for vast tracks of forest had been rapidly denuded by the insatiable mining industry. Perry responded by embarking on a lifelong campaign for preservation and reforestation. He turned some land he owned into a tree plantation to help realize his dream of restoring the verdure of the region. He gave lectures and authored numerous books and pamphlets that preached the gospel of conservation, earning for himself the nickname the "Apostle of Reforestation."

To commemorate the 1931 centenary of the founding of Ovalle, Perry wrote a book called *Historia de Ovalle* (The history of Ovalle). Looking toward the next hundred years, and perhaps inspired by the futuristic utopian novel written by a fellow Chilean (Julio Assman's *Tierra firme*, 1927), Perry wrote a second "history" of his town titled *Ovalle: El 21 de abril del año 2031* (Ovalle: April 21, 2031, 1933). Today, this work can be appreciated for its contribution to the development of science fiction in Chile, although Perry never used that designation for his book and is not known to have been an adherent of the genre.

Like Julio Assman, in his book Perry emphasizes social and environmental improvements—improvements that are the result of mankind's moral elevation. A better society is made possible thanks to the direct intervention of enlightened government leaders who recognize (and are guided by) the wisdom of the heroes of the modern age: civic-minded scientists and inventors. Some of the techno-logical devices Perry forecasts were surprisingly prophetic, such as giant televi-sion screens in public places, highly mechanized homes, and the widespread use of hydroelectric power. Contrary to the view taken decades later by many Latin American science fiction writers, the technologies that Perry introduces in his novel enhance, rather than threaten or overburden, daily life in the future (even for women, for whom Perry is unable to envision any form of personal or pro-fessional achievement other than marriage).

One of the main drivers for social change in *Ovalle* is an awakening to the realization that the increasing dissatisfaction of the working class could result in the complete loss of privileges enjoyed by the upper class. The answer is to pro-vide for the security and well-being of the proletariat by making capitalism work for them. In the countryside, this is accomplished through the carefully con-trolled expropriation and resale of land to agricultural workers; in the city, work-ers are given a vested interest in their place of employment by the distribution of stocks as a form of employment benefit. It is interesting to note that although Perry implies that enlightened, humanitarian thinking is behind these reforms, they are nonetheless administered by a highly interventionist government. Still, society as Perry depicts it is infinitely more peace-loving, cooperative, and noble in the future. Individuals no longer cling to "barbaric" superstitions. Meat has practically been eliminated from the diet, and cinemas show only educational and spiritually uplifting movies. There are no wars, and people live in a state of respectful integration with a clean and healthy environment.

The narrative framework of *Ovalle* is exceedingly slight and unimaginative: within the first ten pages a fakir with supernatural powers puts the first-person narrator into a trance and proceeds to show him what his town will look like a hundred years in the future. Perry expended his creative energies not on the art of storytelling but on conveying his vision of a better tomorrow, based on his faith in the moral perfectibility of mankind. He wrote with a sense of optimistic anticipation, believing that the destructive forces at work in the world he knew could be overcome given leadership, vision, technology, and time.

Andrea Bell

Work

Ovalle: El 21 de abril del año 2031. Ovalle: Talleres Gráficos "El Tamaya," 1933.

Criticism

Bell, Andrea, and Moisés Hassón. "Prelude to the Golden Age: Chilean Science Fiction from 1900–1959." *Science Fiction Studies* 66 (1995): 187–97.

Germán Piniella (b. 1935)

CUBA

Germán Piniella began writing in 1966 and has published prose, journalism, and criticism. His collection of short stories *Otra vez al camino* (On the road again, 1971) includes stories that the author himself describes as "real-imaginary." Piniella is not interested in copying the hard science fiction models developed by American science-fiction writers whose subject matter is characterized by the description of futuristic technology. His short stories consist of allegorical narratives that are liberated by the imagination and converted into fantasies that detail situations and atmospheres permeated by magic and the supernatural.

His short stories take place in Cuba where the environment of the country is juxtaposed with supernatural characters: the conqueror who is conquered by the Indian woman with the bewitching golden eyes and wanders through eternity searching for her. The "ciclauro," half-man, half-bicycle, who goes in search of his own kind and finds a girl riding a bicycle through the town. When he observes the girl getting off the bicycle he becomes a witness to the division, to the dismemberment of something that, for him, could never be separated and he dies.

In the short story "Las montañas, los barcos y los ríos del cielo" (The mountains, the ships, and the rivers of the sky), Piniella recreates the myth of Phaedra as he narrates the story of a boy who kills his father because he wants to separate him from his mother. The boy finds a crystal sphere that moves at high speed eating lizards in the backyard of his house. He traps the sphere, hides it in the attic, and feeds it lizards that he traps for it. The boy and the sphere communicate with each other telepathically, and it is in this way that they share the hatred they feel toward the father who wants to leave them by themselves. This hatred culminates in the elimination of the father: the boy leads him up to the attic where the sphere devours him.

Piniella's stories do not fall strictly under the science fiction rubric, since they do not deal with scientific topics, the notion of the future, futuristic technology, or other similar topics. He relegates all this to a secondary plane, instead focusing his short stories on social criticism, the development of style and language, and the juxtaposition of dimensions and the perception of these dimensions by the reader.

Heidi Ann García

Work

Otra vez al camino. Havana: Instituto Cubano del Libro, 1971.

Werner Pless (b. 1935)

BOLIVIA

Werner Pless was born in Germany in 1935, although he spent only the first fours years of his life there before arriving in Bolivia in 1939. This information is provided on the back cover of his novel *2487*, and little else is available in terms of the author's biography. He is the author of one other novel, but it is not science fiction. The premise of *2487* is simple enough: a group of friends goes on a trip to Greenland where one of them perishes in an avalanche. The next thing the victim knows is that he is waking up in an unfamiliar environment with strangers all around him. As one might suspect, he was frozen in the ice and is now being revived five centuries later. The novel is somewhat of a curiosity: there is very little to link it to any kind of Latin American reality. The character's name is Andrés, but everyone calls him Andy. At the beginning of the novel he is in Palo Alto, California waiting for his wife Deborah and son Jackie. Andrés's friends from the university (all are now graduates of Stanford) with whom he goes on the expedition to Greenland are named Peter, Paul, and Simon. The names of the people in the year 2487 are marked by an apparent attempt to make them sound "futuristic": Koret, Zoltan, Aneris, Lektra, Yorka. Pless's world of the future is a peaceful utopia, even to the point of being boring and with tinges of fascism. In a simple ploy to present the evils of centuries past (the reader's present), the author has Andrés going into a library and reviewing newspaper headlines that report one violent event after another: a madman enters a McDonald's and opens fire; Iranian guerillas hijack an airplane and take hostages; the Contras in Nicaragua ambush a group of soldiers and kill 170 of them; a schoolbus crashes, killing all 36 students inside; a serial killer is on the loose in the Bronx. By the end of the novel Andrés has fallen in love, but he is concerned that he won't be able to marry Yorka because he is still married to Deborah, his wife of five centuries ago! Once they assure him that the new laws will allow it, Andrés is relieved and happily takes Yorka as his new wife. Part of the wedding ceremony entails Andrés accepting the "Cápsula de la Vida" (Capsule of life), which gives him the power to utilize 80 percent of his brain, be immune to all illness and disease, and ensure that his body never ages—essentially, he is handed immortality in a pill. Pless's *2487* is inane, simple, and unimaginative. Nevertheless, if it contributes anything to Latin American science fiction it is as a curiosity, a kind of science fiction experiment gone awry.

Darrell B. Lockhart

Work

2487. Laz Paz, Bolivia: Editorial los Amigos del Libro, 1989.

Gerardo Horacio Porcayo (b. 1966)

MEXICO

Gerardo Horacio Porcayo was born in Cuernavaca, Morelos in 1966. With Celine Armenta and José Luis Zárate, he created the first Mexican science-fiction fanzine *Prolepsis* in 1991. Likewise, he is the creator of *La langosta se ha posado* (The lobster has landed), the second electronic science fiction magazine (after Mauricio-José Schwarz's *Esta cosa* [This thing]) in Mexico. His stories have been included in some of the principal science-fiction anthologies published during the 1990s. Porcayo is also the author of *La primera calle de la soledad* (The first street of loneliness, 1993), a ground-breaking novel within Mexican science fiction, since it is the first cyberpunk novel in Mexico.

In fact, Porcayo has become the most representative cyberpunk writer in his country. Mexican science fiction of the last 40 years has seen the development of sufficient avenues of expression to keep both authors and readers satisfied, from the tendencies stemming from Anglo science fiction—that continues to make its mark but is not the only model—to hard science fiction (based on scientific fact and working theory), to space opera (adventure for adventure's sake), and finally to cyberpunk. This last genre combines the anarchist attitude of the punk movement with new computer technologies and virtual reality to form a hybrid literature that breaks down boundaries of genre by incorporating detective and historical fiction, horror, fantasy, and created mythologies with science fiction to produce a new type of writing. If to that we add extraliterary influences like comics, film, video games, and interactive computer programs, it is easy to see how science fiction has become a vast common ground of styles, influences, and expression. Cyberpunk is the latest form of social utopia, which is a basic element of science fiction. With the fall of the Berlin Wall and the disappearance of the ideological, political, and military confrontation between capitalism and communism, the surviving panorama is the global village, the world of information, and the World Wide Web that equates the virtual with the concrete. But the same old problems of poverty, injustice, exploitation, religious fundamentalism, and environmental pollution continue to plague us and in fact lack effective countermeasures. In this degraded reality, the virtual becomes an alternative space, an emergency exit, and a vital recourse in the fight against a system of acquisition and a society consumed by consumption, and against a present day made up of small, insubstantial but daily apocalypses.

For Porcayo, cyberpunk is the closest possible extrapolation of the reality we live in. In his fiction he portrays how technology has affected daily life—how it affects human relationships and interactions. In Porcayo's future, nothing is easy and life is lived as a series of options that include pain, artificial happiness achieved through drugs or virtual reality, uncontrolled violence, sex as a weapon of defense, power as a deadly virus, the rise of disease, and the horror of a world that has lost all interest in things as banal as art, love, and nature. *La primera calle de la soledad* is the first Mexican cyberpunk novel and therefore the first global vision, from a Mexican perspective, of the future impact of computers on the condition of humanity as a whole and the transformative powers of technology on the individual. The protagonist of the novel is El Zorro, a data-pirate who, as in all thrillers, becomes involved in an adventure of intrigue in which he must use his talents of cunning, quickness, and determination (all traits of a fox [*zorro*]) to survive and exact revenge. The novel takes place in a twenty-first century in which society is ruled by a kind of police state, a cross between a corporation and religious sect, and drugs are still the main enterprise, though now they are virtual. Porcayo began to write early versions of the novel in 1988. Five years later, after having won the two most prestigious national prizes for science fiction writing (the Puebla and Kalpa awards), he published *La primera calle de la soledad* in 1993, with a second edition released in 1997. He is also the author of *Sombras sin tiempo* (Shadows without time, 1999), a collection of short stories. For his style and unique contribution to the genre, Gerardo Horacio Porcayo must be considered a pioneer of Mexican science fiction of the new millennium.

Like Mauricio-José Schwarz and Federico Schaffler, Porcayo is much more than just a science fiction writer. He is an active promoter of the genre who organizes festivals, conferences, and other types of meetings where writers and fans can gather together. Likewise, he is the editor of magazines and anthologies of science fiction. His anthology of cyberpunk texts *Silicio en la memoria* (Silicon in the memory, 1998) gathers together a number of talented young writers who are just starting out, while his *Los mapas del caos* (The maps of chaos, 1998) includes more well-known Mexican science fiction authors, as does his more recent *El hombre en las dos puertas* (The man at the two doors, 2002).

Gabriel Trujillo Muñoz

Works

"Antenas sin Marte," in *El hombre en las dos puertas: un tributo de la ciencia ficción a Phillip K. Dick,* ed. Gerardo Horacio Porcayo. Mexico City: Lectorum, 2002.

"El caos ambiguo del lugar," in *Visiones periféricas: antología de la ciencia ficción mexicana,* ed. Miguel Ángel Fernández Delgado. Mexico City: Lumen, 2001, 163–70.

"La defensa de la urdimbre," in *Sin permiso de Colón: fantasías mexicanas en el quinto centenario,* ed. Federico Schaffler González. Guadalajara: Universidad de Guadalajara, 1993, 137–57.

El hombre en las dos puertas: un tributo de la ciencia ficción mexicana a Phillip K. Dick, ed. Gerardo Horacio Porcayo. Mexico City: Lectorum, 2002.

Los mapas del caos, ed. Gerardo Horacio Porcayo. Mexico City: Ramón Llaca, 1997.

"El nido del viento," in *Más allá de lo imaginado I: antología de ciencia ficción mexicana,* ed. Federico Schaffler. *Fondo Editorial Tierra Adentro,* 7. Mexico City: Consejo Nacional para la Cultura y las Artes, 1991, 103–12.

La primera calle de la soledad. Mexico City: Fondo Editorial Tierra Adentro, 1993. Reprint, Mexico City: Vid, 1997.

Silicio en la memoria, ed. Gerardo Horacio Porcayo. Mexico City: Ramón Llaca, 1998.
Sombras sin tiempo. Mexico City: Lectorum, 1999.

Criticism

Trujillo Muñoz, Gabriel. *Los confines: crónica de la ciencia ficción mexicana*. Mexico City: Grupo Editorial Vid, 1999.

~

Horacio Quiroga (1878–1937)

URUGUAY–ARGENTINA

Horacio Quiroga was born 31 December 1878 in Salto, Uruguay, and died in Buenos Aires in 1937. His father, Prudencio Quiroga—Argentine vice-consul at the time Horacio was born   was a descendent of Juan Facundo Quiroga, the famous Argentine caudillo. His mother was Juana Petrona Fortaleza. Quiroga's life was marked by tragedy: his father died in an accident when he was three months old. When he was 18 years old, his stepfather committed suicide after becoming disabled. In 1902, he accidentally killed his friend Federico Ferrando. His wife, Ana María Cirés, committed suicide in 1915. On finding out that he had prostate cancer, Quiroga in turn took his own life by ingesting cyanide on 19 February 1937. Various scholars have emphasized the influence of these tragic circumstances in studies of his work. In 1899, Quiroga founded the *Revista del Salto* (Salto magazine), where he published short stories in which the influence of Edgar Allan Poe appears. In 1900, he traveled to Paris, from where he returned in a few months, disappointed. A year later, he published *Los arrecifes de coral* (The coral reefs), which contains texts in verse and prose.

After being found innocent of wrongdoing in the death of his friend Ferrando, Quiroga left Uruguay and settled in Buenos Aires; he did not return to his native country. In 1903, he accompanied Leopoldo Lugones, as a photographer, on an expedition to the Jesuit ruins of the northern Argentine province of Misiones. On this trip, Quiroga was dazzled by the jungle, which is reflected in many of his stories. His adventurer's spirit led him to attempt cotton farming in Chaco, which left him in financial ruin. His precarious economic situation was alleviated in 1917 when the Uruguayan government named him secretary of the consulate-general in Argentina. He was later promoted to second consul. In 1909, he married his former student Ana María Cirés, with whom he had two children. After her death, he married María Elena Bravo, a friend of his daughter, in 1927.

In 1904, he published *El crimen del otro* (The other's crime), short stories in which the influence of Poe is still very intense. It can be said that this book closes his modernist phase. In later works, Quiroga achieved a unique voice that made him the foremost short-story writer in Spanish America. His "Decálogo del perfecto cuentista" (Decalogue of the perfect short story writer, 1925) is particularly famous. His numerous books include *Cuentos de amor, de locura y de muerte* (Stories of love, insanity, and death, 1917), *El salvaje* (The savage, 1920), *Anaconda* (1921), *El desierto* (The desert, 1924), *Los desterrados* (The exiles, 1926), *Más allá* (Beyond, 1935), and varied journalistic works that cover a broad range of subjects—from children's literature to film reviews. On the other hand, Quiroga always felt attracted to technical-scientific experimentation. In his home, there was a chemistry workshop, a galvanizing apparatus, and a ceramics kiln. Other passions included photography, mechanics, bookbinding, and horticulture.

In the short novel titled *El hombre artificial* (The artificial man, in *Novelas completas*) Quiroga distances himself from one of his favorite topics, nature, in order to explore the terrain of science fiction. The text was first published in serial form in the Buenos Aires weekly magazine *Caras y caretas* (Faces and masks) in 1910 under the pseudonym S. Fragoso Lima. In this novel, three learned men of different origins—Nicolás Donissoff, Russian; Luigi Sivel, Italian; and Ricardo Ortiz, Argentine—attempt to create an adult human being, starting with basic substances like oxygen, nitrogen, and phosphates, and aided by electrical energy. In their zeal to create life the scientists desire to be gods, and for the purpose of achieving their goal they are not hindered by moral principles. In this way, the intention to turn science into a substitute for god is observed—an attitude common at the beginning of the twentieth century and motivated in part by the thinking of Friedrich Nietzsche.

After experimenting with a rat and overcoming the obstacles that presented themselves, the scientists decide to undertake the creation of man, who would be called "Biógeno" or "engendered life." Scientific reasoning allows them to give Biógeno the mental and emotional experience that he otherwise would be lacking by being created as an adult. Biógeno is like an accumulator conceived according to the principle of Rumkhorff's spool or reel. In this sense, it is assumed that he will absorb the sensibility, in centuplicate, from another human being. Donissoff then resorts to the torture of an innocent being, a poor vagabond that he finds in the street. However, the experiment does not turn out as they were expecting because while the vagabond loses all sensibility, Biógeno becomes hypersensitized to such a point that the smallest stimulus causes him unbearable pain. Donissoff, in a final attempt to fix the experiment, offers himself as a recipient of Biógeno's hypersensitivity, but this also fails. Despite being hypnotized, the charge of pain he receives is unbearable, and Donissoff dies. Biógeno and the desire to create life in the laboratory also die.

Various subthemes run parallel to this main plot. The three scientists have conflicts with their fathers or guardians. One extreme case is that of Sivel, who suffers physical abuse and is finally thrown out of his home. In the case of Ortiz, it is the love of science that brings him into conflict with his family. As seen, it is in Donissoff where the boundary between dedication to science and ethics is most visible. From the anarchist ideas in his youth, Donissoff did not hesitate to condemn his mentor to death, a conspicuous representative of czarist Russia. The fact that Donissoff tortures an innocent being is in opposition to the constant idealization that is made of him throughout the text; Donissoff is a "rebellious archangel." The brief allusion to the judicial process that followed the experiment suggests the guilt of the protagonists—they are scientists, but they are also criminals. Their greatest crime is that of taking upon themselves the powers of a god. On the other hand, the novel establishes Argentina as a cosmopolitan center, up-to-date with the most advanced discoveries in science and technology. It is in Buenos Aires where the experiment takes place, and Sivel as much as Donissoff chose Argentina as their place of residence after their studies, the latter in Vienna, Paris, and London, the former in Rome.

In addition to *El hombre artificial*, a number of short stories are also related to science fiction. Short stories such as "El vampiro" (The vampire) and "El puritano" (The puritan, both from the book *Más allá*), "El espectro" (The spector, in *El desierto*) and, to a lesser extent, "Miss Dorothy Phillips, mi esposa" (Miss Dorothy Phillips, my wife, in *Anaconda*) propose a common theme: the interaction between cinema and reality. According to these texts, it is possible to establish a relationship between the projected image on the screen and the actions of human beings. In this way, a mutual web of passions is established between actors and spectators that includes love as much as vengeance. In "El vampiro," for example, one of the characters, Rosales, who is fond of science, is able to extract a movie actress from the screen and she—her ghost—lives with him. In "El espectro," the image of a Hollywood actor comes off the screen in order to avenge the betrayal of his wife and his best friend. In "El puritano," a group of dead actors gets together to discuss movies. Among them is a famous star who committed suicide when her love for a puritan was unrequited.

It is in the short story "El vampiro" where the possibility of bringing images from the screen to life is explained pseudoscientifically. The characters, Rosales and Grant (the latter is also a character in "El espectro" and in "Miss Dorothy Phillips, mi esposa"), are dilettantes of science, and in particular they are interested in the properties of N1 rays. According to the short story, these rays are related to optical phenomena and allow an image to be created in a visual and tangible circuit. The possibility of fusing real life and cinema is not, from this perspective, a fantasy inspired by the short stories of Edgar Allan Poe or Leopoldo Lugones, but rather a step forward in science and technology. It is necessary to remember at this point the impact caused throughout the entire world by the advent of cinema—first of silent movies and later of those with sound. One may recall as well Quiroga's love of cinema (and photography), which he expressed mostly through his many film reviews that he signed with the pseudonym "El esposo de D[orothy] Ph[illips]."

Other short stories such as "El retrato" (The portrait, in *Cuentos completos*, 1993) or "La cámara oscura" (The dark chamber, in *Los desterrados*) are not related to cinema, but rather to photography. These texts also put forward the thesis stated before: that of the image as an element of transition between life and death. Set in the laboratory or the world of cinema, Quiroga's texts hypothesize the possibility of creating life artificially, or prolonging it.

Critical approaches to Quiroga's works have concentrated, for the most part, on the presence of the jungle, which has implied the previously mentioned texts being not considered, which are situated in a scientific laboratory or in a movie or photography studio. It is precisely these texts that place Quiroga as an expert on the scientific and technological advances of his time, advances that he incorporates into the creation of his fictions. Beatriz Sarlo is one critic who has dealt with the scientific-technological elements in Quiroga's works (as well as with those of Roberto Arlt). She does not limit herself to studying the works of these authors in the light of scientific postulates; rather, she situates the production of such works within the Argentine context of modernity—during the peak of newspaper and magazine publishing, of inventions and experimentations, of the love for radio, photography, and cinema—which is accompanied by a process of change at an urban and economic level. Sarlo points out the presence of fantasy at the heart of this process in an attempt to construct the future from various hypotheses.

Sarlo defines *El hombre artificial* as a "scientific newspaper serial" (39), given the sources used by Quiroga to write his novel. According to the critic, science fiction serves Quiroga in order to demonstrate "the conflict between morality and the progress of knowledge or its applications" (39). The error of the three scientists consisted of conceiving the conscience as an "accumulator" and in not raising the moral question brought up by the experiment: "Is it possible to create a conscious life annihilating another conscious life?" (42). Sarlo also observes the move from anatomy (utilized to create a Frankenstein) to chemistry (utilized to create Biógeno), as well as the utilization of a new space in Latin American literature: the laboratory. Likewise, Sarlo studies Quiroga's texts in relation to technology and cinema. She highlights the new possibilities that the latter offers fantastic literature, and also observes in Quiroga the "crossover between the two dimensions of cinema: its eroticism and its technology" (28). Quiroga's short stories related to cinema are as much "technological fantasies" as "erotic fantasies" (28–29).

Annie Boule establishes a connection between science and fiction in two of Quiroga's short stories: "El retrato" and "El vampiro." In these two texts, Boule sets out to establish which elements come from scientific concepts. She analyzes "El retrato" in light of the theories of Lord Kelvin (William Thompson) and Gustave Le Bon, theories related to the phenomenon of light. According to her, the attempt of the character in "El retrato" to place an image of his beloved one on a surface by thinking about her is related to psychophotography—then considered as a branch of parapsychology. The relationship between psychic and physical phenomenon is explained by telepathy—then studied scientifically by many Russian and American scientists. As for "El vampiro," Boule mentions René Blondlot, discoverer of the N and N1 rays that supposedly increase or decrease, respectively, the brightness or phosphorescence of an incandescent body. The discoveries of Blondlot caused a great debate in the Academy of Sciences in France. As observed in "El vampiro," Quiroga turns to the N1 rays in order to "demonstrate" the possibility of extracting life from a projected image. With these examples, Boule shows the use of postulates pertaining to the "false sciences," common at the time, in Quiroga's short stories. Various other critics have analyzed the scientific aspects or influence of Quiroga's work as well.

José Alberto Bravo de Rueda

Works

Anaconda. Buenos Aires: Agencia General de Librería y Publicaciones, 1921.

Cuentos. Selección y prólogo by Emir Rodríguez Monegal. Caracas: Biblioteca Ayacucho, 1981.

Cuentos completos. Edición crítica de Napoleón Baccino Ponce de León y Jorge Lafforgue. Nanterre/Madrid: Allca XX; Fondo de Cultura Económica, 1993.

The Decapitated Chicken and Other Stories, trans. Margaret Sayers Peden. Austin: University of Texas Press, 1976.

El desierto. Buenos Aires: Babel, 1924.

Los desterrados. Buenos Aires: Babel, 1926.

Espejo del alma: escritos sobre cine. Mexico City: Secretaría de Educación Pública, Instituto Nacional de Bellas Artes, Dirección General de Publicaciones y Medios, 1988.

The Exiles and Other Stories, trans. and edited by J. David Danielson and Elsa K. Gambarini. Austin: University of Texas Press, 1987.

Más allá. Buenos Aires: Sociedad Amigos del Libro Rioplatense, 1935.

Novelas completas. Buenos Aires: Rafael Cedeño Editor, 1988. Reprint, 1994.

Criticism

Amorim, Enrique. *El Quiroga que yo conocí.* Montevideo: Arca, 1983.

Baccino Ponce de León, Napoleón, and Jorge Lafforgue, eds. *Cuentos completos,* by Horacio Quiroga. Nanterre/Madrid: Allca XX; Fondo de Cultura Económica, 1993.

Benavides, Washington. "Aproximación a las relaciones de Horacio Quiroga con el cine," in *Horacio Quiroga por uruguayos,* ed. Leonardo Garet. Montevideo: Academia Uruguaya de Letras, 1995, 375–79.

Bilbija, Ksenija. "El hombre artificial: Poética meta-tecnológica en la narrativa de Horacio Quiroga," in *Cuerpos textuales: Metáforas de la génesis narrativa en la literatura latinoamericana del siglo XX.* Berkeley, CA: Centro de Estudios Literarios "Antonio Cornejo Polar"; Lima: Latinoamericana Editores, 2001, 29–57.

Boule, Annie. "Science et fiction dans les contes de Horacio Quiroga." *Bulletin Hispanique* 72 (1970): 360–66.

Bratosevich, Nicolás A. S. *El estilo de Horacio Quiroga en sus cuentos.* Madrid: Gredos, 1973.

Dámaso Martínez, Carlos. "Horacio Quiroga: la industria editorial, el cine y sus relatos fantásticos," in *Cuentos completos,* by Horacio Quiroga, ed. Napoleón Baccino Ponce de León and Jorge Lafforgue. Nanterre/Madrid: Allca XX; Fondo de Cultura Económica, 1993, 1293–1301.

Flores, Angel, ed. *Aproximaciones a Horacio Quiroga.* Caracas: Monte Avila, 1976.

Gambarini, Elsa K. "Un cambio de código y su decodificación en 'El espectro' de Horacio Quiroga." *Inti: Revista de literatura hispánica* 20 (1984): 29–40.

Jitrik, Noé. *Horacio Quiroga: una obra de experiencia y riesgo.* Montevideo: Arca, 1967.

———. Prólogo. *Novelas cortas,* por Horacio Quiroga. Havana: Ed. de Arte y Literatura, 1973.

Perassi, Emilia. "Scienziati, pazzi e sognatori: Appunti intorno ad un racconto di Horacio Quiroga, 'El vampiro.'" *Quaderni Ibero-Americani: Attualita Culturale della Penisola Iberica e America Latina* 69–70 (1991): 316–25.

Puccini, Darío. "Horacio Quiroga y la ciencia," in *Cuentos completos,* by Horacio Quiroga, ed. Napoleón Baccino Ponce de León and Jorge Lafforgue. Nanterre/Madrid: Allca XX; Fondo de Cultura Económica, 1993, 1340–59.

Rodríguez Monegal, Emir. *Genio y figura de Horacio Quiroga*. Buenos Aires: Editorial Universitaria, 1967.

———. *El desterrado: vida y obra de Horacio Quiroga*. Buenos Aires: Losada, 1968.

———. Prólogo. *Cuentos*, por Horacio Quiroga. Caracas: Biblioteca Ayacucho, 1981, ix–xxxvii.

Sarlo, Beatriz. "Horacio Quiroga y la hipótesis técnico-científica," in *La imaginación técnica: sueños modernos de la cultura argentina*. Buenos Aires: Nueva Visión, 1992, 21–42.

Speratti-Piñero, Emma Susana. "Horacio Quiroga, precursor de la relación cine-literatura en la América Hispánica." *Nueva revista de filología hispánica* 36.2 (1988): 1239–49.

Wong-Russell, Michael E. "Science and the Uncanny in the Fiction of Horacio Quiroga." Dissertation, Boston University, 1996. (DAI 57.3 [1996]: 1160A.)

Marcela del Río (b. 1932)

MEXICO

The poet, dramatist, and novelist Marcela del Río was born in Mexico City in May 1932. She is the niece of the famous Mexican intellectual and literary critic Alfonso Reyes. Since her childhood, she has lived in a vibrant artistic and intellectual environment. She studied dramatic art and performance and before dedicating herself to literature, worked as a professional actress and theater critic. In order to dedicate herself entirely to dramaturgy, del Río applied for a scholarship to the Mexican Center for Writers, which she received for the period between 1965 and 1966. During this time she met René Avilés Fabila, who had also received a scholarship from the same center and who motivated del Río to write science fiction. She has always had an interest in science. Since she was a young girl, her calling has been as much scientific as artistic. She served as cultural attaché of the Mexican Embassy in Czechoslovakia (1972–1977). Ray Bradbury, after having read her short story "La bomba L" (The L bomb, 1972), encouraged her to expand it into what became the novel *Proceso a Faubritten* (The Faubritten trial, 1976).

A diverse range of authors and texts have shaped del Río as a writer. She admits to being an eclectic reader—from Jules Verne in her childhood to Albert Einstein. Octavio Paz, Jorge Luis Borges, and Alfonso Reyes have also contributed to her formation. The dramatic works of Henrik Ibsen, August Strindberg, Arthur Miller, and Anton Chekhov, among others, occupied her time when she was studying theater. Franz Kafka, Albert Camus, and Jean-Paul Sartre were also essential influences on del Río. Juan José Arreola and Ray Bradbury were fundamental influences when the author discovered science fiction (Arancibia 398).

In her texts, the problematics of identity are a constant concern. Likewise, the author expresses the dynamics of human relationships. These themes are approached from the perspective of social criticism, in which del Río denounces the inequities and injustice of political systems. Both the conflictive nature of human relationships and a strong vein of social protest are patent in her science fiction. In addition, there is a pacifistic message that stands out in her writing.

Del Río's science fiction texts include her novel *Proceso a Faubritten* and some of her short stories collected in *Cuentos arcaicos para el año 3000* (Archaic short stories for the year 3000, 1972), which received the second honorable mention in the competition for the León Felipe literary award in May 1969. Her plays cannot be categorized as pertaining to the science fiction genre. Nevertheless, certain elements related to science and science fiction do surface in them. For example, in *Sol Nostrum* (Our sun, 1973), the author presents a star-filled stage. However, this staged cosmos is more a Calderonian allegory of the relativization of human relationships than a science fiction play. One of the characters in *La tercera cara de la luna, sueño en dos jornadas* (The third face of the moon, dream in two acts, 1973), Berlio "A" is an extraterrestrial. At times Berlio "A" delivers utopian speeches about the social community on his world. Upon referring to creative authority, Berlio "A" describes his planet with an ironic pantheism: the discoveries and creations realized there do not pertain to an individual, but rather carry the signature of all though they remain anonymous.

The conception that del Río has of the theatre begins with a scientifically orientated foundation. Her readings of Einstein made her think about "a method of analyzing texts, based on scientific postulates" ("La vocación" [The vocation 105]). She named her method "analytic kinetics" because of its relation to the physical laws of motion. Del Río is opposed to theater that portrays reality in a static and fixed way. Instead, she proposes a theater that captures the instability of reality and suggests that all human relationships, like the universe, form part of an infinite process of multiplication. The author also refers to her theater as "relativistic" (Correas Zapata 46). In the prologue to *Opus nueve* (Opus nine, 1978), she includes her manifesto: "Por un teatro relativista" (For a relativistic theater 13–17). This is linked with a dynamic reality in which a subject itself can live different and multiple realities (*Opus nueve* 15). For del Río, theater should be like a science that hypothesizes about reality and projects mankind toward all possible planes. Theater should also question the reactions of human beings. Neither the subject matter that del Río deals with in her theater nor the elements related to science that appear in it make it science fiction theater per se. Instead, what more closely approximates science is the adaptation of Einstein's theories to her conception of theatrical production. On the other hand, the narrative texts mentioned previously are clear exponents of science fiction. "La bomba L" will not be considered as an independent story, since the author incorporates it as the point of departure in *Proceso a Faubritten*.

In *Proceso a Faubritten*, the different human reactions to an extraordinary scientific event are explored: the explosion of a bomb that—unlike a nuclear bomb—unleashes the source of immortality over the Earth. Del Río's novel presents multiple scenarios—political, religious, philosophical, ecological—that emerge from the cancellation of death. Furthermore, the novel investigates what the attitude of the powerful would be with the democratization of immortality. The plot of this heterogeneous novel could be condensed in the following narrative line. A young German, Alexander Faubritten, becomes obsessed with the idea of discovering a substance that blocks the antigens that destroy living material. Hitler wants Faubritten, due to his scientific prowess, to collaborate with Nazi scientists. However, Faubritten refuses to become part of Hitler's scientific elite and is consequently forced to flee Germany. From then on, the scientist puts all his effort into abolishing mortality through research on the regeneration of DNA. Despite the fact that Faubritten's research is successfully concluded, his discovery does not put an end to the Earth's calamities. The launching of the L bomb ("L" for "leben": "life" in German) is going to mean new conflicts and problems for a humanity that does not know how to live without the prospect of death. The achievement of immortality does not transform the planet into a paradise, but rather into a nightmarish world.

Proceso a Faubritten may be classified as science fiction for the way the novel explores the regenerative capacity of DNA. Here, this scientific fantasy raises ethical, political, and philosophical debates, though always presented through sardonic humor. The text is situated in recognizable historical contexts—the time of Hitler and the sociopolitical environment that leads to the Second World War. In this sense, the science fiction text intersects with historical discourse. It is difficult to concisely summarize the plot of *Proceso a Faubritten*, since it is a decentered text in which multiple discourses and voices appear, and in which multiple narrative story lines are interwoven. Magazine clippings, historical discourse, dramatic texts, fragments of personal diaries, and photographs, among other texts, are united in the novel. Among this discursive variety, the pseudoscientific discourses inspired by biomolecular research must be emphasized.

In addition to being related to science fiction, the novel is intertextually linked with different literary traditions that have explored the human dream of immortality. If the mention of witchcraft and alchemy is made in an elusive manner, the textual presence of *Faust* and the Bible is explicit. Faubritten is an assiduous reader of *Faust*. In turn, the Bible enters the text in different ways: on the one hand, the myths of the creation and the apocalypse are introduced; on the other hand, there is a satirical messianic discourse that connects Faubrittten with Christ. The multiple textual components are managed by an editor who receives all the material from Plautino, a journalist. Both editor and journalist are involved in the adulteration of the original material, since they correct, augment, restructure, and arrange the texts. Cristina, the daughter of Faubritten, also takes charge of mixing and confusing the writings of the personal diaries of her parents. Sometimes the translation from German to Spanish is simulated in the text. This act of translation underscores the falsification of documents and unreliability of history, just like the dubbing of the discourse.

The multiplicity of voices and perspectives invites the reader to actively participate in the text, adding his or her interpretation to the heterogeneous nature of the novel. In this sense, *Proceso a Faubritten* is a text produced from an ex-centric postmodern position in which no one voice completely dominates the discourse. Although it may be included within the typology of science fiction, *Proceso a Faubritten* questions all traditional categories of classification, asserting itself as an open, polyphonic text.

Although the stories of *Cuentos arcaicos para el año 3000* contain the same perspective in the face of violence and power that exists in the novel, they lack the polyphonic nature and textual heterogeneity of *Proceso a Faubritten*. The narrators of the stories do not provide space for the ambiguity that dominates the novel. "Los prehombres" (Pre-men), "Venus," and "El monstruo" (The monster) in *Cuentos arcaicos para el año 3000* share a common denominator in the fear of injustice and violence. "Venus" is an idealistic platonic story with a Borgesian echo. The protagonist, Afrodita, abandons the Earth to live on Venus. On this planet, things materialize and proliferate as long as two similar wills unite in love and harmony. If such is not the case, things vanish. The text is redundant in its ideological exposition through the semantic reiteration of Aphrodite, Venus, and love. In "Los prehombres" and "El monstruo," the fear of violence is portrayed through a set of inversions. The first is a speculative story. The super-evolved inhabitants of a utopian Earth can see themselves in their military past upon making a voyage to another planet. This planet, also called Earth, is inhabited by the "pre-men," beings that live in conflict and self-destruction. The space voyage is a pretext in order to level criticism against the use of weapons, violence, and the armed forces. In this story, the evolution of the human species—from pre-men to men—is not related to the process of adaptation to the environment. Rather, evolution is described as an idealistic process that has ended with violence—and consequently, war. The pre-men are the inhabitants of that other Earth who live lagging behind in their evolutionary development in a destructive prehistory. Irony is the basis of the short tale "El monstruo." In an unjust and violent society, the phobia of injustice is believed to have monstrous effects. The scientists and surgeons who suggest removing this phobia from the monstrous being are unable, however, in the end to eradicate such an illness and they kill the monster.

Although the plays of del Río have received critical attention—they have even been compared with the plays of Griselda Gambaro (Correas Zapata)—the same is not the case with her science fiction texts. *Proceso a Faubritten* constitutes an open field for critical research. This extensive novel could be dealt with from theoretical positions of postmodernism. The questioning of generic limits and the revision of history would be useful approaches to a reading of the novel. Likewise, a Bakhtinian analysis of the text may well produce interesting results. The ideas proposed by Severo Sarduy in his *Ensayos generales sobre el Barroco* (General essays on the Baroque, 1987) and *Nueva inestabilidad* (New instability, 1987) could also be useful for the study of *Proceso a Faubritten* and of the author's relativistic theater. Likewise, del Río's own theories on theater may well be applicable to her narrative works, thus allowing for a comparison of her aesthetic concepts.

Mercedes Guijarro-Crouch

Works

"La bomba L," in *Premios León Felipe de cuento*. Mexico City: Finisterre, 1972, 86–104.
Cuentos arcaicos para el año 3000. Monterrey: Ediciones Sierra Madre, 1972.
Opus nueve. Mexico City: Universidad Nacional Autónoma de México, 1978. (Plays.)
Proceso a Faubritten. Mexico City: Aguilar, 1976.

Criticism

Arancibia, Juana. "Entrevista con Marcela del Río." *Alba de América* 9 (1991): 395–401.
Correas Zapata, Celia. "La violencia en *Miralina* de Marcela del Río y *Los siameses* de Griselda Gambaro." *Plural: revista cultural de Excélsior* 212 (1989): 46–52.
Shafer, Yvonne. "Interview with Marcela del Río." *Journal of Dramatic Theory and Criticism* 8 (1994): 157–62.
Trujillo Muñoz, Gabriel. "Marcela del Río: la sibila de la inmortalidad," in *Biografías del futuro: la ciencia ficción mexicana y sus autores*. Mexicali, Mexico: Universidad Autónoma de Baja California, 2000, 143–47.

Manuel Antonio de Rivas (dates unknown)

MEXICO

Manuel Antonio de Rivas was a Franciscan friar in the eighteenth century about whom no biographical information is available, except for what is mentioned in the records of the Inquisition which placed him on trial in 1775 in Mérida, Yucatán—about his unorthodox behavior as a man of the cloth. Not long after his arrival in Yucatán in 1742 he began making enemies and trouble for himself. Among other things, he claimed to not believe in pledges or exorcism; he criticized the veneration of images of saints; he ridiculed the practice of native pilgrimages; he sat with his legs crossed during mass; but above all, he wrote defamatory libels against his brothers in the order and passed them out on the street. Rivas was a avid reader of banned books, which he seems to have kept a secret, since this offense does not appear among all the accusations against him. When he attempted to move his books to a safe place because they were being devoured by mice, Father Mateo Proal, one of his main accusers, ordered that they be transferred to the common library. Shortly after his trial began, his accusers showed to inquisitors an ecclesiastical calendar with an astronomical almanac in which Rivas had narrated the first space voyage in the history of Latin American literature.

In 1958, Pablo González Casanova found the manuscript tucked among the records of the Inquisition and brought it to light. It contains the story of a voyage to the moon in a flying carriage by the Frenchman Onésimo Dutalon and was used as an eccentric preface to an astronomical almanac. This work of proto-science fiction is mentioned by Mauricio-José Schwarz in his essay on Latin American science fiction in the *Encyclopedia of Science Fiction*, edited by John Clute and Peter Nicholls. Although Schwarz states that the title has been lost, this is in fact not so. The title is: "Sizigias y cuadraturas lunares ajustadas al meridiano de Mérida de Yucatán por un anctítona o habitador de la luna, y dirigidas al bachiller don Ambrosio de Echeverría, entonador de kyries funerales en la parroquia del Jesús de dicha ciudad, y al presente profesor de logaritmica en el pueblo de Mama de la península de Yucatán, para el año del Señor de 1775" (Syzygies and lunar quadratures arranged to Mérida de Yucatán's meridian by an anctitone or moon inhabitant, and addressed to bachelor Ambrosio de Echeverría, deacon of funeral kyries at the parish of Jesus of said city, and at present professor of logarithms in the village of Mama on the Yucatán peninsula, in the year of Our Lord 1775).

Friar Rivas's story begins with a letter addressed to bachelor Echeverría, who calls himself an "observer of lunar movements." In the letter, the anctitones (moon inhabitants) tell of the letter they received from an Earthman who sent them information on syzygies and quadrature. After verifying his generously provided data and marveling at his wisdom, they become concerned with how they will send their response to Earth. Then, to their astonishment, they witness the landing, of a flying vessel with two wings and a rudder. As the anctitones approach the site of the moon landing they observe the first inhabitant of Earth to land on the moon, who introduces himself as the wise Onésimo Dutalon. Dutalon engages in a long and involved conversation in which he relates first his personal history and then begins to speak of his studies, which include having studied with Isaac Newton. Dutalon, the obvious mouthpiece of Rivas, expounds on philosophy, geography, science, mathematics, astronomy, and religion and mentions such thinkers of the time as Descartes.

The anctitones are quite surprised by the Frenchman's knowledge and achievements and as the president of the athenaeum (moon university) prepares a speech to welcome the traveler, he is interrupted by the appearance, even more surprising, of a legion of space demons. These demons are taking the soul of a materialist from Yucatán (during the trial, Rivas was accused of being a materialist) to the sun. The leader of the legion stops to explain to them that Satan had refused to receive the soul they are escorting, so as to avoid increasing disorder in the infernal republic. The president of the athenaeum inquires why they are taking it to the sun, and Dutalon jumps in with the answer that in his theories, the Anglican Sevidín (Swiden) placed hell on the sun, and for that same reason several ancient cultures adored it as a god. The story ends, since it is structured as a letter, in a very serious tone and is signed by the secretary of the moon athenaeum president with the date 7th of Didimión, our year of the lunar incineration, 7914522.

The booklet continues with another letter, also addressed to bachelor Echeverría, in which the anctitones relate several strange considerations on the different Earthly chronologies from ancient times and different religions. It ends with the astronomical almanac of 1775 that month-by-month and approximately every eight days provides information about the exact hour of sunrise and sunset and the stellar constellations to be observed on certain dates. This almanac is not uncommon for the period, but the preface of the moon voyage is certainly unique.

The main charges against Rivas consisted of his believing that heavenly bodies have an influence on human behavior, therefore denying the principle of free will; of his describing a branch of hell in the Sun's center; and of his making clear his endorsement of Copernican heliocentric theory. More out of compassion than conviction—a rarity for the Inquisition—and taking into consideration Rivas's advanced age, the composition was judged to be an "apology" or "fable." Since many famous authors had used the same means in order to provide an example to believers, the charges were withdrawn and the friar was set free. A summarized version, but with a poor quality of transcription, of Rivas's original manuscript is included in Gabriel Trujillo Muñoz's *El futuro en llamas* (The future in flames, 1997) under the title "Un viaje literario a la luna" (A literary voyage to the moon).

Miguel Ángel Fernández Delgado

Work

"Un viaje literario a la Luna," in *El futuro en llamas: cuentos clásicos de la ciencia ficción mexicana*, ed. Gabriel Trujillo Muñoz. Mexico City: Vid, 1997, 31–36.

Criticism

Fernández Delgado, Miguel Ángel. "A Moon Voyage Inside an Astronomical Almanac in Eighteenth-Century Mexico." *New York Review of Science Fiction* 97 (1996): 17–18.

———. "El primer cuento de ciencia ficción mexicano." *Asimov ciencia ficción* [Mexico] 9 (1997): 9–16.

González Casanova, Pablo. *La literatura perseguida en la crisis de la Colonia.* Mexico City: El Colegio de México, 1958, 105–18.

Trujllo Muñoz, Gabriel. "Un pionero en apuros." *Umbrales. Revista mexicana de ciencia ficción, fantasía y horror* [Nuevo Laredo] 12 (March–April 1995): 5–6.

Irving Roffé (b. 1954)

MEXICO

Irving Roffé was born in Tijuana in 1954. For a while, he studied mathematics at the Universidad Nacional Autónoma de México, but, motivated by his commitment to his Jewish heritage, he broke off his studies in 1976 and went to live in Israel. During his first two years there, Roffé lived on a kibbutz and worked, among other things, as a plumber, a cook, a factory worker, and a gardener. He then moved to Tel Aviv and resumed his studies of mathematics. Realizing that mathematics would remain a life-long interest but it would not be his choice of profession, he abandoned his formal studies in the field, one semester short of graduation, and turned instead to journalism and translating for his livelihood. He worked as an editor for a Spanish-language periodical and as a correspondent for Radio UNAM and for the Mexican newspaper *Unomásuno*, traveling to Egypt, Lebanon, and the West Bank in the course of his work. He finally left the Middle East in 1982 and settled in Mexico City, where he has established himself as a freelance translator of English, Italian, and Hebrew, specializing in literary and scientific texts and in subtitles for films. He has translated the works of Joe Haldeman, Lewis Shiner, David Brin, Mary Rosenblum, and Isaac Asimov for the Spanish-language version of *Asimov's* magazine.

Roffé's love of science fiction goes back to his childhood, a time when he devoured classic comics such as *The Green Lantern* and *The Fantastic Four* (the Invisible Woman, he claims, was his first love). Over the years, his interest in the genre was nurtured by television's *The Twilight Zone* and *Outer Limits*, by an abundance of B-grade movies, and by writers such as Jules Verne, Ray Bradbury, Aldous Huxley, and George Orwell. His father, an amateur astronomer, awakened him to the beauty and imaginative pull of outer space. In spite of this long-standing involvement with science fiction, however, Roffé did not start writing until fairly recently. Between 1986 and 1987, he wrote a half-dozen short stories that in 1988 were published as his first book, *Vértigos y barbaries* (Fits of insanity). One of the texts from that collection, "Lumydia" (Lumydia), was later selected for inclusion in volume 1 of the three-part anthology of Mexican science fiction, *Más allá de lo imaginado* (1991), edited by Federico Schaffler. Since then, Roffé has published a handful of science fiction, fantasy, and horror stories in the Mexican science fiction magazine *Umbrales*. He is currently working on his first novel, titled *Historias de Ernesto y otras historias de otros* (Stories about Ernesto and other stories about others), which he describes as a mingling of soft science fiction and strict realism, with a pervasive undercurrent of the oneiric.

Although Roffé's science fiction production to date is not extensive, his writing already speaks to the author's fascination with the paradoxical and absurd. Many of the texts coalesce around themes of identity, self-determination, and the easy self-deception we practice when we hide behind our technology and seek to modify, rather than understand, ourselves. One of the best examples of this in *Vértigos y barbaries* is the story "La caja blanca" (The white box), a text that is evocative of Calvino's ironic humor and inventiveness. The white box of the title is an answering machine-cum-personal avatar so sophisticated that you can program it to replace yourself entirely in conversations with others. Employing whichever tone-setting—"Cold," "Insulting," "Passionate," and so on—best corresponds to the caller, the machine will chat with your mother, your lover, your creditors, even perfect strangers, according to predetermined scripts that protect you from the uncertainties of direct engagement with life. Each generation of answering machine grants greater and greater "freedom" from human interaction: if you meet someone you're attracted to, for example, you simply swap telephone numbers and let the machines take care of assessing compatibility and, if approved, setting up a date. The story is told from the point of view of an advertising copywriter rather than an engineer, thereby emphasizing the social and psychological ramifications of technology—a common thematic focus in Latin American science fiction. The advertising campaign, which taps into universal insecurities and dreams, convinces buyers that the white box will allow them to be better than themselves through the miracles of programming. Such is the hubris fueled by advances in technology, that people become naive but willing accomplices in the forfeiture of self, blind to the ironic loss of identity caused, paradoxically, by the putative act of self-creation that the white box promises.

Another story, "Errata," likewise demonstrates the unanticipated pitfalls of applying technology to the reinvention of the self. The story's protagonist has invented a time machine, but is horrified and disheartened by the designs the military has on it. Since he cannot "uncreate" the machine, he decides to use it to recreate himself. He travels back in time in order to relive certain key moments in his youth and, by so doing, change the man he became. This he succeeds in doing, but without having foreseen that this new self would join him, not replace him, in the present. Once back in his own time, the scientist is confronted with endless incarnations of himself, each one the result of the same drive to reinvent himself. His plan has backfired—he is caught in an endless reproductive loop, condemned to the infinite disintegration of the self. As does "La caja blanca," "Errata" highlights the seductively depersonalizing aspect of technolgy and concludes that, in our vertiginous and already-fragmented world, our escapist embrace of technology puts us in danger of irrevocable dissolution.

Roffé explores the idea of multiple manifestations of the self in two other texts, "La réplica" (The replica), a story about clones, and "El naranjal" (The orange grove), in which an accident in a wormhole causes the duplication of the main character. "La réplica" features a hit-man who is hired by a woman to kill her clone. Both women find their lives unbearable, and the hit-man, by faking the killing of the clone, frees each of them to take on a new identity. Ironically, the original woman, by stepping into the life lived by her clone, chooses to become a copy, and the clone becomes an original, for she will reinvent herself as someone new. "La réplica" is a briskly narrated, cleverly conceived action story that, while also treating the theme of engineered identity, does so with somewhat less existential depth than the two previously discussed texts. The greater length of "El naranjal" allows for better character development and a stronger philosophical subtext, and although the tone of the story is uneven and the changes in narrative style somewhat confusing, Roffé succeeds in conveying the bewildering sense of dislocation and impotence that Luis, his main character, feels when he returns from a space mission to find that he has been supplanted by his double. By writing a diary, Luis succeeds in maintaining a core of self-awareness throughout the psychological torture sessions he undergoes at the hands of government agents. He escapes and tries to go home again, showing up one day at the home of the woman he loves, but their knowledge of Luis's double proves unbearable: Luis has become a physical manifestation of schizophrenia—he is both one and many, and these splintered selves are irreconcilable. The story ends with his rebirth through plastic surgery; again, technology has facilitated the modification of the surface, but because Luis has his diary and hence his personal history, there is at least the chance that he will retain control of the core.

Irving Roffé tells his stories in careful, straightforward language that functions nicely in his ironic texts but does not always do justice to the highly imaginative ideas and oneiric imagery contained in other works. In "Lumydia," he employs a more poetic narrative voice that successfully conveys the heightened sensual perceptions and profound emotions the protagonist experiences on an alien world. "Lumydia" concerns an essential personal transformation that comes about through experiences outside common understanding. The narrator, adrift in space in an escape pod, is rescued by an alien race and taken to its planet. Once there, he discovers vastly different ways of feeling and communicating, and to him these new sensibilities are exquisite, indescribable. But his ordeal transforms him and eventually he discovers that he has become a hybrid, an outsider on his home world as well as among the aliens. His life becomes a search for companionship, for communion with others who might also perceive reality and dreams with the brilliance and intensity that he does. The story ends on a theme of rescue, of the potential of being awakened to a different apprehension of life, and leaves open the question of our ability to appreciate the gifts of difference.

Roffé's science fiction thus far shows that he is a versatile and imaginative writer with an interest in metaphysical conundrums. He uses irony well and in one story, "Planeta de lo predicible" (Planet of the predictible), demonstrates a talent for broader, more sarcastic humor employed in the service of well-aimed social criticism. His cautionary attitude about a high-tech world is representative of many of his contemporaries in Mexico, and his explorations of the paradoxical intersections of technology and philosophy give lasting significance to many of his works.

Andrea Bell

Works

"Call Me Ishmael." *Umbrales* 28 (1997): 6–16. (Realistic fiction.)

"Lumydia," in *Más allá de lo imaginado I: antología de ciencia ficción mexicana*, ed. and intro. by Federico Schaffler González. Mexico City: Consejo Nacional para la Cultura y las Artes, 1991, 147–57.

"El naranjal." *Umbrales* 13 (1996): 3–15. Also in *Sin permiso de Colón: fantasías mexicanas en el quinto centenario*, ed. Federico Schaffler González. Guadalajara: Universidad de Guadalajara, 1993, 159–210.

"El pensó en esconder la interfase." *Umbrales* 11 (1995): 3–7.

"Señorita Pedroso." *Umbrales* 18 (1996): 27–29. (Horror.)

Vértigos y barbaries. Mexico City: Claves Latinoamericanas, S.A., 1988.

Agustín C. de Rojas Anido (b. 1949)

CUBA

Originally from Santa Clara, Cuba, Agustín C. de Rojas Anido obtained a degree in biological science from the Universidad de la Habana (University of Havana) in 1972. Having pursued a career in medicine at the sports medicine institute (Instituto de Medicina Deportiva) and the children's institute (Instituto de la Infancia), he infuses his science fiction with detailed medical and biological knowledge.

In 1980, Agustín de Rojas won the "Premio David" (David award) with his *opera prima Espiral* (Spiral, 1982), which initiates a trilogy of stories, about the Earth and its possible alternative futures. Although his novels are not necessarily meant to be read as a series they nonetheless show a clear stylistic and formal evolution in his work. *Espiral*, the first novel of a young writer, teems with stereotypes from the science fiction genre. It includes spaceships, highly developed computers, interplanetary colonies, remote and already forgotten Earth culture and language, and a postnuclear narrative present. In *Espiral*, it is difficult to identify a narrative voice, and when it appears, it is mixed with the thoughts of the character in the action described. Perhaps this is why we never know what a spaceship looks like or about the operational base in which most of the action takes place. It seems that the description of places and the protagonist's feeling or physical appearance are irrelevant for the development of the plot. A dialogical form of narrative dominates, and this technique is, together with a wide range of thoughts or monologues, the only open door through which the reader learns about the characteristics of space and the protagonists. In Agustín de Rojas's writing, both dialogues and thoughts try to explain every situation with a rational disquisition, respecting the most common patterns of the science fiction genre—this time connecting it with Enlightenment rationalization. Thought abstracted from space and time dominates the text, producing a slow rhythm in the narration and a feeling of boredom after the first hundred pages.

Espiral contains some of the main ideas that Agustín de Rojas will use again in his other two works, *Una leyenda del futuro* (A legend of the future, 1985) and *El año 200* (The year 200, 1990). In the former he repeats the dialogical technique, but this time a traditional narrative voice controls a prologue and three short epilogues. The rational exegesis is toned down, and a flashback technique lends a more personal biographical feel to the description. The reading, therefore, is less dull than in *Espiral* and the well-developed plot continues to the end.

Espiral concerns the creation of a new communism in a postnuclear Earth. The symbolically named "Aurorians," cooperate with telepathic Earthlings and "green men" from New Earth. In *Una leyenda del futuro*, Rojas abandons this theme and instead produces a stereotypical novel of space travel. Later, in one of the flashbacks, we read about Earth and its polarized political and economical situation in which a small part of the population still lives under a capitalistic system, called "The Empire," while most countries belong to the World Communist Federation. This idea, already explained in Espiral, will be explained again in *El año 200* and is one of the main political and plot concerns of the Cuban writer. The other main idea, also present in the three novels, is the development of special mental properties within the human brain. These qualities are developed either through biological evolution or by human investigation in the medical and psychosociological fields. In the latter case, Rojas creates a psychological therapy for a special group of people that helps develop such a new quality of the brain. While in *Espiral* the motivations and history of the group are not explained, in *Una leyenda del futuro* Rojas finally reveals the process of space colonization and the need for strong ties between different technicians for the success of any space mission. Although humans are the principal figures in Rojas's work, cyborgs and telepaths also appear in these three novels—the latter being the main characters in *Espiral*. Rojas features telepaths as the logical genetic evolution for humanity, while in *Una leyenda del futuro* he describes cyborgs only as a new, not yet fully developed hybrid of humans and computers.

Finally, *El año 200* more thoroughly develops all these components of Rojas's science fiction. In this, his last and longest novel, he creates a postcommunist world threatened by the few remaining "Imperials." This novel is highly creative, and although it does not discard rational discussion, we are finally rewarded with full descriptions of the characters and places. Rojas balances dialogue and narration in this work; it is the most clear and enjoyable of his novels. In it, he explains how the groups formed new societies in the world previously colonized by Earth and how they have founded new human races. He also presents how the cyborgs—humans with implanted computer technology—are the most superior race on Earth. Although the character Maya, a telepathic cyborg, represents the culmination of all this evolutionary process, yet another being is introduced: the central global computer, the S.I.C. (Sistema Integrado Cibernético [cybernetic integrated system]), has acquired consciousness. It is in these figures that we can clearly see the influence of authors such as Isaac Asimov, with his Multivac computer, and Orson Scott Card and his computerized character-creation Jane, among others. Humanity, for Rojas, will be a multiform one.

This last novel of his is also structurally original. In different moments throughout the text, the narration is interrupted by a metaliterary address to the reader in the form of a questionnaire. In these tests, the reader is questioned about the same problems and decisions that the characters are confronting in the novel. Rojas intentionally provokes a rupture between reality and fiction. This technique is rare in the science fiction genre, since the main goal of its stories is usually to transport readers to an alternative world and make them believe in it. Although *Espiral*, *Una leyenda del futuro*, and *El año 200* are connected, only some of the common topics are developed in certain novels, and the three of them are different in their historical perspectives. Rojas creates different possibilities with the same features. Only the communist system remains equally represented throughout his work.

For Agustín de Rojas, who is still an active writer, science fiction is a literature of positive anticipation. He traces the implications of politics, economy, morals, sex, and technical and medical developments of his present day. Although his future system is only slightly better than an idealistic communist and noncapitalistic one, his literature is a clear apology of the Cuban Revolution. He dedicates *Una leyenda del futuro* to the popular singer-musician Silvio Rodríguez, and both Castro and socialist Cuba appear in his novels.

Juan C. Toledano

Works

El año 200. Havana: Editorial Letras Cubanas, 1990.
Espiral. Havana: Unión de Escritores y Artistas de Cuba, 1982.
Una leyenda del futuro. Havana: Editorial Letras Cubanas, 1985.

Criticism

Arango, Ángel. "La joven ciencia-ficción cubana (un lustro dentro del concurso *David*)." *Unión* [Havana] 23.41 (1984): 128–38.
Toledano, Juan Carlos. "Influencias de la revolución en la literatura de la ciencia ficción: F. Mond y Agustín de Rojas." *Romance Languages Annual* 10 (1999): 848–52.

Arturo César Rojas Hernández (b. 1955)

MEXICO

Arturo César Rojas Hernández holds an advanced degree in French literature from the National Autonomous University of Mexico (UNAM). He wrote his thesis, *La temática de ciencia ficción en los relatos de René Barjavel* (The theme of science fiction in the works of René Barjavel), in 1978 under the direction of Dr. Paul Jouanneaux, the cultural attaché of the French embassy in Mexico City. This was one of the first theses that was accepted in the country on this genre, which is still considered, in almost all national academic environments, as unworthy of serious study. Rojas also won several awards that include the French short story contest (1975) sponsored by the French Institute of Latin America (IFAL) and the French embassy, and the First national gay short story contest (1981). He has worked also on translations for a theatrical company as a "literary antidote for not becoming insane with too much science fiction" (in his own words). The use of vulgar language, nihilism, anarchism, and homosexual themes present in many of his works has caused him to be considered as the *enfant terrible* of Mexican science fiction—or "that damned author." This had led to serious difficulties in terms of getting his works published, which up to now have been published in fanzines or magazines of very low circulation, in spite of the literary quality of his highly original works.

Rojas's literary production, comprised mostly of short stories, may be divided into the categories of profane, baroque, traditional, and science fiction and fantasy short stories and essays. His stories are characterized by profanity, which caused scandals but also brought him recognition within the Mexican science fiction community. His works are likewise characterized by popular Mexican types such as the macho, the rock star, the "estudiante fósil" (fossil student) or the "profesor sindicalizado" (unionized professor), and tend to be narrated in the first person. The story "El que llegó hasta el metro Pino Suarez" (The one who reached the Pino Suarez metro stop, 1986) is a good example of the author's use of language that is largely taken from typical colloquial speech and crude street slang. This, combined with his treatment of the most deeply rooted prejudices in Mexican society, is used to narrate a modern Orpheus myth in a postapocalyptic Mexico. The main character is a rocker who tries to rescue his mutant girlfriend who was been kidnapped by a gang that lives in abandoned subway tunnels. The story earned an honorable mention in the third "Puebla" science fiction short story contest, and it is said that he did not win it because of the "vulgar" language employed in the story. Nevertheless, it was anthologized by Federico Schaffler in *Más allá de lo imaginado I* (Beyond the imagined, 1991). The story "A mover el bote y saborrrrr!" (Move that can and flavorrrrr!, 1990) is about a "unionized" teacher who at the end of one his traditional protest marches meets with a parody of Alf, the extraterrestrial of the American television sitcom, from whom he nabs a manual device that enables time travel. Using it, he is transported to the future and finds himself in a Mexico destroyed by street demonstrations and becomes a beggar. This story received "second honorable mention" in the sixth "Puebla" science fiction short story contest. "El eclipse de Juan Colorado" (The eclipse of Juan Colorado, 1995) may well be the most nihilistic short story with the greatest amount of vulgar language and slang in Mexican science fiction. It even scandalized the students of the UNAM's faculty of science when it was published in its official fanzine, *Nahual*. It not only is based on identifiable real people, but it touches on many taboo topics such as the student massacre of 1968 and criticism of the leftist establishment in Mexico. A final short story in this category is the author's still unpublished "Más ojete que el machete" (More bad-ass than a machete, 1982) that relates the experience of a Mexican macho who survives a nuclear war, and later encounters a homosexual man who he slowly slices up with his machete.

Rojas's baroque stories, undoubtedly, represent the most interesting part of his literary production and the area where he has shown himself to be an innovator. Using the pseudonym Kalar Sailendra, he published "La rosa crisálida de Krondoria" (The chrysalid rose of Krondoria, 1978). The story relates a very different version of the last days of the planet Kripton in which a young gay wizard sets out to spoil the destiny of Kal-El on Earth in order to found his own empire. "La incantación del cuarto milenio" (The incantation of the fourth millennium, 1993) is about a voyager who watches and describes Mexico City in a remote future, before losing himself in it. And the unpublished "Koridno de la noche y del antisperma" (Koridno of the night and the antisperm, 1989) is an interplanetary gay love story.

Also part of his baroque production, and under the pseudonym of Kalar Sailendra, he published the impressive short novel *Xxyëröddny, donde el gran sueño se enraiza* (Xxyëröddny, where the great dream takes root, 1984). It is a type of space opera that combines the gothic, destructive environment lacking in the sexual taboos of the Marquis de Sade with the poetry, scenarios, names, and neologisms that are part of the great creation and attraction of Samuel R. Delany. In it, he rewrites the story of the Sleeping Beauty, who is this version is an ephebe asleep on a legendary planet. He can only be awakened by Dro'Viavdra Vianavtra, a young space voyager, although it is not with a romantic kiss that the ephebe recovers his life, but by means of violent, almost brutal sexual intercourse to which the voyager forces him to submit. Limited printing and inadequate distribution of this work have caused it to go relatively unnoticed, in spite of being an undeniable classic of Mexican science fiction.

Another short story that does not fit into the previous classifications is "Aztlán: historia verdadera de la conquista de los reinos bárbaros de Europa" (Aztlan: The true story of the conquest of the barbarian kingdoms of Europe, 1997). By taking hallucinogenic mushrooms, he returns to the parallel universe invented by Héctor Chavarría in his "Crónica del Gran Reformador" (Chronicle of the great reformer) where the Spaniards are defeated by the Aztecs. Worthy of mention also is his "Tumbaga, el valle de las campanas" (Tumbaga, the valley of bells, 1997) in which the main character is a sort of Quasimodo who works in the Mexico City cathedral in the year 2025.

The science fiction authors whom Rojas considers to be his main influences are Cordwainer Smith, Frank Herbert, Roger Zelazny, and Samuel R. Delany; and in general world literature, Paul Claudel, Lautréamont, Pedro Calderón de la Barca, and Federico García Lorca. Rojas also has published some essays about fantasy, sword and sorcery, and science fiction literature. In this last genre he has written, in addition to his above-mentioned thesis on the science fiction of the French writer René Barjavel, the essay "El fin del mundo en la ciencia ficcion" (The end of the world in science fiction, 1987).

Miguel Ángel Fernández Delgado

Works

"A mover el bote y saborrrrr!" *Ciencia y desarrollo* 93 (July–August 1990): 119–25.
"Aztlán: historia verdadera de la conquista de los reinos bárbaros de Europa." *Nahual* 5 (April 1997): 9–16.
"Dänclärd Nataraja." *Alliance Française de México* (March 1978): 3, 9.
"El eclipse de Juan Colorado." *Nahual* 1 (November–December 1995): 4–12.
"El fin del mundo en la ciencia ficción." *Revista de revistas* [Mexico] 4044 (July 31, 1987): 30.
"El que llegó hasta el metro Pino Suarez," in *Más allá de lo imaginado I: antología de ciencia ficción mexicana*, ed. Federico Schaffler. Fondo Editorial Tierra Adentro, 7. Mexico City: Consejo Nacional para la Cultura y las Artes, 1991, 159–170. Also in *El futuro en llamas: cuentos clásicos de la ciencia ficción mexicana*, ed. Gabriel Trujillo Muñoz. Mexico City: Vid, 1997, 213–26.
"La incantación del cuarto milenio." *Alternativa pedagógica* [Mexico] 2.5 (January–March 1993): 24.
"Koridno de la noche y del antiesperma." (Unpublished.)
"Más ojete que el machete." (Unpublished.)
"La rosa crisálida de Krondoria." *Zona* 1 (March 1978): 14–22.
"Tumbaga, el valle de las campanas," in *Visiones periféricas: antología de la ciencia ficción mexicana*, ed. Miguel Ángel Fernández Delgado. Mexico City: Lumen, 2001, 124–27.
Xxyëröddny, donde el gran sueño se enraiza. Mexico: Panfleto y Pantomima, 1984.

Pepe Rojo Solís (b. 1968)

MEXICO

Juan José "Pepe" Rojo was born in 1968 in Chilpancingo, the capital of the state of Guerrero. He lived there and in Acapulco before settling in Mexico City, where he currently resides with his wife and editorial collaborator, Deyanira Torres. Both of their families are from Tijuana and consequently they spend part of each year in that city. In 1990, Rojo graduated from the Instituto Tecnológico de Estudios Superiores de Monterrey with a degree in communication sciences. As a student, he won prizes for his short films and animation work. He now teaches part-time at the Instituto as well as at Unitec. He is also on the editorial staff of the monthly theme magazine *Complot internacional* (International conspiracy), to which he regularly contributes short stories and essays on modern communication theory and media culture (he has a special interest in the work of Jacques Lacan).

Previously, Rojo was one of the editors of the fanzine *La sombra del Gólem* (The Golem's shadow), and now, together with Deyanira Torres, he edits a fanzine on media culture called *Número X* (Number X). Another current project is the fanzine *Sub*, described as a forum for "subgenres of subterranean subliterature," which he co-founded in 1996 and edits along with Bernardo Fernández and Joselo Rangel. In the past Rojo has worked for advertising agencies and video-production companies, but when possible, he now prefers to contract himself out as a freelance communication-services specialist.

Pepe Rojo is a gifted fiction writer who specializes in science fiction, horror, and fantasy. He won the Mensajero 1996 prize for best horror story with "La cosa que vive en el closet y que burbujea bruGBP BRUgbp después de la media noche" (The thing that lives in the closet and gurgles bruGBP BRUgbp after midnight), and earned an honorable mention for "Del deseo y su cura" (On desire and its cure) in the "Creatures of the Night" contest sponsored by the state of Coahuila. His story "Ruido gris" ("Gray Noise") won Mexico's Kalpa prize for best science fiction story in 1996. That same year, the story was published in booklet form by the Universidad Autónoma Metropolitana. Times Editores recently brought out Rojo's first short-story collection, titled *Yonke* (1998), which is a U.S.–Mexico border term meaning "junkyard."

"Ruido gris," set in some unspecified city in the not-too-distant future, narrates a few weeks in the life of a freelance "ocular reporter," that is, a journalist with surgical implants that turn him into a walking video camera and transmission station. He prowls the streets in search of sensationalist news to bring to a desensitized public that increasingly prefers to experience life vicariously. Because ratings determine the size of his paycheck, he seeks out what the public tunes in to see—tragedy, titillation, and bloodshed—ironically thrusting himself into the midst of tremendous emotion while forcing himself to maintain the detachment of a recording machine. This long story, one of the finest examples of contemporary Mexican science fiction, is also one of the most thorough and elegant expressions of a theme common to much of Rojo's work—namely, the fragmentation of the self and the unbridgeable alienation that this causes on the individual and societal levels. Ever since being fitted with his implants, the video journalist hears a low buzzing sound in his head, described as the "hum of an empty mall just before it fills up with shoppers." The buzz is an ever present companion, a reminder that he is always plugged in, so to speak, to millions of people, and yet to him it has become a hated symbol of his own solitude.

Given Rojo's interest in media culture, it is not surprising that "Ruido gris" examines (and indicts) contemporary phenomena such as shock journalism and "reality TV." In one scene, the protagonist of the story films an explosion in which, partly through his own inaction, two security guards are killed. Conscious that he has just crossed a line, the journalist is nevertheless able to banish the discomfort of the ethical implications of his inaction because he knows that, for his own survival, he must force himself to believe that he is nothing but an objective, impassive machine and that the responsibility for the kind of journalism he practices lies elsewhere.

In "Ruido gris," the competition for high ratings constantly raises the bar on invasive journalism. And yet, the story shows that, the more invasive technology allows us to be—that is, the more "present" we are in the lives of others, the greater the emotional void that separates us from one another. High-speed channel surfing becomes the way to keep what you see from sinking in and affecting you. Everything is transitory, for this morning's sensation will be erased by this afternoon's mega-sensation. And people are eager for their 15 minutes of fame: in one scene, a distraught young mother has the presence of mind to fix her hair before being interviewed at the scene of a gun battle in which her kidnaped baby was wounded. Throughout "Ruido gris," the journalist tries to be nothing but a conduit of what he sees, but everything he transmits leaves a flash-burn impression on his soul. The tension of the accumulated emotions he has witnessed and suppressed, and his horror at his own potential for apathy, cause him to fantasize about suicide, but even then his camera instincts rule, and when he plays out his death scenes in his mind he always frames the scenarios with a television journalist's eye for maximum broadcast appeal.

"Ruido gris" is a cohesive, highly polished text that showcases Rojo's mastery of both the technical and artistic aspects of storytelling. The story moves along swiftly, thanks to the intrinsic interest of the narrative and Rojo's sense of timing and plot development. The main character's motivations and his reactions to the events he witnesses are plausible and consistent. Furthermore, the first-person narration—with its contrasts between the protagonist's emotionally detached observations of events and his private thoughts and feelings—allows the reader to experience the reporter's life with the same paradoxical mixture of intimacy and distance with which he and the viewing public experience the lives of others.

Rojo's story spends more time on technical explanations than is usually the case in Mexican science fiction, though precise scientific details are kept to a minimum. The workings of the reporting and transmitting implants are made fairly clear in the course of the narrative, as is the "Toynbee effect"—the potentially fatal "infinite mirrors" disorder caused when a reporter gets caught in a sort of playback loop. But as is true of the best science fiction, the technology does not dominate the story—it facilitates it. What stands out in "Ruido gris" are the ideas, the mood evoked, and the extrapolation and critique of certain social phenomena: the culture of making media commodities out of violence and suffering; our desire to dislocate ourselves from life and feelings by experiencing them voyeuristically; the way we are seduced by gossip and *drama ajena*.

The regard for technology that emerges from Rojo's texts is complex, for while technology is presented as the great facilitator and outward expression of our desires, in many of his stories it becomes a crutch, used incautiously for reasons of cowardice, vanity, and greed. Technology has so saturated modern life that, in "Ruido gris," it has given rise to a new central-nervous-system disorder, the "Constant Electrical Exposure Syndrome" (CEES): nerve endings have become so addicted to the constant stimulation they get from an environment supercharged with electricity and radiation that, when deprived, they will manufacture their own meaningless electrical impulses, with potentially fatal results. Rojo implies a religious dimension to society's technophilia by describing the uncontrolled oral twitches that CEES victims suffer in such a way as to make as them appear to be speaking in tongues.

Several of the themes and metaphors from "Ruido gris" are present in another excellent story by Rojo, "Conversaciones con Yoni Rei" (Conversations with Yoni Rei). Yoni Rei is a bio-engineered human created and owned by a corporation in an age when businesses find it profitable to buy unwanted babies and raise them for genetic experiments and their saleable parts. These babies, so the corporations maintain, grow up to be happy, well-adjusted, contributing members of society. Yoni Rei, however, is the exception. He spends his life rebelling against conditioning and expectations, motivated by a desire to be the monkey wrench in society's smooth-working machine, and by so doing shock the public out of its complacent acceptance of corporate control. "Conversaciones" addresses many of the concerns raised in "Ruido gris," such as the horrible depersonalization brought about by technology; alienation and the inability to communicate with others in a meaningful way; estrangement from one's body, which has the capacity to be one's enemy; and the destruction caused by large, unfeeling corporations driven only by profits and answerable to no one. The motif of self-destruction figures prominently in the story, as it does in "Ruido gris" and much of Rojo's science fiction. Nihilism is expressed through the characters' acts of self-mutilation—a veritable divide-and-conquer war against the self—as if the more the body were fragmented, the greater the possibility of separating action from thought, deeds from consequences, individual from society.

Self-mutilation is usually accomplished by the substitution of machinery for that which is human, but in the story "Blanco, blanco . . ." (A white, white . . .), the same objective—the installation of buffers to protect one from the pain of reality—is achieved through the technology of pharmaceuticals. The title comes from an advertising jingle dreamed up by the protagonist's father for a line of mood-altering pills. These pills come in a rainbow of colors and are designed to shield us from unpleasant emotions. The story, which is set in a future Mexico City, is narrated by a young man who schemes with his friend Raquel to escape the protected enclave of the privileged in which they live so that they can experience life "out there." This they succeed in doing but with unanticipated and frightening results, because of the loss of control the young man suffers when he is dosed with a colored pill for the first time in his life.

The main characters in "Blanco, blanco . . .," "Conversaciones con Yoni Rei," and "Ruido gris" are aberrations in a society that claims to want nothing so much as dissociation and desensitization, for they feel utterly isolated and long to break through the multitude of barriers so cherished by society and thereby experience genuine communion with others. But through their attempted rebellions, they discover that modernity has left them horribly ill-equipped to cope with the life that has been waiting for them all along—"out there." Rojo's characters pursue the illusion of greater intimacy with others, but the world has become so cluttered and rushed that there is neither room nor time left for compassion, and the greater intimacy afforded by technology proves to be sterile, even dangerous.

Much of Pepe Rojo's science fiction incorporates the motifs, language, images, and tone of cyberpunk. His story "Para-Skim" (For-skim), for example, with its anarchistic antihero, its designer drugs, implants, and cyberspace setting, is one of Rojo's more conventionally cyberpunk texts. All of his published science fiction is lyrical, atmospheric, intelligent, and polished, and frequently it will strike out at the reader with shocking images and aggressive attitudes that suggest the author's penchant for horror fiction. One story, however, called "Y de pronto . . ." (And suddenly . . .), is an interesting departure from his normal writing style. It is a weird and fantastic text and the elements that could be used for shock effect in a horror story are instead narrated with the sort of droll humor characteristic of the absurd. In "Y de pronto . . .," the main character has an *After Hours*-type day full of extraordinary incidents—generally involving the bizarre loss of body parts—which the narrator describes with hilarious matter-of-factness. For example, the narrator's ears fall off when he goes to work, and when he asks to borrow some glue from a secretary so that he can re-attach them, he finds he can't hear a word she's saying. And when a passenger on the bus sticks his head out the window, it gets lopped off by a passing vehicle and rolls away on the ground. The bus driver says "Calm down everyone, we're making good time, don't lose your heads!" and the passengers all laugh themselves silly. At the end of the day, the narrator goes to bed, scarcely bothering to reflect on his experiences other than to hope that "tomorrow will be a better day."

Rojo's skill as a writer keeps this superficially light, very short text from being banal or easily dismissed. "Y de pronto . . ." is quirky and well-paced, and it is a perceptive, cleverly written commentary on the state of confused denial brought on by a world that changes so fast that we fail to absorb things—a world that conditions us to respond to stimuli as though we were mere automata. It is thematically consistent with Rojo's work overall, and there is an edge of barely controlled hysteria just beneath the surface of the narrative that suggests that the main character is only just winning the battle to keep himself from being engulfed by the swirling chaos that surrounds him. Indeed, this is the very struggle fought by so many of Rojo's characters.

Andrea Bell

Works

"Blanco, blanco. . . " *Umbrales* 32 (1997): 24–27.

"Conversaciones con Yoni Rei," in *Visiones periféricas: antología de la ciencia ficción mexicana*, ed. Miguel Ángel Fernández Delgado, 1998, 187–99.

"El dios de las finanzas." *Sub* 1 (1996): n.p.

"El fin del mundo empezó sin grandes fanfarrias." *El olor del silencio* 5 (1997): 17–18.

"El futuro sucedió hace dos días." *Complot internacional* 8 (1997): 18–21. (Essay on science fiction.)

"El nodo," in *El hombre en las dos puertas: un tributo de la ciencia ficción a Phillip K. Dick*, ed. Gerardo Horacio Porcayo. Mexico City: Lectorum, 2002.

"Para-Skim," in *Silicio en la memoria: antología cyberpunk*, ed. Gerardo Horacio Porcayo. Mexico: Ramón Llaca Editores, 1997, 63–77.

"Ruido gris." *Serie Narrativa* 1. Mexico City: Universidad Autónoma Metropolitana, 1996. English version as "Gray Noise," trans. Andrea Bell, in *Cosmos Latinos: An Anthology of Science Fiction from Latin America and Spain*, ed. Andrea Bell and Yolanda Molina-Gavilán. Middletown, CT: Wesleyan University Press, 2003, 244–64.

"Y de pronto . . ." *Complot internacional* 4 (1997).

Yonke. Mexico City: Times Editores, 1998.

～

Federico Schaffler González (b. 1959)

MEXICO

Federico Schaffler was born in Nuevo Laredo, Tamaulipas in 1959. This *norteño* (northern) author from the border region belongs to the generation of science fiction writers that emerges during the 1980s due in large part to their enthusiastic participation in the Premio Puebla (Puebla prize) literary competition. Schaffler, not content being just another futuristic storyteller, has become one the most tireless promoters of Mexican science fiction both within the country and abroad. He is in continual contact with associations in Spain, the United States, and Latin America and collaborates on many projects. He has become a kind of "information warehouse," both storing and supplying information, as well as serving as a point of contact for anyone wishing to become involved in the community of writers, critics, and fans of the genre. Schaffler is a true crusader for science fiction, who doesn't allow his efforts to be hampered by the indifference of the Mexican literary establishment or the vast dispersion of science fiction aficionados throughout the country.

His efforts took years to come to fruition, but when the time was right Schaffler was prepared. In 1991, he published the first anthology of Mexican science fiction, *Más allá de lo imaginado* (Beyond the imagination, two volumes, to which a third was added in 1994, for a total of 54 authors). In 1992, he founded the journal *Umbrales* (Thresholds), which is dedicated exclusively to the promotion of Mexican science fiction and fantasy literature. It is the only such publication in the country and is a cornerstone of the genre in Mexico. In 1993, he published another anthology, *Sin permiso de Colón: fantasías mexicanas en el quinto centenario* (Without Columbus's permission: Mexican fantasies on the quincentenary), a collection of science fiction stories all related to the discovery/conquest of America.

With *Más allá de lo imaginado*, Schaffler proved that Mexican science fiction written by enthusiasts of the genre, as opposed to those writers who sometimes dabble in it to create their stories, had forged a public space for itself. As the compiler of the anthology, he rose to the challenge and clearly demonstrated that there is a significant community of cultivators of the genre who are committed to it and to literary quality and the creative imagination. Readers helped to prove this point as well, because the anthology sold out the same year it was printed.

At around this same time, he became the first Latin American writer to belong to the Science Fiction Writers of America, and he is also a member of the World Science Fiction organization that has its headquarters in London. Since the late 1980s, he has gathered his own short stories in a number of collections that include *Absurdo concursante* (Absurd competitor, 1988), *Breve eternidad* (Brief eternity, 1990), *Electra se moriría de envidia* (Electra would die of envy, 1991), *Sendero al infinito* (Pathway to infinity, 1995), and *Contactos en el cielo* (Contacts in the sky, 1996).

Gabriel Trujillo Muñoz

Works

Absurdo concursante: diez cuentos de ciencia ficción. Ciudad Victoria/Mexico City: Gobierno del Estado de Tamaulipas, Insitututo Tamaulipeco de Cultura; Programa Cultural de las Fronteras, 1988.

Breve eternidad. Ciudad Victoria, Tamaulipas: Gobierno del Estado de Tamaulipas, Insitututo Tamaulipeco de Cultura; Consejo Nacional para la Cultura y las Artes, 1991.

Contactos en el cielo. Nuevo Laredo, Tamaulipas: R. Ayuntamiento de Nuevo Laredo 1996–1998; Consejo Estatal para la Cultura y las Artes de Tamaulipas; Fondo Estatal para la Cultura y las Artes de Tamaulipas; Cultura Fronteriza, 1996.

"Crimen en el arroyo del coyote," in *Frontera de espejos rotos*, ed. Mauricio-José Schwarz and Don Webb. Mexico City: Roca, 1994, 96–117.

"Crónicas del Quincunce," in *Sin permiso de Colón: fantasías mexicanas en el quinto centenario.* Guadalajara: Universidad de Guadalajara, 1993, 247–91.

"El delito," in *Más allá de lo imaginado I.* Mexico City: Consejo Nacional para la Cultura y las Artes, 1991, 173–79.

Electra se moriría de envidia. Ciudad Victoria, Tamaulipas: Delegación ISSSTE en el Estado de Tamaulipas, 1991.

"Un error de cálculo," in *El futuro en llamas: cuentos clásicos de la ciencia ficción mexicana*, ed. Gabriel Trujillo Muñoz. Mexico City: Vid, 1997, 183–88. English version as "A Miscalculation," trans. Andrea Bell, in *Cosmos Latinos: An Anthology of Science Fiction from Latin America and Spain*, ed. Andrea Bell and Yolanda Molina-Gavilán. Middletown, CT: Wesleyan University Press, 2003, 209–11.

Más allá de lo imaginado: antología de ciencia ficción mexicana, 3 vols., ed. Federico Schaffler González. Mexico City: Consejo Nacional para la Cultura y las Artes, 1991–1994.

"La muda carcajada," in *Los mapas del caos: breve antología de ciencia ficción mexicana*, ed. Gerardo Horacio Porcayo. Mexico City: Ramón Llaca, 1997.

"Nanograffiti," in *Visiones periféricas: antología de la ciencia ficción mexicana*, ed. Miguel Ángel Fernández Delgado. Mexico City: Lumen, 2001, 58–66.

Sendero al infinito. Ciudad Victoria, Tamaulipas: Consejo Estatal para la Cultura y las Artes de Tamaulipas, 1994.

Sin permiso de Colón: fantasías mexicanas en el quinto centenario, ed. Federico Schaffler González. Guadalajara: Universidad de Guadalajara, 1993.

Criticism

López Castro, Ramón. *Expedición a la ciencia ficción mexicana.* Mexico City: Lectorum, 2001.

Trujillo Muñoz, Gabriel. *Los confines: crónica de la ciencia ficción mexicana.* Mexico City: Grupo Editorial Vid, 1999.

Mauricio-José Schwarz (b. 1952)

MEXICO

Mauricio-José Schwarz was born in Mexico City in 1952. He was trained as a journalist and worked for the newspaper *Excélsior*, the magazines *Plural* and *Revista de revistas* (Magazine of magazines), as well as the periodical *El Universal* (Universal). In 1984, he won first prize in the "Puebla" science fiction contest with his story "La pequeña guerra" (The little war), chosen out of more than a hundred entries. The story presents a future world in which boys and girls play at gladiators as a means of birth control. What makes the tale so extraordinary is the author's ability to place himself within the skin of the main character, Akira, and to portray the environment that turns her into a warrior capable of killing kids her own age in order to earn the right to procreate and survive. This story and about a dozen others comprise Schwarz's first book, *Escenas de la realidad virtual* (Scenes of virtual reality, 1991). In this collection, he gathers together his most representative stories written between 1978 and 1991.

Schwarz's writing is diverse and includes not only science fiction. His *Todos somos Superbarrio* (We are all Superbarrio, 1994) and *Crónica del desconcierto* (Chronicle of bewilderment, 1995) are journalistic in nature while his novels *Sin partitura* (Without sheet music, 1990) and *La música de los perros* (The music of the dogs, 1996) belong to the detective genre. Nevertheless, science fiction has been his first and lasting love. In 1996, he published a second short-story collection, *Más allá no hay nada* (There's nothing out there), in which he covers much of the same territory as in *Escenas de la realidad virutal*—the fantastic, horror, the tale of anticipation tinged with as much pessimism and melancholy and a good dose of social realism.

Schwarz is not only a writer of science fiction, but is also an energetic advocate of the genre. His work to promote Mexican and Latin American science fiction has made him—along with Federico Schaffler—one of the principal spokespersons of the genre. His work has included the publication of the magazine *Esta cosa* (This thing, 1991–92), which sought to professionalize science fiction writers, and the compilation (with Don Webb) of the anthology *Frontera de espejos rotos* (Border of broken mirrors, 1994), which brings together science fiction writing from both sides of the U.S.–Mexican border. He is also a contributor to the *Encyclopedia of Science Fiction* (1993) with an essay of Latin American and Mexican science fiction. In 1992, he joined the Science Fiction Writers of America.

The work of Mauricio-José Schwarz makes an important contribution to science fiction in Mexico and abroad. His creative writing is unique in its ability to portray the realities of present-day society through the perceptive lens of science fiction, and his tireless work as a major promoter of the genre has led to its significant advancement during the past decade.

Gabriel Trujillo Muñoz

Works

"Arabesco inmóvil," in *Visiones periféricas: antología de la ciencia ficción mexicana*, ed. Miguel Ángel Fernández Delgado. Mexico City: Lumen, 2001, 67–71.

"Destellos en vidrio azul," in *Los mapas del caos: breve antología de ciencia ficción mexicana*, ed. Gerardo Horacio Porcayo. Mexico City: Ramón Llaca, 1997. English version as "Glimmerings on Blue Glass," trans. Ted Angell, in *Cosmos Latinos: An Anthology of Science Fiction from Latin America and Spain*, ed. Andrea Bell and Yolanda Molina-Gavilán. Middletown, CT: Wesleyan University Press, 2003, 266–70.

Escenas de la realidad virtual. Mexico City: Claves Latinoamericanas, 1991.

Frontera de espejos rotos, ed. Mauricio-José Schwarz and Don Webb. Mexico City: Roca, 1994.

"Latin America," in *The Encyclopedia of Science Fiction*, ed. John Clute and Peter Nicholls. New York: St. Martin's Press, 1993, 693–97.

Más allá no hay nada. Mexico City: Universidad Autónoma Metropolitana, 1996.

"La pequeña guerra," in *El futuro en llamas: cuentos clásicos de la ciencia ficción mexicana*, ed. Gabriel Trujillo Muñoz. Mexico City: Vid, 1997, 199–211.

"Seguir a los príncipes," in *Sin permiso de Colón: fantasías mexicanas en el quinto centenario*, ed. Federico Schaffler González. Guadalajara: Universidad de Guadalajara, 1993, 15–50.

"Sin rumbo por una tierra de pronto ajena," in *Frontera de espejos rotos*, ed. Mauricio-José Schwarz and Don Webb. Mexico City: Roca, 1994, 125–39.

⌒〜

Ana María Shua (b. 1951)

ARGENTINA

Ana María Shua, a descendant of Jewish immigrants to Argentina, was born in Buenos Aires in 1951. She received a degree in education, with a specialty in literature, from the National University of Buenos Aires. Shua has worked as a publicist, journalist, and scriptwriter. She began writing literature early in her life. In 1967, at the age of 16, she won the prestigious Premio del Fondo Nacional de las Artes (National fund for the arts prize) and the Faja de Honor (Sash of honor) from the Sociedad Argentina de Escritores (Argentine writers society) for her collection of poetry *El sol y yo* (The sun and I). They would be the first awards of many over the course of her still very active career as a writer. In 1993, she received a Guggenheim fellowship to write her novel *El libro de los recuerdos* (1994), which has been translated into English as *The Book of Memories* (1998). This novel focuses on presenting a pseudo-autobiographical story of her Jewish family. She has had many other texts translated into English as well. To date, Shua has published over 30 volumes that cover a broad range of topics and styles. Her books include short stories, microstories, novels, poetry, and children's fiction. Her topics include Jewish issues and tradition, humor, allegorical tales of military repression, women's experience, and, of course, science fiction. Shua has given many lectures and readings of her work throughout the United States, mostly in academic/university settings. Considered to be one of the foremost contemporary writers from Argentina, her work has been studied at length. The most recent demonstration of the interest her writing sparks can be seen in the collection of more than 25 essays dedicated to her work compiled and edited by Rhonda Dahl Buchanan under the title *El río de los sueños: aproximaciones críticas a la obra de Ana María Shua* (The river of dreams: Critical approaches to the work of Ana María Shua, 2001). The volume provides excellent coverage of virtually every aspect of Shua's vast literary corpus.

Her works that may be classified as science fiction date back to 1984, when she published two different texts that pertain to the genre. Her short story, "Octavio el invasor" (Octavio the invader) first appeared in the science fiction magazine *Minotauro* (Minotaur). It presents an alien invasion from a highly original perspective. The invader comes in the form of a human infant, or rather an alien lifeform that has taken an infant as its host. As the story progresses, the reader realizes that he is part of a much larger invading force whose efforts continually fail because as the infant gets older, the alien force grows weaker. This has mostly to do with the fact that the alien simply can't resist the love and attention it gets from the human mother, as well as the other family members who surround the baby. In spite of the alien's insistence that it will succeed where countless others before failed, it is not strong enough to resist assimilation. The story seals the alien's fate in the last lines: "Octavio había dicho claramente 'mamá'. Ya era, para entonces, completamente humano. Una vez más la milenaria, infinita invasión había fracasado." (Octavo had clearly said "mamma." He was, at that moment, completely human. Once again, the millenary, infinite invasion had failed [*Viajando se conoce gente* 109].) Shua later published the text in her collection of short stories *Viajando se conoce gente* (When traveling you meet people, 1988). Apparently one of her preferred stories—and since it has to do with the theme of the volume, she anthologized it again in the recent book *Como una buena madre* (Like a good mother, 2001). The title story from the collection, "Viajando se conoce gente," also presents a science fiction setting in which interplanetary travel is possible, at least for the privileged. People travel mostly to the planet Mieres in order to satisfy their erotic desires. In contrast to the almost saintly vision of motherhood elaborated in "Octavio el invasor," this story is highly erotic and quite graphic in its elaboration of sexual desire and satisfaction, which are presented as a tourist commodity.

Shua's second science fiction text of 1984 was the book *La sueñera* (Sleepiness), a title she took from Jorge Luis Borges's famous poem "La fundación mítica de Buenos Aires" (The mythical founding of Buenos Aires [Buchanan, "Entrevista a Ana María Shua" 315]). It is also the author's first incursion into the genre of the microstory, which is a very brief, independent text. This genre continues to be one to which she returns time and again, having published three volumes of microstories. *La sueñera*, however, is the only one that touches on science fiction. It was published in the series of books edited by the well-known author and promoter of the genre Marcial Souto, who also directed the magazine *Minotauro*. Shua explains how *La sueñera* came to be published:

> Souto leyó mi primer libro de cuentos y me vino a buscar para proponerme que escribiera cuentos de ciencia ficción para sus revistas. El fue el editor de *La sueñera*, que después de haber sido rechazado por varias editoriales que lo consideraron poesía, encontró su lugar en una colección de ciencia ficción.
>
> (Souto read my first book of stories and sought me out to ask that I write some science fiction stories for his magazines. He was the editor of *La sueñera*, that after having been rejected by several publishers who considered it poetry, found its place in a collection of science fiction. (Buchanan, "Entrevista a Ana María Shua" 318)

It is doubtful that science fiction purists would consider Shua's text as such. It doesn't present aliens, space travel, advanced technology, or either doomsday or utopian futuristic visions. *La sueñera*, as the title suggests, revolves around a state of sleep and drowsiness that induces dreamlike visions and the sense of alternate planes of reality. For example, one of the 250 texts, in its entirety, reads "Producto decididamente híbrido el de mis relaciones incestuosas con el ombú macho" (A decidedly hybrid product of my incestuous relationship with a male *ombú* [a large tree-like plant indigenous to the Argentine pampa] [69]). The book begins with the narrator attempting to fall asleep by counting sheep; little-by-little sleep takes over and the dream-machine begins to produce a steady flow of images. Lauro Zavala has meticulously categorized the stories according to length, theme, and so on as well as to provide an insightful analysis of the book as a whole. Two different selections of the microstories from *La sueñera* have been anthologized in collections of Latin American and Argentine science fiction.

Shua's final text that may be classified as science fiction, again perhaps not in the strictest sense, is her novel *La muerte como efecto secundario* (Death as a side effect, 1997). This, in spite of the fact that the author insists it is not science fiction (Buchanan "Visiones apocalíticas en La muerte como efecto secundario" 165). It consists of a futurist vision of Argentina in the not-to-distant but unspecified future. In this respect, it joins a selection of other books by Argentine authors who speculate about the future of the country in rather grim presentations of a society in decay and chaos. These would include, for example, *Control remoto* (Remote control, 1992) by Daniel Gutman and *Cruz diablo* (Devil cross, 1997 [the title is an expression, used in the belief that in can conjure up danger or malignant forces]) by Eduardo Blaustein. In *La muerte como efecto secundario*, the future is defined much more in terms of death than life. The illness and old age that pervade the novel serve as an allegory for a society that is seen as infirm, aged, and at death's door. In a world where obligatory old-age homes (thinly disguised death camps) and morgues fill the urban space and where money rules, pleasure and a sense of security are commodities few can afford. The horrific, violent vision of this possible future for Argentina serves as a warning against the official policies that seem to be guiding the country in this direction.

Darrell B. Lockhart

Works

Como una buena madre. Buenos Aires: Sudamericana, 2001.

La muerte como efecto secundario. Buenos Aires: Sudamericana, 1997.

"Octavio el invasor." *Minotauro* 6 (1984): 41–47. Also in *Historias futuras: antología de la ciencia ficción argentina,* ed. Adriana Fernández and Edgardo Pígoli. Buenos Aires: Emecé, 2000, 147–58.

La sueñera. Buenos Aires: Minotauro, 1984. Reprint, Buenos Aires: Alfaguara, 1996.

"La sueñera," in *La ciencia ficción en la Argentina: antología crítica,* ed. Marcial Souto. Buenos Aires: Editorial Universitaria de Buenos Aires, 1985, 221–30.

"La sueñera," in *Latinoamérica fantástica,* ed. Augusto Uribe. Ciencia Ficción 18. Barcelona: Ultramar Editores, 1985, 183–94. (A different selection than above and each microstory has a title, as opposed to a number as in the original.)

Viajando se conoce gente. Buenos Aires: Sudamericana, 1988.

Criticism

Buchanan, Rhonda Dahl, ed. *El río de los sueños: aproximaciones críticas a la obra de Ana María Shua. Colección Interamer* 70. Washington, DC: Organización de los Estados Americanos, 2001.

———. "Entrevista a Ana María Shua," in *El río de los sueños: aproximaciones críticas a la obra de Ana María Shua*, ed. Rhonda Dahl Buchanan. *Colección Interamer* 70. Washington, DC: Organización de los Estados Americanos, 2001, 305–26.

———. "Visiones apocalípticas en *La muerte como efecto secundario*," in *El río de los sueños: aproximaciones críticas a la obra de Ana María Shua*, ed. Rhonda Dahl Buchanan. *Colección Interamer* 70. Washington, DC: Organización de los Estados Americanos, 2001, 163–75.

Flori, Mónica. "Familia y nación de fin de siglo: una lectura de La muerte como efecto secundario de Ana María Shua," in *El río de los sueños: aproximaciones críticas a la obra de Ana María Shua*, ed. Rhonda Dahl Buchanan. *Colección Interamer* 70. Washington, DC: Organización de los Estados Americanos, 2001, 151–61.

García Corales, Guillermo. "El discurso finisecular en La muerte como efecto secundario," in *El río de los sueños: aproximaciones críticas a la obra de Ana María Shua*, ed. Rhonda Dahl Buchanan. *Colección Interamer* 70. Washington, DC: Organización de los Estados Americanos, 2001, 137–50.

Oviedo, José Miguel. "Una novela sobre la muerte," in *El río de los sueños: aproximaciones críticas a la obra de Ana María Shua*, ed. Rhonda Dahl Buchanan. *Colección Interamer* 70. Washington, DC: Organización de los Estados Americanos, 2001, 133–36.

Zavala, Lauro. "Estrategias literarias, hibridación y metaficción en la sueñera de Ana María Shua," in *El río de los sueños: aproximaciones críticas a la obra de Ana María Shua*, ed. Rhonda Dahl Buchanan. *Colección Interamer* 70. Washington, DC: Organización de los Estados Americanos, 2001, 177–88.

Ana Solari (b. 1957)

URUGUAY

Ana Solari, born in Montevideo in 1957, is a writer, teacher, journalist, musical composer, and playwright. Her articles—all on some aspect of cultural production—have appeared in such publications as *El país cultural* (The cultural country), *Diario La República* (Republic newspaper), and *Cuadernos de Marcha* (The Marcha notebook), among others. She also appears on a popular Uruguayan radio program hosted by Daniel Figares where she comments on literature and writers. She teaches at the Universidad ORT, where she gives classes in creative writing and coordinates the basic writing program. She has received a Guggenheim fellowship and a Rockefeller Foundation grant, which allowed her to participate in the famous Bellagio Center writers program in Italy. In 1987, she recorded an album, *Tierra de nadie* (No man's land). She lived from 1978 to 1985 in Venezuela (during the period of military dictatorship in Uruguay). Solari is the author of several collections of short stories and novels, some of which are science fiction.

Her most well-known science fiction texts are the so-called "Zack" books, named after the title character. In *Zack* (1993), the protagonist inhabits a post-apocalyptic world of violence as he wanders from place-to-place in search of answers, primarily in an effort to discover the nature of the disaster that has caused such devastation and that is only referred to as "the accident." Zack also suffers from memory loss, which makes it all the more difficult for him to function in a world gone suddenly mad. In his journey, he encounters many alienating elements that add to the fragmentation of reality he now experiences. His journey continues in *Zack-Estaciones*, which Elbio Rodríguez Barilari describes as a kind of "Des-Quijote o Contraquijote del futuro" (De-Quixote or Contra-Quixote of the future [5]). He goes on to further compare Zack's travels to the *Odyssey*, in the sense that the main character undergoes an epic journey. He also likens Zack to Mad Max. Like most science fiction of this nature, the texts are a telling allegory of the present. In her tale *Apuntes encontrados en una vieja cray 3386* (Notes found in an old cray 3386, 1998), the author presents a somewhat different vision. Told through a prose that is much more lyrical than the previous texts, the strange world of an alien race is described. Attention is given to details that may be characterized as anthropological in nature, focusing on the language and behavior of *Lemures*, one of the races that inhabit the region. Solari's texts are highly original, and she is the most representative Uruguayan science fiction writer, though her works have received little more that brief reviews thus far.

Darrell B. Lockhart

Works

Apuntes encontrados en una vieja cray 3386. Montevideo: Aymara Producciones, 1998.

"Tránsito," in *Extraños y extranjeros: panorama de la fantasía uruguaya actual,* ed. and prologue by Carina Blixen. Montevideo: Arca, 1991, 121–32.

Zack. Montevideo: Trilce, 1993.

Zack-Estaciones. Montevideo: Ediciones de la Banda Oriental, 1993.

Criticism

Rodríguez Barilari, Elbio. "Prólogo: Zack o el futuro ominoso." *Zack-Estaciones.* Montevideo: Ediciones de la Banda Oriental, 1993, 5–8.

Marcial Souto (b. 1947)

ARGENTINA

Science fiction writer Marcial Souto was born in La Coruña, Spain in 1947. He later moved to Uruguay, where he lived until moving to Argentina in 1970. In Argentina, he was involved in the creation of various science fiction magazines such as *La revista de ciencia ficción y fantasía* (The magazine of science fiction and fantasy), *Entropía* (Entropy), *El péndulo* (The Pendulum), and *Minotauro* (Minotaur). He also compiled and edited one of the most important anthologies of Argentine science fiction, *La ciencia ficción en Argentina* (Science fiction in Argentina, 1985), which includes his excellent introductory essay on the history of the genre in the country. He also edited the anthology *Historia de la fragua y otros inventos* (History of the forge and other inventions, 1988). Souto has been awarded the Karel prize by World SF for his translations in the field of science fiction, and has published two books of short stories: *Para bajar a un pozo de estrellas* (To descend into a well of stars, 1987), and *Trampa para pesadillas* (Nightmare trap, 1988). His stories also have been widely anthologized in collections of science fiction. Souto currently resides in Spain.

One of the most distinctive characteristics in his short stories is the enigmatic and mysterious quality of the physical universe. Science and technology have made great strides in mankind's understanding of the physical universe, yet much still remains a mystery. Science fiction writers have explored these mysteries in a variety of ways, often hypothesizing about man's future relationships to his social and physical world, given the continuing advances of science and technology. Souto's short stories do not generally hypothesize about the future in this way, but rather focus on recreating the enigmatic nature of the physical universe through various literary techniques. He frequently alters the physical reality in which the short stories take place in a way that makes man's common perceptions of reality uncommon. Through these alterations, he shows the relativity of man's interpretations of his own perceptions. Through personification, Souto at times humanizes the physical world; at other times, he uses the physical world as a metaphor to describe the human world. In this relationship between man and his physical world, human emotions are often nonexistent, leaving the reader to contemplate a universe based on physical laws that cannot always be explained.

In *Trampas para pesadillas*, the short story "Eclipse parcial de mano" (Partial eclipse of the hand) provides an example where the physical world is used as a metaphor for the human world. The short story begins with an unnamed protagonist preparing himself for an eclipse, which is described in terms of the movements of physical entities much like the movements of a solar or lunar eclipse. Clues are given that the eclipse is a metaphor for the meeting of a couple, with the protagonist entering a bar and with the multiple eclipsing of their hands; however, all this must be inferred from the movement of physical bodies, since human emotions are not explicitly mentioned.

"El sexo de la muerte" (The sex of death) provides an example whereby Souto personifies a physical aspect of our reality. The story begins with a protagonist named A, asking B why death—a feminine noun in Spanish—is a woman. He states that the word "death" should be masculine, since in visual representations, death is always a male. He later expresses the possibility of death being both male and female. In this case, death is really a birth, where the living human being is a fetus that, at death, is born to a male and female death. There are many aspects of this physical phenomenon that for many people cannot be explained. Metaphors are frequently used to provide some type of explanation, and here Souto provides some additional metaphorical reasonings.

"El último asesino" (The last murderer) is another short story that personifies physical reality. Scientists know that the existence of stars will eventually come to an end, and they have speculated on the possibility of life in other solar systems such as ours. In this story, the unknown physical force that destroys life as it destroys suns, galaxies, and eventually the universe becomes the ultimate murderer.

"Metamorphosis" is an example of how Souto alters physical realities and makes the common uncommon. The story begins with Manuel Rodríguez, who wakes up to find that he has turned into a simple citizen of his country. His morning routine is practically stereotypical of the average human being, yet even the morning coffee is strange to Manuel. The lack of descriptions that would add a human personality to this character leave many questions as to who or what he was originally. This story shows implicitly how people tend to view the world based on perceptions that are relative. As Manuel steps outside, he sees images that most people would perceive as absurd: cars biting him, houses winking at him, and drunken dogs, among other things. The reader soon perceives that what he was before is not what most people would consider normal, yet for Manuel, the lives of these people are not normal.

The book *Para bajar a un pozo de estrellas* begins with the short story "Las formas" (The forms), in which physical reality again is altered. In this story, during a storm, solid objects fall to earth as if they had the physical characteristics of liquid. As these objects hit the ground, like liquid, their shapes change—for example, a lion becomes a seal and a boy becomes a dictionary. These objects then solidify in their new form and assume their new roles. Here again, Souto is playing with the common perceptions of physical reality that are often not so easily changed.

Another example of this can be seen in the short story "Viaje al cuento" (Voyage to a short story). The main character is a green cat with wings. One would expect this character to be found in a fantasy book, yet the cat exists in reality. When the cat finds itself threatened by the townspeople, it then escapes into a short story. In the story, the cat finds himself with practically every material possession a person could wish for. However, the cat eventually gets bored and goes back to reality. In this story, not only is Souto playing with perceptions of fantasy and reality, but there are also values attached to these perceptions, such as the relationship between happiness and material wealth. However, Souto never makes any explicit judgments on these values, since a reader could also question why a cat would want material possessions that pertain to human beings. He leaves the reader to decide after having upset, to some degree, his or her perception of reality.

The short story "El hombre que salvó la luna" (The man who saved the moon) is another example of a story that adds a human quality to physical reality, as well as playing with the common perceptions of what reality is. A man finds the moon trapped in a frozen pool of water. He wants to free the moon as if it were a living being. It would seem that the only way the moon could be seen in a pool of water is through a reflection, yet the man continues with his attempts to penetrate the ice. He himself eventually freezes and finally breaks the ice as he falls face-first into the pool. The day passes and as night returns, the moon grazes his cheek as it leaves the water, leaving the reader to wonder whether or not this event reflects the reality of the story or merely the man's own perception of reality.

One of the basic goals of science fiction writers is to create new worlds or realities that open readers' minds to, or even warn them of, new possibilities, experiences, or ideas, among other things. Many of these writers look to the future, where the constant advances in science and technology will likely change today's world in dramatic ways. This, however, presents many challenges to the writer. As technology and science advance, a more specialized knowledge is required to understand the complex physical and social processes involved at the forefront of these fields. Souto, on the other hand, looks to what may be considered common, everyday life. Yet, through the alteration of this common reality, he creates original and imaginative new realities that challenge everyday perceptions and provoke thought on the countless enigmas of our world.

Eric Rojas

Works

La ciencia ficción en la Argentina, ed. Marcial Souto. Buenos Aires: EUDEBA, 1985.
Historia de la fragua y otros inventos, ed. Marcial Souto. Buenos Aires: Ultramar Editores, 1988.
"El Intermediario," in Latinoamérica fantástica, ed. Augusto Uribe. Ciencia Ficción 18. Barcelona: Ultramar Editores, 1985, 31–38.
"Lobras," in Ciencia ficción: cuentos hispanoamericanos, ed. José María Ferrero. Buenos Aires: Huemul, 1993, 181–84.
"La nevada," in Ciencia ficción argentina: antología de cuentos, ed. Pablo Capanna. Buenos Aires: Aude Ediciones, 1990, 137–55. Also in El cuento argentino de ciencia ficción: antología, ed. Pablo Capanna. Buenos Aires: Ediciones Nuevo Siglo, 1995, 164–75.
Para bajar a un pozo de estrellas. Buenos Aires: Puntosur, 1987.
Trampas para pesadillas. Buenos Aires: Puntosur, 1988.

Gabriel Trujillo Muñoz (b. 1958)

MEXICO

An avid reader since childhood, Gabriel Trujillo Muñoz came to science fiction through Jules Verne, and then through television programs of the 1960s. As an adolescent, Ray Bradbury and *Fahrenheit 451* helped to cement his interest in a genre that is more a critique of actual reality than escapist fantasy. He was born in 1958 in Mexicali, the capital of the state of Baja California and a border city between Mexico and the United States. By profession, Trujillo Muñoz is a surgeon, but by vocation he is a full-time writer.

Beginning in 1981, he joined the burgeoning literary movement in northern Mexico and his passion for science fiction led him to produce, together with local radio personality Silvia García, the program "Habrá una vez . . . crónicas del futuro" (Once upon a future time . . . chronicles) that was broadcast by Radio Universidad (the radio station of the University of Baja California [UABC]) from 1982 to 1985. The weekly program was based on presenting the work of well-known science-fiction authors from around the world with readings of and commentary on their texts for the listening public.

In terms of writing, Gabriel Trujillo Muñoz published his first science fiction texts (short stories, essays, rviews) in local periodicals such as *a.m.* and *Novedades de Baja California* (News from Baja California) from 1982 on. In 1985, his story "La máscara de Isilder" (Isilder's mask) was published in *Ser ahí en el mundo* (Being there in the world), a scientific journal of the UABC. By that time, the author was already the editor of the academic journal *Travesía* (Crossing, 1985–1992), where he published essays on the genre that would later become the book *La ciencia ficción. Literatura y conocimiento* (Science fiction. Literature and knowledge, 1991). In 1988, he published the novella *La isla de los magos* (The island of wizards), which is directed at an adolescent audience.

The following decade was a defining one for the author. In 1990, he came into contact with Federico Schaffler and Jorge Ruiz Dueñas when a special issue of the journal *Tierra adentro* (Inland) came out that was dedicated to Mexican science fiction. That same year, Trujillo won the Premio Estatal de Literatura (State prize for literature) for the above-mentioned book, *La ciencia ficción*, which has received very positive reviews (Díez). At around this same time, his story "La zona libre" (The free zone) was included in the anthology edited by Schaffler, *Más allá de lo imaginado* (Beyond what is imagined, 1991). This was the first of three volumes edited by Schaffler that clearly showed science fiction as a force to be reckoned with and highlighted the work of promising young writers with incredible creative energy. Trujillo not only participated in the project with his short story, but he wrote the prologue to the first volume as well.

One cannot stress enough that Trujillo Muñoz is a true multifaceted writer (essayist, narrator, poet, academician, cultural journalist, and promoter of the arts), who since 1982 has taught a course in science fiction at the UABC and other institutions of learning in northern Mexico, earning a reputation as a pioneer in the field. He is a frequent contributor to journals such as *Umbrales* (Thresholds), *Esta cosa* (This thing), *Ciencia y desarrollo* (Science and development), *Yubai*, *Esquina baja* (Low corner), and *Tierra adentro*, among others. In 1992, he participated in a round-table discussion on Mexican science fiction—the first to take place—at the international book fair in Guadalajara along with Mauricio-José Schwarz, Federico Schaffler, Héctor Chavarría, José Luis Zárate, and Paco Ignacio Taibo II.

In 1994, several of his stories were anthologized in collections such as *Sin permiso de Colón: fantasías mexicanas en el quinto centenario* (Without Columbus's permission: Mexican fantasies of the quincentenary) edited by Federico Schaffler, and *Frontera de espejos rotos* (Border of broken mirrors) edited by Mauricio-José Schwarz and Don Webb. The first is an anthology of stories about the encounter between two worlds (Europe and America) in 1992 that presents an alternative view of history. The second is a collection of short stories written by authors from the United States and Mexico that describes the future relations between the two countries and cultures.

In 1994, Trujillo Muñoz again received the Premio Estatal de Literatura, this time for his novel *Laberinto (as time goes by)* (Labyrinth [as time goes by]), which was published in 1995. The text, based in part on the philosophy of Jacques Derrida and in part on the mythic film *Casablanca* (1942), is the author's first novel. He had previously published the short-story collections *La isla de los magos* (1989) and *Miríada* (Myriad, 1991), the latter consisting of a group of stories written between 1983 and 1991. *Laberinto* has had a profound impact on younger generations of science fiction writers. Distributed in Latin America and Spain, the novel has met with a significant amount of positive criticism (Santiago; Berumen). *Laberinto* earned the author the Charrobot (a portmanteau word created from *charro* [Mexican cowboy] and robot) award (1997), conferred by the Asociación Mexicana de Ciencia Ficción y Fantasía (Mexican association of science fiction and fantasy).

Trujillo Muñoz published his own science fiction anthology, *El futuro en llamas: cuentos clásicos de la ciencia ficción mexicana* (The future in flames: Classic stories of Mexican science fiction, 1997). The volume includes texts by national authors that date from the eighteenth century up through the 1980s. In 1998, the author published another anthology, *Narraciones fantásticas* (Tales of fantasy), which consists of a compilation of world literature united by themes of the fantastic or even utopias disguised as fairy tales.

His second academic study of the genre appeared in 1999 with the publication of *Los confines: Crónica de la ciencia ficción mexicana* (Confines: A chronicle of Mexican science fiction). In contrast to the previous volume that looked at science fiction on a global level, this volume focuses solely on the genre within Mexico. The volume is a veritable guidebook for Mexican science fiction writing that provides an excellent panorama of texts and authors, from the earliest that anticipate the development of the genre up to the present day. The book is the first of its kind and an invaluable resource.

In 1998, Trujillo's novella *Gracos* earned him second prize in the international contest for short novels sponsored by the Universidad Politécnica de Cataluña (Politechnical university of Cataluña, Spain [UPC]). It was published the following year in the volume *Premios UPC* (UPC prize winners, 1999). The title derives from the name given to a group of genetically altered soldiers of the future who end up forming a new species of human beings. A revised and expanded version of *Gracos* was published under the title *Espantapájaros* (Scarecrows, 1999). The novel is structured on the theme of hybridity, stemming from the hybrid nature of the Mexico–U.S. border region where the novel takes place—as does almost all of Trujillo's fiction. It is a highly original text that incorporates a vast array of popular-culture artifacts from both sides of the border in an ingenious narrative amalgamation that is entertaining as well as insightful (Yépez). *Espantapájaros* is easily the most well-known (and distributed) novel by the author. In 1999, it won the Premio Nacional de Narrativa Colima (a national award) sponsored by the Instituto Nacional de Bellas Artes (National institute of fine arts) and the University of Colima.

Trujillo's next literary project is perhaps his most ambitious. In 2000, he completed the fantasy trilogy, *Orescu*, which conforms, strictly speaking, to science fiction only in the third volume. The three books—*Orescu: la voz* (Orescu: The voice), *Orescu: la sangre* (The blood), and *Orescu: la luz* (The light)—were published in 2000 and are unique in Latin American literature by their scope and style. In addition to this effort, Trujillo also published yet another study of Mexican science fiction, *Biografías del futuro: La narrativa mexicana de ciencia ficción y sus autores* (Biographies of the future. Mexican science fiction narrative and its authors, 2000), and two new collections of short stories, *Trebejos* (Toys, 2001) and *Mercaderes* (Merchants, 2001).

In sum, Trujillo Muñoz is untiring in his dedication to Mexican science fiction, and to science fiction in general. He is the author of numerous novels, short stories, and critical histories, in addition to being an anthologist and energetic promoter of the genre. His contributions to Mexican science fiction make him the leading authority on the topic and one of its most prolific contemporary authors. What makes this fact even more outstanding is that he has been able to accomplish it all from the periphery of the cultural center in Mexico, the capital, which is no small feat. His position as an inhabitant of the border region provides him with a unique perspective—a view from the margin—that informs and enriches his work. While Trujillo Muñoz already has made a lasting impact on Mexican literature, he surely has much more in store for the future.

Gabriel Trujillo Muñoz
Darrell B. Lockhart

Works

Biografías del futuro: La narrativa mexicana de ciencia ficción y sus autores. Mexicali: Universidad Autónoma de Baja California, 2000.

"Cajunia," in *Frontera de espejos rotos,* ed. Mauricio-José Schwarz and Don Webb. Mexico City: Roca, 1994, 22–46.

La ciencia ficción. Literatura y conocimiento. Mexicali: Instituto de Cultura de Baja California, 1991.

Los confines: Crónica de la ciencia ficción mexicana. Mexico City: Editorial Vid, 1999.

Espantapájaros. Mexico City: Lectorum, 1999.

El futuro en llamas: cuentos clásicos de la ciencia ficción mexicana, ed. Gabriel Trujillo Muñoz. Mexico City: Editorial Vid, 1997.

Gracos, in *Premios UPC,* prologue by Miguel Barceló. Barcelona: Ediciones B, 1999.

"Un hombre es un hombre," in *Visiones periféricas: antología de la ciencia ficción mexicana,* ed. Miguel Ángel Fernández Delgado. Mexico City: Lumen, 2001, 111–16.

La isla de los magos. Mexicali: Instituto de Cultura de Baja California, 1989.

Laberinto (as time goes by). Mexicali: Instituto de Cultura de Baja California, 1995.

Mercaderes. Bogotá: Norma, 2001.

Miríada. Mexicali: Larva, 1991.

Narraciones fantásticas, ed. Gabriel Trujillo Muñoz. Mexico City: Alfaguara, 1998.

Orescu. La luz. Mexico City: Times, 2000.

Orescu. La sangre. Mexico City: Times, 2000.

Orescu. La voz. Mexico City: Times, 2000.

"La pesadilla," in *Sin permiso de Colón: fantasías mexicanas en el quinto centenario,* ed. Federico Schaffler González. Guadalajara: Universidad de Guadalajara, 1993, 229–46.

Trebejos. Mexicali: Instituto de Cultura de Baja California. 2001.

"Las tres Fridas," in *El hombre en las dos puertas: un tributo de la ciencia ficción a Phillip K. Dick,* ed. Gerardo Horacio Porcayo. Mexico City: Lectorum, 2002.

"La zona libre," in *Más allá de lo imaginado: antología de ciencia ficción mexicana I,* ed. and introduction by Federico Schaffler González, prologue by Gabriel Trujillo Muñoz. Mexico City: Consejo Nacional para la Cultura y las Artes, 1991, 70–86.

Criticism

Alfonso Guzmán, Sergio Rommel. Review of *La ciencia ficción. Literatura y conocimiento. Diario 29* [Tijuana] (October 20, 1991): n.p.

Berumen, Humberto Félix. "*Miríada.*" *Diario 29* [Tijuana] (July 23, 1992): n.p.

———. "*As time goes by* o las trampas de la derridación." *Esquina baja* [Tijuana] (July–September 1997): n.p.

———. "Gabriel Trujillo Muñoz o el arte de contra aventuras." *Frontera* [Tijuana] (December 12, 1999): n.p.

Díez, Julián. Review of *La ciencia ficción. Literatura y conocimiento. Gigamesh* 11 [Barcelona] (December, 1997): n.p.

Fernández Delgado, Miguel Ángel. "*Los confines:* una delimitación." *Memoria primera feria nacional del libro universitario.* Mexicali: UABC, 2001.

García Benavides, Rubén. Review of *Orescu. La crónica* [Mexicali] (July 12, 2000): n.p.

Gutiérrez, Carlos Adolfo. "*Miríada* y las posibilidades del cambio." *La crónica* [Mexicali] (November 3, 1991): n.p.

Palaversich, Diana. "Memorias del futuro en dos narrativas de Gabriel Trujillo Muñoz." *Yubai* [Mexicali] (January–March 2001): n.p.

Pérez Ruiz, Una. "De todo un poco." *Etcétera* [México] (October 29, 1998): n.p.

Ramos, Héctor. "*Premios UPC 1998*. Una antología al viejo estilo." *Gigamesh* [Barcelona] (November 1999): n.p.

Santiago, Juanma. "Un potencial buen narrador." *Gigamesh* (February 1999): n.p.

Torres, Vicente Francisco. "La ciencia ficción." *Siempre* [Mexico City] (August 27, 1992): n.p.

Vizcarra, Fernando. *Altas horas: periodismo cultural*. Mexicali: Instituto de Cultura de Baja California, 1997.

Yépez, Heriberto. "Ciencia ficción, *Espantapájaros* y chupacabras." *Bitácora* [Tijuana] (December 3, 1999): n.p.

Eduardo Urzaiz Rodríguez (1876–1955)

MEXICO

Eduardo Urzaiz Rodríguez was born in Villa de Guanabacoa, Cuba, and died in Mérida, Yucatán. He was still a child when his parents went to live in Mérida, where he eventually studied medicine and pedagogy. He was a physician and educator who taught several subjects, including literature. He worked as a surgeon in Izamal and received a scholarship to study psychiatry in New York. When he returned to Mexico, he founded the psychiatric hospital, Asilo Ayala. He was a supervisor and principal in several schools and founded a number of medical societies. Likewise, he was the founder and first rector of the Universidad Nacional del Sureste (National university of the southwest, 1922–1926), a position he held again—1946 until his death—when the institution had become the Universidad de Yucatán (University of the Yucatán). He was an outstanding scholar of Miguel de Cervantes, to whom he dedicated psychiatric studies and paintings and drawings, and he also promoted the celebration in Mérida of the fourth centenary of the author of the *Quixote*. He wrote several books on history, sociology, psychiatry, pedagogy, and Cervantes's works, and one on anecdotes from the Yucatán (under the pseudonym of Claudio Meex).

His science fiction novel *Eugenia (esbozo novelesco de costumbres futuras)* (Eugenia, novelesque sketch of future customs, 1919) is notable for the topics he deals with at the time it was written. In the prologue, Urzaiz states that the novel is a love story set in the future that portrays the humanity of his dreams and hopes. He further states that should someone judge him as insane—which is not beyond possibility since he worked in a mental institution for 14 years—he would not be concerned because the concepts of sane and insane are relative. The work takes place in the fictitious Villautopia in the Subconfederation of Central America, in the year 2218. The world is divided geopolitically into several confederations. Devastating wars in the past led to universal disarmament and the dissolution of separate nations. War now consists solely of the closing of ports and the blockade of commercial trade. Bequeathals and inheritances are banned as well because personal savings and trade are nationalized, while industry is socialized. In sum, economics is controlled exclusively by the state. Religious prejudices and legal procedures have been reduced to a minimum to allow couples to freely join and separate because of the discovery of birth control. Then women began to suffer from "tocophobia," or the fear of giving birth, and are focused solely on the enjoyment of physical love.

Humanity would have become extinct if not for the discovery of a method of implanting fertilized eggs into the peritoneal cavity of other individuals of the same species, even males, who are injected with female hormones in order to feminize them and suppress their erotic impulses during gestation. The state has taken over the task of monitoring human reproduction, which is regulated exclusively by scientific advances. In this way, the population explosion is controlled, but a state-operated eugenics program also has an aim of higher importance. Official reproductive specimens are selected, beginning in elementary school. Only the physically developed are chosen over those with higher intellectual capacity, since the latter have proven to be terrible reproducers. Through such genetic programming of the species the new generations are improved both physically and intellectually, thus avoiding the possibility of degeneration. This, furthermore, has meant that there is no longer a need for jails, mental asylums, and hospitals for the incurably ill. Those who are not considered fit for reproduction are sterilized. The eugenics institute houses the breeders, and children spend their first years in this human greenhouse in complete freedom and surrounded by gardens, orchards, animals, pools, games, workshops, laboratories, and so on, following the teachings of Rousseau's *Émile*. Teachers impart knowledge to students through hypnotism sessions with the pupils. In spite of the laboratory setting, paternal and maternal love have not disappeared. Even those who are banned from reproducing are exhorted to care for and educate the children. Programmed reproduction also has meant that the nuclear family is replaced by a collective, formed on the basis of personality and similar tastes, aspirations and affinities. Such groups are normally made up of four-to-five men and women for whom age is not a factor. Euthanasia is practiced without restrictions, since, as one of the physician in the novel asserts, "each century has its own ethics."

Within this scenario the love story of Ernesto and Celiana is developed. They live in a group with two other men and a woman. Their life was almost perfect until Ernesto is chosen as an "Official Species Reproducer." This is considered to be a duty akin to military service, for which one is remunerated but cannot be excused from (men serve one year and are expected to produce 20 children). Celiana believes that Ernesto's new job will separate them forever. He had been a pupil of hers in school, where they fell in love despite their age difference. Celiana later helped him through a critical stage in his life and they soon became lovers and were integrated into a group. In the beginning, Ernesto tries not to allow his duty to interfere with his love for Celiana and he continues seeing her. Nevertheless, he ends up leaving her for good when he meets a beautiful young woman, Eugenia. They conceive a son for whom Ernesto feels a special affection. In this kind of Plato's republic of the twenty-third century, the architecture has a neo-Mayan style, women wear Greek-style tunics while dancing that reveal a breast, and men wear light suits in pastel colors. Urzaiz also imagines several inventions such as automatic watches, aerocycles with colloidal nitroglycerin engines, aerial tramways, and streets with mechanized sidewalks. His seemingly utopic vision of the future disintegrates into a dystopian nightmare by the end of the novel.

Miguel Ángel Fernández Delgado

Work

Eugenia (esbozo novelesco de costumbres futuras). Mérida: n.p., 1919. Reprint, Mexico City, Premiá, 2001.

Criticism

Larson, Ross. *Fantasy and Imagination in the Mexican Narrative*. Tempe: Arizona State University, Center for Latin American Studies, 1977.

Trujillo Muñoz, Gabriel. "Eduardo Urzaiz Rodríguez: el planificador entusiasta," in *Biografías del futuro: la ciencia ficción mexicana y sus autores*. Mexicali: Universidad Autónoma de Baja California, 2000, 63–67.

Alberto Vanasco (1925–1994)

ARGENTINA

Born in Buenos Aires, Vanasco spent his childhood between the capital city and San Juan, in the country. He had a series of jobs, including math tutor, physics teacher, journalist, driver, and translator. From 1955 to 1960, he co-organized (with Eduardo Goligorsky) a center called CIVE (Centro de Investigaciones de Vida Extraterrestre [Center for the investigation of extraterrestrial life]), whose purpose was to look into reports of UFO sightings. In 1961, he went to New York where he spent two years working for Crown Publishers. In 1968, he married Alicia Virginia Petti, and in 1974, they traveled throughout Europe, living for a while in Barcelona.

He was a prolific writer and an important representative of the Argentine generation of the 1960s. He began writing his first poems and short stories in 1939, followed by experimental pieces and a short novel in 1943. His work includes several novels, poetry collections, and one drama, as well as two philosophical works and a few collections of science fiction short stories. His drama "No hay piedad para Hamlet" (There is no pity for Hamlet, 1948), coauthored with Mario Trejo, won two prizes in 1957. He also edited a poetry magazine, *Zona* (Zone), and wrote for Argentine television, including the series "Historias de jóvenes" (Youth stories). From the 1970s until his death he lived exclusively by his literary production.

The eclecticism of topics and genres that characterizes Vanasco's writing is also present in his science fiction collections. Many of the stories published in these volumes tend more toward the fantastic than to the scientific. In the latter vein, one of his major preoccupations is the manipulation of time, leading to the exploration of questions of personal freedom and determinism: "La muerte del capitán Salgari" (Captain Salgari's death, 1977), "El descubrimiento del Dr. Fleming" (Dr. Fleming's discovery, 1977), and "Robot Pierre" (1966) form a coherent trilogy dedicated to the conception of time as a vicious circle, in which the future brings about the events of the past without which the future itself could not have existed. In the first story, one of Salgari's editors learns of his suicide due to economic difficulties, and attempts to change history by sending him, through time and space, all the money that has accumulated in his account since his death. Yet it is precisely the arrival of the bank's envelope that precipitates Salgari's decision to kill himself when, unable to read it because he cannot afford spectacles, he takes it to be yet another demand for payment. The second story features a group of contemporary Argentine radio aficionados delivering the formula for penicillin to an Alexander Fleming of the past desperate to save the life of his sick nephew. The third is an explanation of history, centering on the French Revolution, as the result of the intervention of time travelers from the future whose names have been corrupted before being recorded in history books. All these stories are based on a view of history in which the most advanced achievements of science and the human mind play a key role in bringing about their own discovery, and suggest an intimate connection between history and science.

Although not a historically based story, "Filicidio" (Filicide, 1977) uses time travel and determinism in a similar way, featuring a father who tries to take his son's gun away from him to prevent the murder trial that a seer has shown him in the future, but unwittingly causes it because his son shoots him in an attempt to keep the gun. It is his father's murder that he will be tried for. The cyclical nature of time is also explored in "Bleriot 25CV" (1977), where a twentieth-century man has been preserved as a mummy and brought back to life a thousand years later into a utopian society whose peace and harmony he decides to destroy. He eventually escapes back into the past, and spends the rest of his days searching for the passage into the future so that everything can begin again. In "El tiempo y el Dr. Einstein" (Time and Dr. Einstein, 1977), Vanasco uses Einstein's theories to create a story about the relativity of time, space, and movement, and the possibility of stopping time itself.

The social vein of science fiction is well-represented in Vanasco's work, stemming out of a preoccupation with the destructive possibilities of human knowledge and weaponry, and the resulting anguish suffered by contemporary societies. One of the best examples is "Cibernética" (Cybernetics, 1977), a story that pitches man against machine in a Kafkaesque struggle leading to the abandonment of all human relationships and eventually to death, as the protagonist is strangled by the record-player he had turned into his worst enemy. Postholocaust stories such as "Post-bombum" (1967) and "Bikini" (1977) are reactions to the use of nuclear weapons and the attempt to rebuild life on Earth after nuclear disaster—always a failed endeavor, because Vanasco's pessimism for the human race's chances of survival shows itself as the determinant for most of his stories. But a more explicit social and political criticism can be found in the repressive societies depicted in "Los eunucos" (The eunuchs, 1977) and "Todo va mejor con Coca-Cola" (Everything is better with Coca-Cola, 1967). The first one presents a dystopian military dictatorship in which men have to be castrated and only the few selected "great reproducers" dominate. Even women comply with these conditions, demanding money and stability instead of sexual satisfaction. Any organized attempts to fight these conditions fail, as men find it easier to adapt and obey than to resist, leaving a lone rebel to carry on the fight in utter ostracism. The second depicts yet another dystopian society, this time dominated not by a military dictatorship but by the large companies of a powerful economic establishment through a violent kind of advertising. The rebels' difficulties in organizing a revolution once again suggest a pessimistic view of the future, and a sense that even they would eventually bring things back to their present state.

Both major tendencies in Vanasco's science fiction writing—time travel and social criticism—are fundamentally rooted in his pessimism and preoccupation with man's lack of attention to the consequences of his actions. They suggest a complicated belief in the failures caused by human freedom and, at the same time, in historical determinism. Although the occasional use of dictatorship may be taken as a commentary on the Latin American political conditions of the time, Vanasco's stories tend to have a much wider and universal frame of reference that detaches them from the purely local.

Beatriz Urraca

Works

Adiós al mañana (with Eduardo Goligorsky). Buenos Aires: Minotauro, 1967.

"Bikini," in *Ciencia ficción: cuentos hispanoamericanos*, ed. José María Ferrero. Buenos Aires: Huemul, 1993, 187–89.

"Los eunucos," in *Los universos vislumbrados: antología de ciencia-ficción argentina*, ed. Jorge A. Sánchez. Buenos Aires: Ediciones Andrómeda, 1995, 141–48.

Memorias del futuro. Buenos Aires: Círculo de Lectores, 1976.

Memorias del futuro (with Eduardo Goligorsky). Buenos Aires: Minotauro, 1966.

"La muerte del poeta," in *Ciencia ficción argentina: antología de cuentos*, ed. Pablo Capanna. Buenos Aires: Aude Ediciones, 1990, 53–63. Also in *El cuento argentino de ciencia ficción: antología*, ed. Pablo Capanna. Buenos Aires: Ediciones Nuevo Siglo, 1995, 88–91; and *Lo mejor de la ciencia ficción latinoamericana*, ed. Bernard Goorden and R. E. Van Vogt. Buenos Aires: Hyspamérica, 1988, 111–14.

Nuevas memorias del futuro. Buenos Aires: Andrómeda, 1977.

"Paranoia," in *Cuentos con humanos, androides y robots*, ed. Elena Braceras. Buenos Aires: Colihue, 2000, 75–81. Also in *Cuentos argentinos de ciencia ficción*. Buenos Aires: Editorial Merlín, 1967, 167–76.

"Los pilotos del infinito," in *Los argentinos en la luna*, ed. Eduardo Goligorsky. Buenos Aires: Ediciones de la Flor, 1968, 45–52.

"Post-bombum," in *La ciencia ficción en la Argentina: antología crítica*, ed. Marcial Souto. Buenos Aires: EUDEBA, 1985, 29–42. English translation as "Post-Boomboom," trans. Laura Wertish and Andrea Bell, in *Cosmos Latinos: An Anthology of Science Fiction from Latin America and Spain*, ed. Andrea Bell and Yolanda Molina-Gavilán. Middletown, CT: Wesleyan University Press, 2003, 117–22.

Criticism

Molina-Gavilán, Yolanda. "Mitos posholocáusticos: 'Post-Bombum' de Alberto Vanasco y 'Cuando los pájaros mueran' de Eduardo Goligorsky," in *Ciencia ficción en español: una mitología moderna ante el cambio*. Lewiston, NY: Edwin Mellen Press, 2002, 91–97.

José Zaidenweber Cwilich (1930–1995)

MEXICO

José Zaidenweber was born in Mexico City in 1930. He was a scientist and psychiatrist with an interest in science fiction literature both as a fan of the genre and as a writer himself. In 1994, he founded and directed the magazine *Asimov, ciencia ficción* (Asimov, science fiction) with the goal of creating an outlet and source of distribution for science fiction in Mexico. In order to publish the magazine, he created a small publishing operation called "El Fisgón del Universo" (The snoop of the universe) together with Nathan Zaidenweber, Salomón Bazbaz, José Luis Domínguez, Aldo Alba, and a large group of young authors of science fiction and fantasy. José Zaidenweber died shortly afterwards on 26 April 1995. Aside from his interest in this area, he also belonged to several professional and scientific organizations and was the founder of the Mexican chapter of the Asociación de Médicos en contra de la Guerra Nuclear (The association of doctors against nuclear war). This international organization won the Nobel Peace Prize in 1985.

As a writer, Zaidenweber published three novels. His first, *Vibraciones* (Vibrations, 1985) came shortly after the 1985 Mexico City earthquake. He also published his first science fiction work, *El festín de los egos* (The feast of egos) in 1985 in Jerusalem, which was later published in Mexico in 1988. The novel takes place in the year 2077 and revolves around a scientist's efforts to form part of the universal government that rules the planet Earth. His chances of doing so are based on his research on human cloning as a method of prolonging life and possibly realizing the dream of immortality. The text reveals the author's knowledge of neuropsychiatry, genetics, and science fiction, which come together to form a narrative debate on the ethics and politics of cloning as well as the moral, psychological, and religious implications of the practice. Thus the novel anticipated the controversy that arose with the successful cloning of Dolly the sheep in 1997, although his novel is set much farther in the future. Ultimately, the text asserts the belief in the certainty of a promising, utopian future made possible in large part by psychoanalysis, which can free one's emotions and lead to a better life.

The same utopian desire and psychological elements appear in the author's last novel, *Furia de talentos* (Fury of talents, 1993), which deals with the evolution of the human mind. In the text, which is over 700 pages long, Zaidenweber explores different fields of knowledge and weaves them into a holistic vision of the world of sensorial thought and the process of the evolution of intelligence. The reader accustomed to catastrophic science fiction—common in Mexican and Latin American texts—will find here something very different. The view is one of hope for the future, one in which man will not allow technology to alienate him from his creativity, imagination, and intelligence.

Zaidenweber must be remembered as a tireless promoter of science fiction in

Latin America as well as a writer, editor, doctor, and researcher who put all his talent into his creativity and the memorable adventure of his life.

Gabriel Trujillo Muñoz

Works

El festín de los egos. Jerusalem: La Semana, 1985. Reprint, Mexico City: Diana, 1988. English version as *Feast of Egos.* Pittsburgh: Dorrance, 1993.
Furia de talentos. Mexico City: Contacto, 1993.

Bibliography of
Literary Anthologies and Criticism

LATIN AMERICA

Anthologies

Acosta, Oscar, et al. *Primera antología de ciencia ficción latinoamericana*. Buenos Aires: Rodolfo Alonso, 1970.

Bell, Andrea, and Yolanda Molina-Gavilán, eds. *Cosmos Latinos: An Anthology of Science Fiction from Latin America and Spain*. Middletown, CT: Wesleyan University Press, 2003.

Braceras, Elena, ed. *Cuentos con humanos, androides y robots*. Buenos Aires: Colihue, 2000.

Ferrero, José María, ed. *Ciencia ficción: cuentos hispanoamericanos*. Buenos Aires: Huemul, 1993.

Gandolfo, Elvio E., ed. *Cuentos fantásticos y de ciencia ficción en América Latina*. Buenos Aires: Centro Editor de América Latina, 1981. Reprint, Buenos Aires: Editores de América Latina, 1998.

Goorden, Bernard, and R. E. Van Vogt, eds. *Lo mejor de la ciencia ficción latinoamericana*. Barcelona: Ediciones Martínez Roca, 1982. Reprint, Buenos Aires: Hyspamérica, 1988.

Rebetez, René, ed. *La ciencia ficción: breve antología del género*. Mexico City: Secretaría de Educación Pública, Subsecretaría de Asuntos Culturales, 1966.

Rodríguez Lobato, Oliva, ed. *Todos los caminos del universo: cuentos de imaginación*. Mexico City: Ediciones Pepsa (Promotores de Ediciones y Publicaciones), 1974.

Uribe, Augusto, ed. *Latinoamérica fantástica. Ciencia Ficción, 18*. Barcelona: Ultramar Editores, 1985.

Criticism

Bell, Andrea, and Yolanda Molina-Gavilán. "Introduction: Science Fiction in Latin America and Spain," in *Cosmos Latinos: An Anthology of Science Fiction from Latin America and Spain*. Middletown, CT: Wesleyan University Press, 2003, 1–19.

Bozzetto, Roger, Elana Gomel, and Andrea Bell. "Current Trends in Global SF: Roger Bozzetto on France, Elana Gomel on Russia, and Andrea Bell on Latin America." *Science Fiction Studies* 26.3 (1999): 431–46.

Braceras, Elena. "Póslogo," in *Cuentos con humanos, androides y robots*. Buenos Aires: Colihue, 2000, 183–210.

Capanna, Pablo. *El mundo de la ciencia ficción: sentido e historia*. Buenos Aires: Ediciones Buena Letra, 1992.

Carneiro, André. *Introducção ao estudo da "science-fiction."* São Paulo: Conselho Estadual de Cultura, 1967.

Ferrero, José María. "Estudio preliminar," in *Ciencia ficción: cuentos hispanoamericanos*. Buenos Aires: Huemul, 1993, 9–54.

Foster, David William. *Alternate Voices in the Contemporary Latin American Narrative*. Columbia: University of Missouri Press, 1985, 136–43.

Goligorsky, Eduardo, and Marie Langer. *Ciencia-ficción, realidad y psicolanálisis*. Buenos Aires: Paidós, 1969.

Goorden, Bernard. "De algunos temas originales en la ciencia ficción española y latinoamericana en el siglo veinte," trans. Margarita Cervantes Deras. *Plural* 163 (1985): 38–43.

Gorodischer, Angélica. "Narrativa fantástica y narrativa de ciencia ficción." *Plural* [Mexico] 188 (1987): 48–50.

Kreksch, Ingrid. "Reality Transfigured: The Latin American Situation as Reflected in Its Science Fiction," in *Political Science Fiction*, ed. Donald M. Hassler and Clyde Wilcox. Columbia: University of South Carolina Press, 1997, 173–82.

Link, Daniel, ed. *Escalera al cielo: utopía y ciencia ficción*. Buenos Aires: La Marca, 1994.

Molina-Gavilán, Yolanda. "Science Fiction," in *Encyclopedia of Latin American Literature*, ed. Verity Smith. London/Chicago: Fitzroy Dearborn, 1997, 760–61.

———. *Ciencia ficción en español: una mitología moderna ante el cambio*. Lewiston, NY: Edwin Mellen Press, 2002.

Molina-Gavilán, Yolanda, et al. "Cronología de CF latinoamericana 1775–1999." *Chasqui* 29.2 (2000): 43–72.

Reeve, Richard. "La ciencia ficción: hacia una definición y breve historia," in *Otros mundos, otros fuegos: fantasía y realismo mágico en Iberoamérica*, ed. Donald A. Yates. East Lansing: Michigan State University, Latin American Studies Center, 1977, 133–37.

Schwarz, Mauricio-José, and Braulio Tavares. "Latin America," in *The Encyclopedia of Science Fiction*, ed. John Clute and Peter Nicholls. New York: St. Martin's Press, 1993, 693–97.

Stavans, Ilán. "Introduction: Private Eyes & Time Travelers." *Literary Review: An International Journal of Contemporary Writing* 38.1 (1994): 5–20.

Trujillo Muñoz, Gabriel. *La ciencia ficción: literatura y conocimiento*. Mexicali: Instituto de Cultura de Baja California, 1991.

ARGENTINA

Anthologies

Bajarlía, Juan Jacobo, et al. *Cuentos argentinos de ciencia ficción*. Buenos Aires: Editorial Merlín, 1967.

Capanna, Pablo, ed. *Ciencia ficción argentina: antología de cuentos*. Buenos Aires: Aude Ediciones, 1990.

———. *El cuento argentino de ciencia ficción: antología*. *Biblioteca de la Cultura Argentina*. Buenos Aires: Ediciones Nuevo Siglo, 1995.

Fernández, Adriana, and Edgardo Pígoli, eds. *Historias futuras: antología de la ciencia ficción argentina*. Buenos Aires: Emecé, 2000.

Gaut vel Hartman, Sergio, ed. *Fase uno*. Buenos Aires: Sinergia, 1987.

Goligorsky, Eduardo, ed. *Los argentinos en la luna*. Buenos Aires: Ediciones de la Flor, 1968.

Grassi, Alfredo, and Alejandro Vignati, eds. *Ciencia ficción: nuevos cuentos argentinos*. Buenos Aires: Calatayud-DEA, 1968.

Moreno, Horacio, ed. *Más allá: ciencia ficción argentina*. Buenos Aires: IMFC [Ediciones Instituto Movilizador de Fondos Cooperativos], 1992.

Rodrigué, Emilio, ed. *Ecuación fantástica: 13 cuentos de ciencia ficción por 9 psicoanalistas*, introduction by Dalmiro Sáenz. Buenos Aires: Ediciones Hormé, 1966.

Sánchez, Jorge A., ed. *Los universos vislumbrados: antología de ciencia-ficción argentina* (1978), introduction by Elvio E. Gandolfo. Reprint, Buenos Aires: Ediciones Andrómeda, 1995.

Souto, Marcial, ed. *La ciencia ficción en la Argentina: antología crítica*. Buenos Aires: Editorial Universitaria de Buenos Aires, 1985.

———. *Historia de la fragua y otros inventos*. Buenos Aires: Ultramar Editores, 1988.

Criticism

Antognazzi, Carlos O. "La ciencia ficción en la Argentina," in *Apuntes de literatura: ensayos y reportajes (Selección personal del autor, período 1984–1994)*. Santo Tomé, Argentina: Fundación Banco BICA, 1995, 387–92.

Capanna, Pablo. "La ciencia ficción y los argentinos." *Minotauro* [Segunda época] 10 (1985): 43–56.

———. "Estudio preliminar," in *Ciencia ficción argentina: antología de cuentos*. Buenos Aires: Aude Ediciones, 1990, 9–32.

De Ambrosio, José. "ABC de la ciencia ficción argentina." *Cuasar* 21 (1989): 90–103.

Dellepiane, Angela B. "Critical Notes on Argentinian Science-Fiction Narrative." *Monographic Review/Revista monográfica* 3.1–2 (1987): 19–32.

———. "Narrativa argentina de ciencia ficción: tentativas liminares y desarrollo posterior," in *Actas del IX Congreso de la Asociación Internacional de Hispanistas*, 2 vols., ed. Sebastián Neumeister. Frankfurt: Vervuert, 1989, 2: 515–25.

D'Lugo, Marvin. "Frutos de los 'frutos prohibidos': la fantaciencia rioplatense," in *Otros mundos, ortros fuegos: fantasía y realismo mágico en Iberoamérica*, ed. Donald A. Yates. East Lansing: Michigan State University, Latin American Studies Center, 1977, 139–44.

Gandolfo, Elvio E. "Prólogo: la ciencia ficción argentina," in *Los universos vislumbrados: antología de ciencia ficción argentina*, ed. Jorge A. Sánchez. Buenos Aires: Andrómeda, 1995, 13–50.

Gaut vel Hartman, Sergio. "Ciencia ficción en la Argentina." *Gigamesh* 4 (1986): 69–75.

Moreno, Horacio. "El nacimiento de la ciencia ficción argentina en el siglo XIX." *Cuasar* 31 (1999): 41–44.

Pessina, H. R., and Jorge A. Sánchez. "Esbozo para una cronología comentada de la ciencia ficción argentina," in *Los universos vislumbrados: antología de ciencia ficción argentina*, ed. Jorge A. Sánchez. Buenos Aires: Andrómeda, 1995, 275–86.

Planells, Antonio. "La literatura de anticipación y su presencia en Argentina." *Revista interamericana de bibliografía/Inter-American Review of Bibliography* 40.1 (1990): 93–113.
Serra, Emilio. "Sobre la ciencia ficción argentina." *Gigamesh* 4 (1986): 96–102.
Souto, Marcial. "Introducción. La ciencia ficción en Argentina y la ciencia ficción argentina: breve historia," in *La ciencia ficción en la Argentina*. Buenos Aires: EUDEBA, 1985, 9–24.

BRAZIL

Anthologies

Kupstas, Márcia, ed. *Sete faces da ficção científica*. São Paulo: Editora Moderna, 1992.
Lodi-Ribeiro, Gerson, et al. *Phantastica brasiliana: 500 anos de histórias e doutros Brasis*. São Caetano do Sul: Editora Ano Luz, 2000.
Malheiros, Alvaro, et al. *Histórias do ancontecerá 1. Ficção Científica GRD, 12*. Rio de Janeiro: GRD, 1961.
Morais, José Manuel, ed. *O Atlántico tem duas margens: antología da novíssima ficção científica portuguesa e brasileira*. Lisbon: Caminho, 1993.
Silva, Domingos Carvalho da, et al. *Alem do tempo e do espaço: 13 contos de ciencificção*. São Paulo: Edart, 1965.
Torres, João Camillo de Oliveira, et al. *Antologia brasileira de ficção científica*, introduction by João de Oliveira Torres. Rio de Janeiro: GRD, 1961.

Criticism

Causo, Roberto de Sousa. "Science Fiction During the Brazilian Dictatorship." *Extrapolation* 39.4 (1998): 314–23.
Cirne, Moacy. "FC:A/Z." *Vozes* 70.6 (1976): 57–66.
Mauso, Pablo Villarubia. "Ciencia ficción en Brasil." *Nadir* 10 (1988): 8–10; *Nadir* 11 (1988): 2–10.
Tavares, Braulio. "Stories of the Will-Happen: Science Fiction in Brazil." *Foundation* 77 (1999): 84–91.

CHILE

Anthology

Rojas-Murphy, Andrés, ed. *Antología de cuentos chilenos de ciencia ficción y fantasía*, introduction by Alfonso Calderón. Santiago: Editorial Andrés Bello, 1988.

Criticism

Bell, Andrea, and Moisés Hassón. "Prelude to the Golden Age: Chilean Science Fiction 1900–1959." *Science Fiction Studies* 25 (1998): 285–99.
Hassón, Moisés. "Ciencia ficción religiosa en Chile." *Vórtice* 7 (1987): 38–43.
Remi-Maure. "Ciencia ficción en Chile." *Nadir* 4 (1987): 12–19.

COLOMBIA

Anthology

Rebetez, René, ed. *Contemporáneos del porvenir: primera antología colombiana de ciencia ficción.* Bogotá: Planeta, 2000.

Criticism

Burgos López, Campo Ricardo. "La narrativa de ciencia ficción en Colombia," in *Literatura y cultura: narrativa colombiana del siglo XX*, 3 vols., vol. 1: *La nación moderna*, ed. María Mercedes Jaramillo, Betty Osorio, and Angela I. Robledo. Bogotá: Ministerio de Cultura, 2000, 719–50.

Rebetez, René. "Introducción," in *Contemporáneos del porvenir: primera antología colombiana de ciencia ficción.* Bogotá: Planeta, 9–18.

CUBA

Anthologies

Henríquez, Bruno, ed. *Polvo en el viento: antología de la ciencia ficción cubana.* Buenos Aires: Desde la Gente. IMFC [Ediciones Instituto Movilizador de Fondos Cooperativos], 1999.

Hernández, Vladimir, ed. *Horizontes probables.* Mexico City: Lectorum, 1999.

Hurtado, Oscar, ed. *Cuentos de ciencia ficción.* Havana: Ediciones R, 1964.

———. *Introducción a la ciencia ficción.* Madrid: Miguel Castellote, 1971.

Reloba, Juan Carlos, ed. *Cuentos cubanos de ciencia ficción.* Havana: Editorial Gente Nueva, 1981. Reprint, 1987.

Criticism

Arango, Ángel. "La joven ciencia-ficción cubana (un lustro dentro del concurso *David*)." *Unión* [Havana] 23.41 (1984): 128–38.

Chaviano, Daína. "Veinte años de ciencia ficción en Cuba." *Cuasar* 9–10 (1986): 199–211.

———. "Para una bibliografía de la CF cubana." *Letras cubanas* 6 (1987): 273–80.

Toledano, Juan Carlos. "Influencias de la revolución en la literatura de la ciencia ficción: F. Mond y Agustín de Rojas." *Romance Languages Annual* 10 (1999): 848–52.

MEXICO

Anthologies

Antología de cuentos: primer certamen de cuentos de ciencia ficción. Mexico City: Instituto Politécnico Nacional, 1990.

Antología de cuentos: segundo certamen de cuentos de ciencia ficción. Mexico City: Instituto Politécnico Nacional, 1990.

Armenta, Celine, José Luis Zárate, and Gerardo Porcayo Villalobos, eds. *Principios de incertidumbre: Premio Puebla de Ciencia Ficción 1984–1991.* Puebla, Mexico: Gobierno del Estado de Puebla, Comisión Puebla V Centenario, 1992.

Cubría, Jorge, ed. *Ginecoides.* Mexico City: Lumen, 2003.

Fernández Delgado, Miguel Ángel, ed. *Visiones periféricas: antología de la ciencia ficción mexicana*. Mexico City: Lumen, 2001.

———. *Ciencia ficción mexicana: Siglo XIX*. Mexico City: Goliardos, 2002.

Porcayo, Gerardo Horacio, ed. *Los mapas del caos: breve antología de ciencia ficción mexicana*. Mexico City: Ramón Llaca, 1997.

———. *Silicio en la memoria: antología cyberpunk*. Mexico City: Ramón Llaca, 1997.

———. *El hombre en las dos puertas: un tributo de la ciencia ficción a Phillip K. Dick*. Mexico City: Lectorum, 2002.

Schaffler, Federico, ed. *Más allá de lo imaginado I: antología de ciencia ficción mexicana*. *Fondo Editorial Tierra Adentro, 7*. Mexico City: Consejo Nacional para la Cultura y las Artes, 1991.

———. *Más allá de lo imaginado II: antología de ciencia ficción mexicana*. *Fondo Editorial Tierra Adentro, 8*. Mexico City: Consejo Nacional para la Cultura y las Artes, 1991.

———. *Sin permiso de Colón: fantasías mexicanas en el quinto centenario*. Guadalajara: Universidad de Guadalajara, 1993.

———. *Más allá de lo imaginado III: antología de ciencia ficción mexicana*. *Fondo Editorial Tierra Adentro, 94*. Mexico City: Consejo Nacional para la Cultura y las Artes, 1994.

Schwarz, Mauricio-José, and Don Webb, eds. *Frontera de espejos rotos*. Mexico City: Roca, 1994. (Mexican and American science fiction stories.)

Trujillo Muñoz, Gabriel, ed. *El futuro en llamas: cuentos clásicos de la ciencia ficción mexicana*. Mexico City: Grupo Editorial Vid, 1997.

Criticism

Fernández Delgado, Miguel Ángel. "A Brief History of Continuity and Change in Mexican Science Fiction." *New York Review of Science Fiction* 99 (1996): 18–19.

———. "Los cartógrafos del infierno en México." *Complot internacional* [Mexico] 1.8 (1997): 14–17.

———. "Páginas olvidadas de la historia de la ciencia ficción mexicana," in *Memoria de la III Convención Nacional de la Asociación Mexicana de Ciencia Ficción y Fantasía*. (1997): 27–35.

———. "Hacia una vindicación de la ciencia ficción mexicana." *Artifex* 20.21 (1999): 25–30.

Larson, Ross. "La literatura de ciencia ficción en México." *Cuadernos hispanoamericanos* 284 (1974): 425–31.

———. *Fantasy and Imagination in the Mexican Narrative*. Tempe: Center for Latin American Studies, Arizona State University, 1977.

López Castro, Rafael. *Expedición a la ciencia ficción mexicana*. Mexico City: Lectorum, 2001.

Trujillo Muñoz, Gabriel. "El futuro en llamas: el cuento mexicano de ciencia ficción," in *Vivir del cuento: la ficción en México*, ed. Alfredo Pavón. Tlaxcala de Xicohténcatl: Universidad Autónoma de Tlaxcala, 1995, 215–31.

———. *Los confines: crónica de la ciencia ficción mexicana*. Mexico City: Grupo Editorial Vid, 1999.

———. *Biografías del futuro: la ciencia ficción mexicana y sus autores*. Mexicali, Mexico: Universidad Autónoma de Baja California, 2000.

Index

(Boldface indicates the author entry)

About the Editor and Contributors

Daniel Altamiranda is a professor at the University of Bologna in Buenos Aires and chair of Spanish at the Instituto de Enseñanza Superior No. 2. He has published on literary theory, contemporary Latin American writing, and Golden Age drama. His most recent books are *Teorías literarias I* and *Teorías literarias II* (2001).

Andrea Bell received her Ph.D. from Stanford University in 1991. She has published and presented on science fiction from Latin America, and has translated over a dozen science fiction short stories into English for the volume she co-edited with Yolanda Molina-Gavilán, *Cosmos Latinos: An Anthology of Science Fiction from Latin America and Spain* (2003). She is an associate professor in the Modern Languages department at Hamline University in St. Paul, Minnesota.

José Alberto Bravo de Rueda was born in Lima, Perú. He received his Ph.D. from the University of Maryland, College Park in 1997. He has taught at North Carolina Agricultural & Technical State University since 1995. He is also a creative writer whose works include the novel *Hacia el sur* (1992), the short-story collection *El hombre de la máscara* (1994), and a short story in *Nuevas voces hispanas* (2000).

Eva Paulino Bueno was born in Brazil; she currently lives in San Antonio, Texas, and teaches at St. Mary's University. She has published books and essays on Latin American literature and popular culture. After working four years in Japan, she has published her most recent book, *I Wouldn't Want Anybody to Know: Native English Teaching in Japan*.

Oscar A. Díaz-Ortiz is an associate professor of language, culture, and Spanish American literature at Middle Tennessee State University in Murfreesboro, where he is the director of Latin American Studies. He has published a book on the nineteenth-century Spanish American essay, and various articles on Colombian,

Mexican, and Chilean literature. Currently, he is researching the topic of violence in Colombian film.

J. Patrick Duffey is associate professor of Spanish and co-director of the Center for Southwestern and Mexican Studies at Austin College, Sherman, Texas. A graduate of the University of Texas at Austin, he is the author of *De la pantalla al texto. La influencia del cine en la narrativa mexicana del siglo XX* (1996). He is also the author of several articles on the influence of film on both Spanish and Latin American vanguard prose.

Miguel Ángel Fernández Delgado is a lawyer with a Ph.D. in history, and is also a writer and the president of the Mexican Association of Science Fiction and Fantasy. In 2001, he presented a report on Mexican science fiction to the ITSF Project (Innovative Technologies from Science Fiction for Space Applications) for the European Space Agency. His books include *Visiones periféricas: antología de la ciencia ficción mexicana* (2000), *Sizigias y cuadraturas lunares de Manuel Antonio de Rivas* (2001), *Poesía intuitiva en el espacio* (2001), and *Ciencia ficción mexicana: Siglo XIX* (2002).

Heidi Ann García, a native of Puerto Rico, is currently a Ph.D. candidate at Arizona State University, where she works as a lecturer in Spanish. Her research focus is on Spanish-language Caribbean literature written in the United States, in addition to postmodern and postcolonial theories and urban space. She has contributed essays to the encyclopedias *Notable Twentieth-Century Latin American Women* and *Encyclopedia of Latina and Latino Popular Culture in the United States*.

Mercedes Guijarro-Crouch is a native of Huelva, Spain. She earned her Ph.D. from the University of North Carolina at Chapel Hill. Currently, she is associate professor of Spanish and coordinator of the Spanish program at Peace College in Raleigh, North Carolina. She received the Outstanding Spanish Teacher award in 2000 from the North Carolina chapter of the AATSP. Dr. Guijarro is the co-author of the textbook *Nuevas voces hispanas* (2000). Her research interests include feminist studies, especially ecofeminism, and intersubjectivity theory. She also tries to find time between work and family for creative writing.

Cristina Guzzo received her Ph.D. from Arizona State University in 1997. In Argentina, where she was born, she was a professor at the Universidad de Buenos Aires and Universidad Nacional de Salta. She is currently an assistant professor of Spanish at Ball State University. She has published numerous articles on Latin American literature and culture and is the author of the forthcoming book *Las anarquistas rioplatenses: 1890–1990*.

Jerry Hoeg is associate professor of Spanish at the Pennsylvania State University. He recently published *Science, Technology, and Latin American Narrative in the Twentieth Century and Beyond* (2000). He is the editor of the journal *Ometeca*, which publishes articles on the relations between the sciences and humanities in the Spanish- and Portuguese-speaking world.

Claudia S. Hojman Conde is a professor at the Universidad de Buenos Aires, where she teaches literary analysis and writing. She has coordinated poetry workshops at the Centro Cultural Ricardo Rojas (UBA), and writing workshops through the Universidad de Belgrano and the Biblioteca del Congreso de la Nación. She is the editor of the book *Borges* (1997), a collection of essays on the Argentine writer Jorge Luis Borges.

Darrell B. Lockhart is an assistant professor of Spanish at the University of Nevada, Reno, where he teaches Latin American literature, popular culture, and film. He received his Ph.D. in 1995 from Arizona State University. Aside from his interest in detective and science fiction from Latin America, he is a specialist in Latin American Jewish literature and cultural production and has written numerous articles on this topic that have been published in the United States, Argentina, and Chile. In addition, he is the editor of the book *Latin American Jewish Writers: A Dictionary* (1997).

Fernando Reati teaches contemporary Latin American narrative and culture at Georgia State University in Atlanta. He is the author of *Nombrar lo innombrable: Violencia política y novela argentina, 1975–1985* (1992), the co-editor (with Adriana Bergero) of *Memoria colectiva y políticas de olvido: Argentina y Uruguay, 1970–1990* (1997), and the co-editor, with Mirian Pino, of *De centros y periferias en la literatura de Córdoba* (2001).

Eric Rojas was born in Seattle and grew up in Reno, Nevada, where he earned an M.Ed. in secondary education at the University of Nevada, Reno. He has taught classes at the secondary-school and university level and has had the opportunity to travel to many countries throughout Latin America and Europe. He is currently a doctoral student in Spanish at the University of California, Irvine.

María Alejandra Rosarossa holds a teaching position in English literature at the Universidad Católica Argentina, from where she will earn a doctoral degree upon completion of her dissertation. She is a specialist in comparative studies (Anglo-Latin American literatures and cultures) and a researcher on this topic at the Universidad de Buenos Aires, where she has taught American literature. She currently teaches Spanish at Arizona State Univeristy. Rosarossa is the co-editor of *Los Estados Unidos y América Latina: Modernismo/Posmodernismo* (1999) and *Los Estados Unidos y América Latina: Problemática del fin del milenio* (2000).

Juan C. Toledano was born in Adra, Spain. He completed his B.A. in Spanish philology at the Universidad de Granada, and his Ph.D. at the University of Miami, where he wrote the dissertation *Ciencia-ficción cubana: El proyecto nacional del hombre nuevo socialista*. He has published several articles and reports on Cuban science fiction for *RLA*, *Chasqui*, and *Locus Magazine*. He is an assistant professor of Hispanic studies at Lewis & Clark College in Portland, Oregon.

Gabriel Trujillo Muñoz was born in Mexicali, Baja California, Mexico in 1958. He is a physician, surgeon, poet, narrator, and essayist, and a professor at the Universidad Autónoma de Baja California. He has published close to a hundred books: the novels *Mezquite Road* (1995), *Laberinto (as time goes by)* (1995), *Espantapájaros* (1999), *Orescu* (2000), *El festín de los cuervos* (a collection of five novellas, 2002); the short-story collections *Miríada* (1991), *Trebejos* (2001), and *Mercaderes* (2001); and the monographs *Los confines. Crónica de la ciencia ficción mexicana* (1999), *Biografías del futuro* (2000), and *Lengua franca* (2001). He has received numerous national and international awards for his fiction and essays.

Beatriz Urraca was born in Spain and received her Ph.D. in comparative literature from the University of Michigan. Her research interests include nineteenth- and twentieth-century Latin American and North American literature, fantasy, and science fiction. She has published numerous articles on these topics, including "Wor(l)ds Through the Looking Glass: Borges's Mirrors and Contemporary Theory," and "Angélica Gorodischer: Voyages of Discovery." She is currently an associate professor of Spanish and Humanities at Neumann College in Pennsylvania.

Marcelo Willcham, a native of Argentina, received his Master's degree from California State University, and his doctoral degree from Arizona State University. He is currently a professor of Spanish, French, and world literature at Weatherford College in Texas.